THE GEOPOLITICS OF REGIONAL POWER

The International Political Economy of New Regionalisms Series

The International Political Economy of New Regionalisms series presents innovative analyses of a range of novel regional relations and institutions. Going beyond established, formal, interstate economic organizations, this essential series provides informed interdisciplinary and international research and debate about myriad heterogeneous intermediate level interactions.

Reflective of its cosmopolitan and creative orientation, this series is developed by an international editorial team of established and emerging scholars in both the South and North. It reinforces ongoing networks of analysts in both academia and think-tanks as well as international agencies concerned with micro-, meso- and macro-level regionalisms.

The Geopolitics of
Regional Power
Geography, Economics and Politics
in Southern Africa

SÖREN SCHOLVIN
Leibniz Universität Hannover, Germany

ASHGATE

Published by
Ashgate Publishing Limited
Wey Court East
Union Road
Farnham
Surrey, GU9 7PT
England

Ashgate Publishing Company
110 Cherry Street
Suite 3-1
Burlington, VT 05401-3818
USA

www.ashgate.com

British Library Cataloguing in Publication Data
A catalogue record for this book is available from the British Library

The Library of Congress has cataloged the printed edition as follows:
Scholvin, Sören.
  The geopolitics of regional power : geography, economics and politics in Southern Africa / by Sören Scholvin.
      pages cm. -- (The international political economy of new regionalisms series)
  Includes bibliographical references and index.
  ISBN 978-1-4724-3073-1 (hardback) -- ISBN 978-1-4724-3074-8 (ebook) -- ISBN 978-1-4724-3075-5 (epub) 1. Regionalism--Africa, Southern. 2. Geopolitics--Africa, Southern. 3. Middle powers. 4. South Africa--Foreign relations--Africa, Southern. 5. Africa, Southern--Foreign relations--South Africa. I. Title.
  JQ2720.A38R437 2014
  327.68--dc23

2014018286

ISBN 9781472430731 (hbk)
ISBN 9781472430748 (ebk – PDF)
ISBN 9781472430755 (ebk – ePUB)

Printed in the United Kingdom by Henry Ling Limited, at the Dorset Press, Dorchester, DT1 1HD

Contents

List of Figures and Maps

Figures

Maps

List of Tables

Preface

Halford Mackinder once wrote that each century has its own 'geographical perspective'. The rise of heartlandic powers, Russia and the German Reich, and their challenge to the British Empire, was the dominant paradigm of Mackinder's time. The geographical perspective that the era required for understanding and interpreting international relations centred on the presumed vast resources of the interior parts of the Eurasian continent, their newly gained accessibility via railway lines and the fact that control of this pivotal region of world politics lay beyond the reach of the Royal Navy. Using a term attributed to James Fairgrieve, 'the world that counts' was shifting from maritime Europe to continental Eurasia.

It appears that we are presently witnessing another shift in the world that counts. As demonstrated by the process of enlarging the G8, emerging powers have become members of the international institutions that deal with major global challenges – ranging from climate change to the current financial crisis. Brazil, China, India and South Africa have, meanwhile, also set up parallel institutions such as the BASIC Group, the BRICS Summit and the IBSA Dialogue Forum. Their political influence results from their growing economic strength, as Goldman Sachs' publications on the performance of the BRIC nations unintentionally show. This realignment of international relations is not, however, limited to the global level; regional international relations have become somewhat detached from global international relations. In some parts of the world, warfare remains a means of interstate rivalry. In others, it does not.

One may, therefore, convincingly argue that the logic of international relations varies from one region to another. The independence of the regional level reinforces the importance of the rise of regional powers. States such as Brazil, Nigeria, South Africa and Venezuela have become drivers of regional cooperation and integration. Even in the Middle East, Iran, Saudi Arabia and Turkey each independently pursue their own agendas, albeit within certain limits, so do some states in East and Southeast Asia. Regional powers tie their neighbouring countries together economically and interlink them globally – they function as regional economic hubs and as hinges between their respective periphery and the cores of the global economy. Political advisors hence stress that overall regional economic development depends upon the economic performance of the respective regional power. Regional security policy is also affected by regional powers: Nigeria was the most important actor in West African security interventions during the 1990s. In their competition for influence, the policies of Iran and Saudi Arabia are currently destabilising the Middle East. Brazil has been the pioneer of a security community in South America. South Africa has intervened and mediated in many sub-Saharan African conflicts, ranging from Ivory Coast to Sudan to Zimbabwe.

In spite of all these changes that have characterised the early twenty-first century, there appear to be many well-known patterns in international relations: material structures in a given geographical space shape those international relations. Energy resources are of prime relevance for the foreign policy of emerging powers. South Africa's intervention in Lesotho in 1998 was driven by fears for the safety of the Katse Dam, which is vital for supplying water to Gauteng. There has been significant friction between Bolivia and Brazil because of the renationalisation of Bolivia's natural gas industry. Brazil's support for Nicolás Maduro after the death of Hugo Chávez is partly due to the investment by Petrobras in Venezuela's Orinoco Delta. Shrinking energy resources and the need to decarbonise their energy sectors push emerging powers towards an active foreign policy and regional cooperation, as demonstrated by South Africa's efforts to import hydropower from its neighbouring countries. Transport infrastructure – ranging from harbours, railway tracks and roads to pipelines and transmission lines for electricity – remains a key strategic tool, as the central role of Brazil in the Initiative for the Integration of the Regional Infrastructure in South America, or IIRSA, demonstrates. In Central Asia, one may even reasonably explain the cooperation and confrontation between major intra- and extraregional powers by the pipelines that they each envisage laying for accessing the region's landlocked natural gas reserves.

These observations suggest that international relations are shaped, at least partly, by forces that outlast the rise and fall of economically and politically powerful nation-states and empires. For adherents to realist approaches in Political Geography, the geographical setting of international relations constitutes the essential force that endures. However, in this day and age few scholars still pursue realist approaches in Political Geography. The discipline is nowadays shaped rather by a constructivist agenda. Whilst constructivist approaches certainly shed light on important aspects of international relations, they cannot capture the eternal forces addressed by realist approaches and hence fail to take into consideration the most basic conditions of international relations – those provided by geography. Conceptualising the geographical setting as a set of conditions – that is, as a set of naturally given and manmade material structures in geographical space – allows us to better grasp the sometimes striking continuity of international relations. Nicholas Spykman famously wrote 'ministers come and go, even dictators die, but mountain ranges stand unperturbed'. But how much of present-day international relations can we explain by geographical setting alone? How do nongeographical factors, which seemingly matter in some way or another, interact with geographical factors? And, coming back to Mackinder, which geographical perspective is an adequate one for emerging powers?

In this study, I strive to answer these questions. I bring a geopolitical perspective into research on emerging powers and revitalise realist approaches in Political Geography. This study was written and researched between 2009 and 2013, when

I worked first as a research assistant at the Institute of Geography at the University of Hamburg and then as a research fellow at the German Institute of Global and Area Studies.

At the German Institute of Global and Area Studies, my research benefitted greatly from my participation in Daniel Flemes's research team on 'Foreign Policy Strategies in the Multipolar System'. My work was also strongly influenced by two field trips to Southern Africa, undertaken in 2010 and 2011, and the numerous discussions that I had with businesspeople, politicians and researchers there. I would particularly like to thank Fritz Becker (University of Namibia, Windhoek), Anton Bösl (Konrad Adenauer Foundation, Windhoek), Peter Draper (South African Institute of International Affairs, Johannesburg), Deon Geldenhuys (University of Johannesburg), Neuma Grobbelaar (South African Institute of International Affairs, Johannesburg), Trudi Hartzenberg (Trade Law Centre, Stellenbosch) and Philip Nel (University of Otago, New Zealand) for their support of my field research and/or helpful suggestions on the most suitable empirical and theoretical framework for this study. Last but not least, realising this research project would not have been possible without the continuous and skilled support of Jürgen Oßenbrügge (University of Hamburg) and Joachim Betz (German Institute of Global and Area Studies, Hamburg), both of whom I am particularly grateful to.

Stade, Germany
19 January 2014

List of Abbreviations

ANC	African National Congress
AU	African Union
CMA	Common Monetary Area
COMESA	Common Market for Eastern and Southern Africa
CONSAS	Constellation of Southern African States
DBSA	Development Bank of Southern Africa
EAC	East African Community
ITCZ	Intertropical Convergence Zone
LHWP	Lesotho Highlands Water Project
MISP	Maputo Iron and Steel Project
NP	National Party
NEPAD	New Partnership for Africa's Development
OAU	Organisation of African Unity
OPDS	Organ for Politics, Defence and Security
QCA	Qualitative Comparative Analysis
SACU	Southern African Customs Union
SADC	Southern African Development Community
SADCC	Southern African Development Coordination Conference
ZANU PF	Zimbabwe African National Union Patriotic Front

Chapter 1

Introduction

Core Question and Purpose of this Study

Emerging powers are new key players in international affairs. Most prominently, China and India have been labelled 'new drivers of global change', with their rise restructuring global governance (Humphrey and Messner 2005; Kaplinsky 2005). The rapid economic growth of certain countries poses a challenge to the Global North. The BRIC grouping – that is, Brazil, Russia, India and China – is likely to dominate the global economy in terms of output by 2050 (O'Neill 2001; O'Neill et al. 2005; Wilson and Purushothaman 2003). Smaller emerging economies – the so-called 'N-11' – are also predicted to overtake some of the major economies from the Global North in terms of gross domestic product in the first half of the twenty-first century, although they will not reach the size and importance of BRIC (Wilson and Stupnytska 2007).

There are various theoretical concepts that capture the potential that emerging powers have to be partners of the West. In development studies, the former are referred to as 'anchor countries' by the German Development Institute (Stamm 2004) and as 'pivotal states' by Chase, Hill and Kennedy (1996, 1999). Both terms revolve around the idea that the economic and political development of these states determines the relative development of their neighbourhoods. Scholars of the German Institute for International and Security Affairs examine states that are able to shape specific policies either constructively or detrimentally, the so-called 'leading powers', as partners for Germany (Husar et al. 2008; Husar and Maihold 2009). Barnett (2003, 2004, 2005), a former consultant for the Pentagon, proposes a new form of cooperation between the United States, its European partners and emerging powers. Huntington (1996) writes that the dominant states of what he calls 'civilisations' may help to solve regional conflicts. Their intervention is more easily accepted by the minor states of their region than the intervention of external powers is. Brzezinski (1997) and Huntington (1999) argue almost identically that states such as South Korea and Ukraine that possess a strategically important location constitute essential partners for great powers. Khanna (2008) suggests that what he calls the 'Second World' is about to become the stage upon which the future of the global order will be decided. Second World states are, accordingly, potential key allies of three global empires – China, the European Union and the US.

The concept of 'regional powers', which stresses the regional level, was originally coined by scholars of the German Institute of Global and Area Studies. Based on case studies on Brazil, China, India, Russia and South Africa, Flemes and Nolte (2010) define regional powers as states that are part of a delimited region. They are ready to assume regional leadership, and furthermore possess the necessary material and ideational capacities to do so. As a consequence, they are highly influential in their respective region. Close cultural, economic and political ties, the provision of collective goods for the region, an ideational project of leadership and regional followership are all mentioned as criteria for the classification of different types of regional powers.

The geographical criterion as it is included in the definition of regional powers highlights that such research is grounded in a misunderstanding of geography and regionness. For instance, it is argued that Venezuela cannot be considered a full regional power because its leading role is limited to a group of states that do not share common borders and that they do not, therefore, constitute a region (Flemes and Lemke 2010). Yet, regional powers create their sphere of influence by tying other states economically and politically to them. Shared borders are thus not necessarily a defining criterion of regionness. Furthermore, Flemes and Lemke (2010) argue that Brazil, China, India and South Africa are each part of their own geographically delimited region because they are located in South America, East Asia, South Asia and Southern Africa respectively. Yet they do not elaborate on the nature and characteristics of these regions, apparently being convinced that South America, East Asia, South Asia and Southern Africa constitute naturally given entities. They ignore that there is interaction between geography and regional powers: geography influences the policy options of regional powers; by their policies, regional powers influence the geography of their respective region.

In order to advance a geographical perspective on regional powers, I thus address in this book the following core question: how do geographical factors – taken to mean the structures both manmade and naturally given that exist in geographical space – influence the economic and political relations of regional powers? Given the absence of geographers from research on regional powers and their silence when it comes to nonconstructivist Political Geography, answering this question has, first of all, an explorative purpose. I intend to build inroads into a realist geopolitical analysis of regional powers. The objective of this study is, therefore, to provide a sound picture of to what extent, and how, geographical factors influence economics and politics in the specific case of regional powers. I will show not only that geography matters, but also how it does. In order to answer the core question, I first provide an overview of the state of research on emerging powers. Second, I summarise and evaluate, in a rather broad manner, the state of the art in Classical Geopolitics. Based on this, I incorporate, third, additional geopolitical literature in order to unearth the concepts that suit my analytical needs. These concepts and the review of the state of the art in Classical Geopolitics lead me to indicators for the impact of geographical factors on the economic and political relations of regional powers. I elaborate, fourth, on suitable methodologies. Reviving Classical Geopolitics, identifying the necessary indicators and adapting methodologies to them, I thus advance what I term 'Realist Geopolitics'. I then, fifth, test this theory for the South African case.

Theoretical Context

Having once been a key subject for geographers, Geopolitics was for the most part abandoned by them after the Second World War because of its discrediting of its self in the context of National Socialism. German geographers especially rejected the inclusion of Geopolitics as a part of their academic discipline from these years on (Schöller 1957; Troll 1947). Political Geography in the US had already turned rather descriptive in the 1930s and was difficult to distinguish from Regional Geography, as exemplified by Derwent Whittlesey's main work *The Earth and the State* (1944). In the 1980s, Taylor (1985) made some initial efforts to revitalise Political Geography as the analysis of the interplay of geography and power. Critical Geopolitics was launched as a constructivist approach a decade later (Ó Tuathail 1989, 1996; Ó Tuathail and Dalby 1998). Today, constructivism predominates in Political Geography to an extent that practically makes it the exclusively used approach.

It is apparent, however, that the way material structures in geographical space shape economics and politics cannot be examined from a constructivist perspective. My investigation requires a materialist approach – that is, one which is based on scientific realism. Classical Geopolitics is such an approach. Classical Geopolitics is characterised by three features (Lacoste 1976): first, international relations are conditioned by the spatial configuration of naturally existing and manmade material objects. These objects have an impact on states that is independent from social construction. As I show in Chapter 2.2, many scholars conceptualise material reality as a frame that limits the feasible options for human decision makers. Some even argue that it guides courses of action. Second, Classical Geopolitics is policy-oriented. It is most suitable for elaborating rational strategies for states to pursue, done by deriving these policies from the geographical conditions that affect the respective state. Third, Classical Geopolitics incorporates the dynamic nature of politics. Despite the common reproach that its adherents claim to articulate timeless truths, most scholars of Classical Geopolitics acknowledge the temporal contextuality of their work. This temporal contextuality results from the fact that manmade material objects in geographical space evolve in the long run. So does mankind's ability to use nature. Location and physical geography are contrariwise seen as constants.[1] Therefore, Classical Geopolitics is the most suitable approach for explaining long-term patterns in international relations.

The only noteworthy geographers who stand in the tradition of Classical Geopolitics today are Cohen (2009), Grygiel (2006) and Gray (1991, 1996). Regardless of the quality of their analyses, the fact that there remain only these three renowned scholars indicates that a vast gap exists between geopolitical theory, methodology and practice. In order to revive Classical Geopolitics, I refer

---

1 One may also argue, however, that the temporal variation of physiogeographical factors contributes to explaining economic and political processes, as climate change exemplifies.

to Mackinder (1887, 1890, 1904), Fairgrieve (1917) and Spykman (1938a, 1938b, 1942; Spykman and Rollins 1939a, 1939b). Halford Mackinder is probably the most famous representative of Classical Geopolitics because of his 'Heartland Theory' (1904, 1919, 1943). On a meta-level, the essential feature of his thinking is the explanation of economics and politics by geographical location and physical geography. For Mackinder, physical geography was the one constant in human history and geographers always had to study its effects on mankind. Nicholas Spykman, who adapted the Heartland Theory to the political constellation of the Second World War (1942, 1944), pursued the same approach. He derived foreign policy strategies from location and physical geography and coined the famous phrase 'ministers come and go, even dictators die, but mountain ranges stand unperturbed' (1942: 41). James Fairgrieve advanced similar ideas. He explained that geography provides conditions that enable human societies to advance economically – coal deposits in England were, for example, a necessary precondition for the Industrial Revolution. In comparison to Mackinder and Spykman, Fairgrieve went even further regarding the strength of geographical forces. He suggested that the human mind was shaped by geographical factors and argued that such forces also accounted for the patterns of recurring foreign policy strategies, which generate a dynamic of their own.

The early adherents of Classical Geopolitics explained social phenomena exclusively by natural causes – to be precise, by location and physical geography. Referring only to natural causes often leads, however, to crude forms of geodeterminism. I do not think that one should try – or indeed that it is even possible – to explain everything by location and physical geography. What I seek to show here is rather that geographical factors have to be taken as necessary but insufficient explanatory conditions for many social phenomena that occur. Hence, I refer to INUS causality (Mackie 1974). For example, one may argue that coal-fired power stations will dominate electricity generation in emerging economies if they both possess this fossil fuel in large quantities and if the need for electricity for their rapid economic growth is great. Such reasoning keenly applies to China, India and South Africa. It shows that geographical conditions, large coal reserves, must be combined with nongeographical conditions, such as a growing electricity demand. This combined factor is part of a larger set of combined factors. Each of them is unnecessary but sufficient for the outcome. This means that there are various paths that lead to the outcome. Coal may also dominate electricity generation in a high-growth economy because there are no alternative technologies available and coal can be imported. As I show in this book, geographical factors alone rarely cause anything – but many of the causes of phenomena that matter to Political Geography and Political Science do, however, include geographical factors as necessary conditions.

Hypotheses, Operationalisation and Methodologies

Based on Realist Geopolitics, I develop three hypotheses. They revolve around the opportunities and constraints posed by geographical factors vis-à-vis the policy options of regional powers:

H1 Location and physical geography set a frame that guides economics and politics. The patterns of expansion of regional powers – meaning the directions in which they focus their crossborder influence – result from location and physical geography.

This hypothesis is intended to verify whether, as expected, geographical factors guide economics and politics in the sense that they limit the number of available options. In other words, I argue that geographical factors dictate which courses of action can be realised and which ones cannot. In most cases, geographical factors do not reduce the number of feasible options to only one. Whenever there is more than one feasible option, one might investigate whether courses of action occur that are, from a geopolitical perspective, rational.

H2 Manmade material structures in geographical space that cannot be altered in the short term – like railway lines – guide economics and politics in a way similar to how naturally given structures – such as mountain ranges – do.

A realist approach to geopolitics is materialist and therefore needs to include not only location and physical geography but also the material structures in geographical space that have been built by humans. Manmade structures differ from location and physical geography insofar as their existence can only partly be explained by location and physical geography. They are thus, to a certain degree, rather the outcome of human decisions.

H3 The sphere of influence of a regional power reflects geographical conditions, meaning that the range of its influence is delimited by geographical forces. Geographical limitations will be partly overcome if the regional power invests disproportionately in the expansion of its influence.

I argue that geographical factors propose a possible region of influence for every regional power, meaning that there are geographically rational limits to the expansion of its influence. Yet, courses of action do not have to be rational. Provided that a regional power possesses sufficient capacities to withstand the pressures exerted by geographical factors, it may push any geographically determined limits. This means that recognition is given here to the fact that regional powers shape their region of influence – they shape geography.

The first step in the operationalisation of the hypotheses for the case of South Africa is to show what location and physical geography imply as rational strategies. Therefore, I draw expectations about this from South Africa's location relative to other African countries, elaborate on the effects of physical geography on the movement of people and goods and show where natural resources of interest to South Africa – ranging from oil, gas and raw minerals to crops and water – are located. As a second step, I take into consideration manmade geography – which can be defined as core zones of population and economic activity, as well as the interactions between them. These interconnections materialise, most importantly, as transport networks. Together with location and physical geography, manmade material geography reveals the patterns that should be expected to mark regional interactions and the projection of power by South Africa. The third step is to then compare these predictions with the de facto situation and dynamics on the ground. In order to do this, I investigate patterns of trade and investment in Central, East and Southern Africa, and the role that South Africa and South African businesses play in and for neighbouring countries. I shed light on South Africa's relevance for intergovernmental organisations in Southern Africa and the political strategies of the regional states, and analyse how geographical factors matter to South Africa's regional security policy.

Working with a medium-sized number of cases – South Africa is, in terms of regional economics and politics, closely linked to roughly a dozen other states – I use Qualitative Comparative Analysis (QCA) as a first methodology. The purpose of QCA is to bring together the advantages of quantitative analysis with those of qualitative analysis. Doing this allows generalisation and case-oriented depth (Ragin 1987). In QCA, cases are seen as configurations or combinations of conditions, which replace what are otherwise called 'independent variables' (Rihoux and De Meur 2009). All possible configurations of the conditions are shown in truth tables in order to find out, by using Boolean algebra, which combinations theoretically lead to the outcome or the dependent variable. This way, necessary and sufficient conditions are revealed (Berg-Schlosser et al. 2009; Dion 1998; Ragin 1998). The use of QCA is highly suited to my study because it reflects the fact that I do not consider geographical factors to be the only conditions that determine economic and political outcomes. Since this method aims at uncovering the paths that lead to the outcome and starts with complexity instead of with the mere correlation of two phenomena, it is most helpful to reveal INUS causalities. Yet, QCA does not explain the paths to the outcome. Elaborating on the causal relations between them is an additional responsibility of the researcher (Rihoux and De Meur 2009).

Given that I am interested in the steps between the initial cause and the final outcome – not just in correlations on a macro-level – the second method I apply is Process Tracing. This enables me to plausibly explain the mechanism at work when a cause leads to an outcome (Checkel 2005; Reilly 2010). Process Tracing is comparable to the putting together of a jigsaw puzzle without knowing whether I possess all the pieces of that puzzle or, indeed, whether all the pieces in my hands are even part of it (George and McKeown 1985). I search for pieces of evidence that can make plausible my reasoning on the causal relationship between geographical factors on the one side and economics and politics on the other. Hence, whilst QCA reveals the necessary and sufficient conditions, tracing processes means elaborating on the causal mechanisms relevant to the three hypotheses.

QCA and Process Tracing, moreover, fit the case selection for my study. As summarised in Chapter 7, South Africa appears to be a typical case for the impact of material structures in geographical space on economics and politics. Typical cases are best suited for explaining the causal mechanisms at work. Finding plausible causal mechanisms renders the theory tested conceivable. The absence of plausible causal mechanisms, meanwhile, indicates that it will be necessary to modify or even discard altogether the theory in question (Seawright and Gerring 2008). By searching for a plausible causal mechanism that links geographical factors to economics and politics, I test Realist Geopolitics – thereby not only examining whether geography matters but also how so.

Structure of this Book

Alongside the Introduction (Chapter 1) and Conclusion (Chapter 7), this book contains five further chapters. Chapter 2 provides the theoretical and methodological framework for my study. In Chapter 2.1, I explain the regionalisation of international relations, which forms the background to Political Science research on regional powers. Following on, I then summarise the major concepts currently in play about emerging powers and illuminate the gaps that exist in related research on geography and regionness. Chapter 2.2 serves to develop Realist Geopolitics as a key strand of theory. I start with an overview of the different varieties of Classical Geopolitics, and then analyse the contributions of Mackinder, Spykman and Fairgrieve to this discipline with regard to theoretical premises and methodologies. Addressing the shortcomings of Classical Geopolitics whilst also refuting the fundamental criticism of it that is advanced by adherents of Critical Geopolitics, I afterwards modify and revitalise Classical Geopolitics as what I call henceforth 'Realist Geopolitics'. Since several present-day scholars refer to geographical factors as independent variables in their quest to explain social phenomena, I contextualise Realist Geopolitics accordingly in the last part of Chapter 2.2.

In Chapter 2.3, I present different concepts for geopolitical analyses that are representative of the tradition of Classical Geopolitics. After having shown how they can be applied to the study of regional powers, I elaborate on the indicators that fit with these concepts and reveal the impact of geographical factors on the economics and politics of regional powers. I also explain which sources of information appear appropriate to my case study. In the last main section of Chapter 2.3, I present QCA and Process Tracing and adapt them to the needs of my study.

In chapters 3–6, I apply Realist Geopolitics to a case study of South Africa and its regional relations. Following the aforementioned steps of the operationalisation, herein I first examine location and physical geography (Chapter 3) and second address the transport infrastructure and socioeconomic characteristics of East and Southern Africa (Chapter 4). These two chapters cover the conditions underpinning my QCA. Third, I apply Process Tracing to South African regional cooperation on water, electricity and transport, showing how geographical and nongeographical factors interact (Chapter 5). Fourth and finally, I examine the de facto economic and political interaction between South Africa and its neighbouring states, which covers the outcome of my QCA. Alongside this, Process Tracing is also applied to South Africa's regional security policy (Chapter 6).

Chapter 2
Theoretical and Methodological Framework

In this chapter, I first present the various policy-related concepts on emerging powers. This overview reveals the lack of clearly delimited spheres of influence and a current disregard of geographical factors in the academic literature. Second, I analyse methodological and theoretical considerations in Classical Geopolitics, sketch Realist Geopolitics as a new strand of theory and contextualise it within contemporary physiocratic approaches. Third, I operationalise Realist Geopolitics for the study of the international relations of regional powers, present guiding questions that cover the independent and dependent variables, and outline the two methodologies that I apply – QCA and Process Tracing.

2.1 Emerging Powers: State of Research

Regionalising International Relations

Dividing the international system into subsystems and thusly regionalising international relations is a long-standing tradition. Gulick (1955), Morgenthau (1954) and Wight (1978) reasoned about interacting subsystems that are supposedly marked by a regional balance of power. Bull (2002) argued that regional balances of power prevented minor states from being absorbed up by regional hegemons whilst Waltz (1979, 2000) – the godfather of structural realism, an approach which seems to be at odds with regionalising politics – suggested that minor states could interact with each other independent of great powers, forming regional systems that follow the same logic as the international one. The consensus appears to be that analysing regional subsystems will be a useful pursuit if subsystems represent distinct theatres of operation (Thompson 1973). Whilst the aforementioned scholars only hinted at the relevance of the regional level, Väyrynen (1984) – whose analyses from the mid-1980s come fairly close in nature to the current research on emerging powers – referred to the efforts of the Frontline States to end their economic subordination to South Africa through regional cooperation, doing so in order to show that the independence of the regional level decreases with its closer integration into the global economy. He suggested using regional institutions and regionally dominant states as well as the economic, geographic and political proximity of closely interrelated states as indicators both for the existence of subsystems and for their delineation.

The regionalisation of international relations has grown tremendously since the early 1990s. The erosion of the Westphalian nation-state system and growing economic interdependence across state borders, two consequences of neoliberal globalisation, are frequently named – along with the more recent decline of US hegemony – as developments that account for the regionalisation of politics (Hettne and Söderbaum 2000). Hurrell (2007) writes that regions are the main setting for the production and management of (in)security, due to interference by external powers having by now become rare. States that dominate a region are the producers and managers of that (in)security. New Regionalism, meanwhile, has steadily built an entire subdiscipline of Political Science on the basis of regions being understood as socially constructed communities and, thus, as an independent level of analysis (Breslin et al. 2002; Hettne, Inotai and Sunkel 2000).

The most prominent work on political regionalisation published since the early 1990s is certainly Samuel P. Huntington's *The Clash of Civilizations* (1996). Huntington depicts a multipolar world in which the West struggles to maintain its dominance. According to him, the core factor that divides peoples and determines their political orientation has, since the end of the Cold War, been neither economic nor ideological. Mankind is, rather, divided into 'civilisations', which makes culture – and therein religion – the essential criterion for sociopolitical identification. Huntington furthermore argues that core states may assume the role of the leaders of their civilisation and therefore possess the capacity to stabilise their neighbourhood. Civilisations that lack a core state face more difficulties to solve internal conflicts than those that are dominated by a core state do. A less culture-based approach is Thomas Barnett's *The Pentagon's New Map* (2003). A former professor at the US Naval War College and former consultant at the Pentagon, Barnett divides the world into two parts: the 'functioning core' consists of the Global North and some stable emerging powers, for instance India, Mexico and South Africa; the 'nonintegrated gap' comprises everything else. Whilst the functioning core is characterised by prosperity, democratic governance, a high level of security and stability, the nonintegrated gap bears the opposite features: poverty, authoritarian rule, a low level of security and instability. Barnett traces this sharp contrast back to the fact that, in his view, only the core participates in globalisation. US security policy should, therefore, aim at exporting stability to the gap and integrating it into globalisation (Barnett 2004).

The best-known purely academic approach to regionalising politics is Buzan's and Wæver's (2003) theory of 'regional security complexes'. The key idea behind regional security complexes is that international relations theory must adapt to regional contexts. In Buzan's words:

> [the] security implications of the anarchic structure [of international relations] do not spread uniformly throughout the [international] system. Complex patterns of alignment and enmity develop […] in all types of anarchic systems […] and it is they, rather than the grosser system structure overall, which define the security environment of most states. (1983: 105)

Being rooted in the English School of International Relations, which distinguishes between systems and societies of states, Buzan's and Wæver's approach implies that the world consists of various regions that function according to different logics or that are at different stages of the evolution from systems to societies of states. A simplified version of regional security complexes is Singer's and Wildavsky's (1993) division of the world into 'zones of peace' and 'zones of turmoil', which resembles Barnett's model. Singer and Wildavsky argue that military means are no longer used in interstate conflicts in Europe, North America and parts of East Asia. The practice of international relations in the zones of peace is, therefore, different than it is in the zones of turmoil.

In an article in *Beiträge zur Internationalen Politik und Sicherheit* (2012) on South Africa–Southern Africa relations since 1994, I previously took up the idea that the logic of international relations varies from one region to another and furthermore linked this idea to regional powers. I showed herein that Nelson Mandela's agenda of democratisation and human rights led to confrontation between South Africa and the states across the African continent. The status quo approach of his successors Thabo Mbeki and Jacob Zuma – with their paradigmatic shift towards national sovereignty as the cornerstone of foreign policy – favours cooperation between regional neighbours, a practice that is more advanced in Southern Africa than in many other parts of the world. Hence, a key determinant for the varying logic of international relations from one region to another is the grand strategy of regional powers – be it a revisionist or status quo-oriented one.

Strategic Partners of the West

In his best-seller *The Second World* (2008), Parag Khanna argues that there is a new stage upon which the future global order will be decided: the Second World. Second World states – ranging from Egypt and Kazakhstan to Mexico – are also potential key allies of the world's three empires – China, the EU and the US.[1] Brzezinski points out that some countries, so-called 'geopolitical pivots', matter more because they possess a strategically important location, 'either in defining access to important areas or [by] denying resources' to great powers (1997: 41). The geopolitical pivots identified by Brzezinski face stronger neighbours – China in the case of Indonesia, Russia in the case of Ukraine for instance. To balance these regional rivals, the geopolitical pivots need strong partners – primarily the US. Huntington's (1999) thoughts on 'secondary regional powers' are based on the same logic. These states seek to balance primary regional powers in collaboration

---

1   As I argue elsewhere (Scholvin 2009b), Khanna's book is full of bizarre notions. For example, the author explains Latin America's political instability by the character of the Latin American people, who lack, according to him, respect for their fellow citizens. His methodology is strangely unscientific: Khanna appears to have only spoken to people from each country's cosmopolitan elite, whose thoughts are passed off as representative of those of the entire population.

with the US. For the latter, a sound foreign policy strategy relies on cooperation with secondary regional powers because that alliance allows them to balance potential challengers.

Chase, Hill and Kennedy (1996, 1999) argue that nine 'pivotal states' – Algeria, Brazil, Egypt, India, Indonesia, Mexico, Pakistan, South Africa and Turkey – should become the focal points of US commitment to the Global South. The pivotal states are believed to determine the development of their respective region because of their economic and political relevance to it. Similarly, the term 'anchor countries', as used by the German Development Institute, is meant to encompass former Third World countries that play a central role on both a global and regional scale. The one criterion that determines whether or not a state is an anchor country is its share of the regional economic output. In order to divulge which countries qualify as anchors, Stamm (2004) selects those with the largest gross domestic product from each region delimited by the World Bank in its frequent studies. Then, the share of the largest economy is subtracted from the regional gross domestic product and the relative contributions of the remaining countries are compared. All countries providing at least 20 per cent of the remaining gross domestic product are also considered anchor countries. Scholars of the German Development Institute associate a state having a high economic output with it also having a determining role in its regional economic development. They argue that that anchor countries are, moreover, economically more diversified and possess a larger share of industrial production than other former Third World countries do. For this reason, they are regional growth engines. Prosperity in anchor countries is expected to lead to regional prosperity, recession in anchor countries to regional recession.

The central problem in the definition of anchor countries, as well as of pivotal states, is that the economic relevance of these countries to their neighbourhood has barely been tested. Their supposed effects on regional economic dynamics are uncertain and not spatially delimited. As a side note, the true purpose of the anchor country concept appears to be providing justification for preferential cooperation between Germany and emerging markets (Scholvin 2009a). The same premise can be said to apply both to the pivotal state concept and to that of the so-called 'leading powers', which the German Institute for International and Security Affairs examines. Its scholars argue that Germany must cooperate with leading powers from the Global South in order to henceforth realise its own national interests. Leading powers are defined as the states that can shape specific international policies constructively or detrimentally – either alone or by mobilising other state and nonstate actors. In addition to sharing common goals, the political capacities of each leading power and them having special relations with Germany are relevant considerations in the policy advice given by this think tank (Husar et al. 2008; Husar and Maihold 2009).

New Drivers of Global Change

Emerging powers not only play an important role on the regional level. For this reason, some scholars from the German Development Institute add further characteristic features to the defining criteria of anchor countries. Conceptualised as global actors, anchor countries are thus members of the G20, possess a permanent seat in the United Nations Security Council (or strive for one at least), assume an increasingly relevant military role in the global arena, are new donors of foreign aid, invest in international cooperation and are, generally speaking, leaders of the Global South in international negotiations. Despite these commonalities, anchor countries are not at all alike. They vary considerably in terms of governmental systems, prosperity and economic size, as well as policy preferences (Humphrey and Messner 2005). China, a global great power of tremendous relevance to climate change concerns, falls into this group of states. So does Nigeria, an underdeveloped rentier state whose importance beyond West Africa is questionable. Even there, it appears to be in reality a source of instability rather than a driver of political cooperation and economic progress (Scholvin 2014a).

Amongst all the emerging powers, China and India play a special role. Because of their enormous impact on issues of key global relevance, Humphrey and Messner (2006) label them 'new drivers of global change'. They argue that the rise of China and India cannot be compared to the rise of the so-called 'tiger states' – Hong Kong, Singapore, South Korea and Taiwan – because of the exceptionally large population sizes of the former. Growing production and trade, alongside vast financial reserves, are the central features of their economic rise – developments that are fundamentally changing the global distribution of power. High emissions of carbon dioxide being generated by China's and India's industrialisation further demonstrate the growing relevance of these two powers to issues of global concern (Humphrey and Messner 2006; Messner 2007).

In contrast to China and India, Brazil and South Africa tend to be regarded by political scientists as states that matter primarily for the policies practiced in their respective regions (Mayer 2009). This distinction, which implicitly arises as part of the concept of new drivers of global change, is, however, problematic. Brazil and South Africa are as much involved in global networking as China and India are (Flemes, Scholvin and Strüver 2011). Enlarging thus the group of new drivers of global change, one can see that the specific ways in which these states are changing the international system vary considerably. India pursues a defensive course, opposes economic liberalisation and assumes a Third World attitude aimed at limiting the influence of the Global North. South Africa promotes neoliberalism under the condition that the Global North lifts import barriers and stops subsidising its own exports. In general, South Africa follows a reformist path of moderately challenging established powers on individual issues. It uses multilateral coalitions to balance the Global North but refrains from calling the entire global order into question – something that is, rhetorically at least, part of India's foreign policy. Brazil occupies a middle-of-the-road position. It tries to balance the dominance of the US multilaterally and has acquired the role of a spokesperson for the Global South in this way. Yet, Brazil does not seek to change Western dominance in essence and pursues a course of economic liberalisation for its own benefit (Nel and Stephen 2010). With regard to the overall impact of emerging powers on the international system, these differences between them do not matter that much. Borrowing an idea from Hurrell (2006), emerging powers are, rather, crucial not because they are alike but because they exert a comparable effect on the international system. Their rise is slowly bringing to an end the dominance of the Global North and undermining the long-held conviction that there are no viable alternatives to Western models of governance.

BRIC(S)

The acronym BRIC – standing for Brazil, Russia, India and China – originates from the publications of scholars working for the investment bank Goldman Sachs. They predict that these four countries, which are already today the world's growth engines, will dominate the global economy in terms of gross domestic product by 2050 provided that they pursue sound policies (O'Neill 2001; O'Neill et al. 2005; Wilson and Purushothaman 2003). South Africa was considered a potential candidate for membership of this exclusive club, but was eventually left out because of its low growth rates and relatively small economy (Wilson and Purushothaman 2003). In addition to BRIC, there is the 'N-11' – that is, the next 11 of Bangladesh, Egypt, Indonesia, Iran, Mexico, Nigeria, Pakistan, Philippines, South Korea, Turkey and Vietnam. They will not reach the economic size of BRIC and will not have the same impact on the global economy. Only Indonesia and Nigeria are comparable to the smaller BRIC countries because of their vast populations and considerable economic growth rates. Meanwhile Mexico and South Korea, and to a lesser degree Turkey and Vietnam, possess the potential to catch up with the Global North in terms of per capita income (Wilson and Stupnytska 2007).

O'Neill and his colleagues certainly did not have political analysis in mind when they started their research on BRIC – their aim has been to show which markets are most lucrative for investment and only rarely do they draw political conclusions. Political scientists have, nonetheless, enthusiastically adopted the acronym. Some even argue that BRIC as a political concept makes more sense than it does as an economic one (Armijo 2007). As part of this scholarly embracing of the term, Mexico and even Indonesia are sometimes included in a group of emerging powers that shape global governance – the acronym thus changing to BRICSAM (Cooper, Shaw and Antkiewicz 2008).

BRIC(S) has also turned from an analytical concept into a political network. The foreign ministers of Brazil, Russia, India and China first jointly met in New York in September 2006. The first formal BRIC Summit took place in Yekaterinburg two years later. South Africa joined the grouping in 2010. Even though the institutional framework and purpose of BRICS remains vague, key issues of current global relevance have been discussed at the annually held summits – mostly economics and the global financial architecture, but also the tensions over Iran's nuclear programme. In spite of serious differences between the member states – most importantly Russia's vision of turning the grouping into an anti-US platform, something to which China is strongly opposed – BRICS has been quite successful as a network. It has brought together the voices of emerging powers and caused changes in established institutions of global governance such as the World Bank. Given that emerging powers appear to cooperate in flexible networks rather than fixed alliances (Flemes, Scholvin and Strüver 2011), several further groupings have arisen out of BRICS: India, Brazil and South Africa have initiated economic and political cooperation as IBSA; with regard to climate change, meanwhile, Brazil, South Africa, India and China are currently cooperating closely as BASIC.

Regional Powers

As the previous sections show, the research on regional powers undertaken by the German Institute of Global and Area Studies stands in the context of other economist and political-scientific concepts on emerging powers. Not surprisingly, the first ever definition of regional powers was put forward a long time before the scholars at the German Institute of Global and Area Studies began carrying out research on regional powers. Østerud (1992) wrote in the early 1990s that regional powers were part of a delineated region and able to withstand any intraregional coalitions. They, furthermore, were said to exert a high degree of influence in all regionally important affairs and to have the potential to become global great powers.

Drafting an initial research agenda at the German Institute of Global and Area Studies, Nolte (2006) adds many further characteristic features: regional powers are part of a geographically, economically and politically delimited region. Within this region, regional powers claim a leadership role. They therefore significantly influence both the delineation of the region and its ideational construction. Regional powers moreover need extensive material, organisational and ideational capacities in order to be able to successfully project their power. A simple surplus of power as compared to neighbouring countries is a necessary but not a sufficient condition for regional powerhood. Regional powers have to be closely culturally, economically and politically linked to their neighbouring countries. Given all of the aforementioned characteristics, regional powers are very influential in regional affairs: they shape, for instance, the regional security agenda. Apart from that, regional powers also use regional governance structures in order to realise their goals. Their leading role is accepted or at least respected by relevant intra- and extraregional powers. Regional powers are integrated in global governance structures, wherein they represent the interests of their region at least in part.

Whilst Nolte's original list of characteristics covers numerous aspects that certainly matter to regional powerhood, it is ultimately too demanding. Being implicitly derived from the Brazilian case, in their totality these characteristics do not even apply to the other most readily identifiable regional powers, namely India and South Africa. They, furthermore, render research on regional powers in the Middle East impossible. That all said, the present definition of regional powers that is used by scholars at the German Institute of Global and Area Studies is less demanding. Accordingly, they argue that regional powers are:

- part of a geographically delimited region;
- ready to assume leadership;
- in possession of the necessary material and ideational capacities to do so; and
- consequently are highly influential in their region (Flemes and Nolte 2010).

Summarising Schirm's (2005) definition, one may also say that regional powers are rule makers at the regional level. They possess a power over resources that they transform into a power over outcomes. Close cultural, economic and political ties, the provision of collective goods for the region, an ideational project of leadership and regional followership are mentioned as further, noncompulsory criteria for classifying different types of regional powers (Flemes and Nolte 2010). Based on the findings of an international conference on regional powers held in Hamburg in September 2008, Flemes and Lemke (2010) draw the conclusion that Brazil, China, India, Russia and South Africa fully comply with the proposed criteria for being a regional power. Iran, Israel and Venezuela – three other states analysed at the same conference – only meet some of the defining features, meaning that they represent 'defective' regional powers (of which there are probably many more).

The application of the geographical criterion by Flemes and Lemke reveals one of the weaknesses of research hitherto on regional powers. It does not make sense to argue that Brazil, China, India and South Africa are part of geographically delimited regions simply because they are located in South America, East Asia, South Asia and Southern Africa respectively. Flemes and Lemke appear to be convinced that these continents and subcontinents are given entities and, hence, they do not address what actually defines the region in each case. In other words, they do not elaborate on the organising forces that are exerted by regional powers and that bring coherence to their respective sphere of influence. Claiming that Venezuela cannot be considered a full regional power because it possesses a leading role only amongst a group of states that do not share common borders is an even less convincing argument. The authors fail to explain why having common borders is a defining feature of regionness. They disregard the fact that regional powers create their sphere of influence by tying other states economically and politically to them. What is more, they do not shed light on the geographical factors that affect the power potentialities and possible range of influence of regional powers – examining such factors would help integrate the geographical component to definitions of regional powerhood and lead to a more accurate delineation of spheres of influence. In order to fill this research gap, the next subchapter will present a theoretical basis for the analysis of how geographical factors influence international relations.

2.2 Realist Geopolitics: Historical Roots and Contemporary Tie-ins

Classical Geopolitics

The varieties of Classical Geopolitics
German geographer Friedrich Ratzel established Geopolitics as a science, although he himself did not use this nomenclature. His books *Anthropogeographie* and *Politische Geographie*, first published in the 1880s and 1890s, were considered fundamental works in the field by other geographers. Ratzel (1897) conceptualised states as growing organisms bound to their soil. He claimed that the natural environment – or, more precisely, soil – determined the power of states and, therefore, their fate: states grow by acquiring more soil; they decline by losing soil.[2] It was Ratzel's Swedish colleague Rudolf Kjellén who coined the term Geopolitics in 1916, defining it as the science of states considered as geographical organisms. For him, states were actual life forms fighting for survival. They were thus subject to a cycle of birth, growth, maturity and death. As distinct from Ratzel's earlier work, Kjellén also incorporated demographics, economics, social aspects and political authority into his research.

Practically all German scholars of Geopolitics in the first half of the twentieth century referred to the concepts that had been elaborated by Ratzel and Kjellén. They analysed politics in the context of historical evolutions supposedly determined by the organic nature of states. They combined social Darwinism and geographical determinism. Maull (1936) conceptualised states as organisms going through a life cycle. Vogel (1921), meanwhile, depicted the evolution of states as a struggle for survival. He argued that the power of every state, and their political strategies, thus resulted from location and physical geography. Haushofer and his colleagues from the *Zeitschrift für Geopolitik* accordingly defined Geopolitics as the science of the 'geo-fixedness of the political processes' (1928: 27). They added a strong policy orientation to the ill-conceived analytical concept that they had adopted from Ratzel and Kjellén: that Geopolitics should be a tool of nationalist and revisionist propaganda. Haushofer (1928) explicitly recommended the use of suggestive maps in order to influence nonscientific audiences in public debates. Stressing this policy turn in Geopolitics, Maull (1936) refined the aforementioned definition by Haushofer and his colleagues – he now distinguished between Geopolitics and Political Geography. The former, aiming at concrete political action, addressed

---

2 Throughout his entire work, Ratzel never operationalised soil. It thus remains unknown how the quantity and quality of soil – the basis of national power – can actually be measured.

the spatial requirements of states for their existence whereas the latter was, rather descriptively, about their geo-fixedness.

In sharp contrast to social Darwinism and geodeterminism in Germany, early Geopolitics in France was founded on and followed the concept of 'possibilism' (Sprout and Sprout 1965). For possibilists, the environmental milieu was seen to create opportunities and constraints. It does not determine human action. Reasonable proponents of realist versions of Geopolitics would not object to this idea. They would examine the impact of geographical opportunities and constraints on mankind. For some possibilists, however, even the mere notion that the environmental milieu makes certain courses of action more likely than others because they are better adapted to geography was an unpalatable one (Febvre 1922). Brunhes and Vallaux (1921) more moderately reasoned that Napoléon's famous statement about the politics of states resting in their geography was accurate but also incomplete. They showed that geographical conditions guide the course of history. However, humans also change their physical surroundings. They make geography in this way. Manmade geography constitutes, following Brunhes and Vallaux, an explanation for human action but geography is not something beyond human control.

Pioneering British and US scholars in the field often occupied a middle position between their German and French colleagues. They sought to explain history by its geographical conditions. Cornish (1923), for example, associated the location of capital cities with physical geography, especially topography. Semple (1903) presented location and topography as determinants of movement and, hence, of the expansion of states. Mahan (1890), meanwhile, described the geographical conditions – both human and physiogeographical – that enable a state to become a maritime power. Turner (1920) went a step further. He argued that physical geography had shaped the character of the people of the US. He identified, for example, the characteristic features of the US political system, such as democratic governance, as being derived from the Frontier experience. What distinguished British and US forms of geodeterminism from the German variant of it was that – regardless of the degree of geodeterminism claimed – the former aimed at objective analysis. The latter was, however, partisan and manipulative (Kelly 2006). Mackinder and Spykman, and to a lesser extent Fairgrieve, were the outstanding representatives of objective geodeterminist research. In the following sections, I thus focus on the methodological and theoretical foundations laid by them in order to revive realist approaches in Political Geography.

Mackinder's Geopolitics
At the dawn of the twentieth century, Halford Mackinder gave a speech at the Royal Geographical Society in London entitled *The Geographical Pivot of History* (1904). He divided the world into three zones: the pivot area or heartland, located in the centre of the Eurasian land mass; the inner crescent, a semicircle at the rim of Eurasia; and, the outer crescent, comprising the larger Eurasian islands, Africa,

the Americas and Australia.[3] The most important difference between the outer crescent and the heartland is that the former permits the movement of goods and people via open seas and navigable rivers, whereas the latter remains inaccessible to naval forces – and its inhabitants are thus limited to using land-based modes of transport instead. Those from the outer crescent rely on naval power in order to protect their trading power and routes. Their continental counterparts focus, in contrast, on land-based military forces. This geographical setting frames the struggle between continental and maritime powers, which has, according to Mackinder (1904, 1919), shaped the history of mankind thus far.

Mackinder believed that a fundamental geostrategic change could be observed in his own lifetime. What he called the 'Columbian Age' was about to end. The Columbian Age had been marked by the dominance of maritime powers due to the ease of movement across the world's waterways. From the beginning of European expansion in the fifteenth century until Mackinder's time, maritime powers had controlled the coastlines of all continents and ruled the world. Great Britain was the country that most rapidly industrialised and that was able to create a worldwide empire because of locational and physiogeographical advantages: proximity to transatlantic trade routes and the warm Gulf Stream; having natural resources close to open seas; and, rivers being available as a means of transport, opening up the interior of the country (1909). Beyond the British Isles, naval trade routes constituted the backbone of Britain's economic superiority to the rest of the world – Mackinder (1922) reasoned that the dominance of maritime powers was totally dependent upon their control of the open seas. Yet, in the early twentieth century, new means of transport – and especially the railway – now made landlocked resources accessible. The advantages of commercial shipping were vanishing. Troops could be transferred easily by land across enormous distances. Mackinder (1904, 1905, 1919) concluded that in the post-Columbian Age, continental powers would be able to make use of the tremendous resources that he expected they would find in the heartland. As a consequence, he believed that continental powers would industrialise faster than maritime powers and build stronger armies and navies, thereby eventually replacing the maritime powers as the rulers of the world.

After the First World War and the revolution in Russia, Mackinder's attention shifted to East Europe because it had become the key to containing the heartlandic powers – that is, the German Reich and, more importantly, the Soviet Union. He famously wrote that 'who rules East Europe commands the heartland[,] who rules the heartland commands the world-island [and] who rules the world-island commands the world' (1919: 150). Although Mackinder capitalised on the anti-Bolshevik sentiment of this time in order to stress the necessity of applying the strategies he suggested, his reasoning was based on locational and physiogeographical grounds.

---

3   In his book *Democratic Ideals and Reality* (1919), Mackinder briefly elaborated on Africa as the southern heartland with it having structural patterns similar to those of the northern heartland: its scenery is marked by wide, open grasslands and local people depend on animals for transport.

It did not matter whether the German Reich or the USSR longed for continental hegemony – what was important was the heartland and its geography. Thirty-four years later, Mackinder re-emphasised the insurmountable defensive advantage of the heartland, labelling it 'the greatest natural fortress on Earth' (1943: 601). Further to that, he elaborated on a maritime alliance consisting of Britain as 'a Malta on a grander scale' (1943: 601), France as the European bridgehead and Canada and the US as the industrial reserve and strategic depth of this alliance. He added to his geopolitical model a 'mantle of vacancies', consisting of African and Asian deserts as well as the subarctic zones of Eurasia and North America. He suggested that these areas formed a natural buffer between the continental and maritime blocs.

The cornerstone of Mackinder's Geopolitics is the assumption that 'geographical features govern or, at least, guide history' (1890: 78). For him, geography was a science about the effects of nature on mankind. He emphasised that the relationship between mankind and nature can only be understood by taking into consideration how technology allows the former to interact with the latter (1887, 1890). Nature establishes a framework for human action and mankind's reshaping of nature. Technology indicates the extent to which nature can be reshaped but nature always guides human behaviour by throwing up forces to be overcome and opportunities to be taken; it makes some courses of action rational. This does not mean, however, that nature mechanistically dictates the decisions taken by humans. Using Mackinder's own words, 'man and not nature initiates, but nature in large measure controls' (1904: 422).

Knowledge about geographical conditions hence enables geographers to predict which strategies, for example in foreign policy, will be successful. Nongeographical variables do play a certain role in shaping the courses of human action, but they are nevertheless not the object of analysis in the studies carried out by geographers. Mackinder accordingly declared that 'my concern is with the general physical control [of social processes]' (1904: 422). This was also the premise of his speech *On the Scope and Methods of Geography* (1887). He argued therein that geographers had to explain the environment first and, based on this, ask how it affects mankind. This means that physiogeographical research provides information on the independent variables that are relevant to Human Geography, including Geopolitics.

Based on these theoretical fundaments, Mackinder (1890) proposed an analytical scheme or sequence of three steps. First, humans have certain needs and interests. They are taken as given. Affluent people living in Europe in the Middle Ages, for example, wanted to purchase silk from China. They longed for a transport route from China to Europe. Second, nature sets a framework of possible options. It determines what is feasible and rational. Geographers draw conclusions by analysing this independent variable. Third, technology, being an intervening variable, influences the frame provided by nature.

For instance, the only available means of transport from China to Europe in the Middle Ages were caravans, which passed through Central Asia and the

Middle East. People living in certain topographically favoured places – mostly natural harbours and oases along the transport route – thus attained power and wealth because of the interplay between human needs, the frame set by nature and available technologies. When technological progress made transport by ship around Africa a more efficient option, the interaction between mankind and nature changed. Small islands and coastal trading stations positioned along the new sea lane to the Far East became crucial. The wealth and power of Italian merchants and Middle Eastern rulers now waned. The history of the Old World has, accordingly, to be told as the evolving history of the trade routes between Europe and the Far East. What matters to world history is the Sahara as a natural barrier, the Red Sea as a transport route and the technological advances in navigation that made the expeditions of Portuguese and Spanish sailors possible (1900a, 1900b).

Spykman's Geopolitics
Almost identically to Mackinder, Nicholas Spykman (1942, 1944) divided the world into three zones: the heartland, its rimland and the maritime world. Comparing the Heartland Theory and the Rimland Theory, a fact that is often overlooked is that Spykman's rimland states are able to act independently. Mackinder's world, on the other hand, is shaped by the eternal struggle between continental and maritime powers; he only hinted at states from the inner crescent being a third category of actors in his article *The Round World and the Winning of Peace* (1943). Spykman (1942, 1944) contrariwise suggested a shifting pattern of great power rivalry: continental and maritime powers sometimes fight over the rimland but also work together at other times in order to counter emerging rimland powers. Spykman drafted his geopolitical theory during the Second World War, and accordingly regarded the German Reich and Japan as enemies of the US. Yet, his thoughts could easily also be applied to the Cold War era. Already in 1942, he declared that Soviet control from the Urals to the North Sea was no better than German control from the North Sea to the Urals, indicating that constant geographical factors matter – and not fluctuating politics.

His central geostrategic advice was that the defence of the US had to begin beyond the Americas. In contrast to Mackinder, Spykman thought that the containment of the heartland was sufficient to secure the maritime world. He rephrased Mackinder's dictum, arguing that 'who controls the rimland rules Eurasia [and] who rules Eurasia controls the destinies of the world' (1944: 43). The balance of power in Eurasia had to be preserved by the US to prevent one power from gaining control of the heartland, maritime Europe and the Far East. For the containment of the heartland, the great powers located just beyond the edge of the rimland, Britain and Japan, were long-term geostrategic partners of the US. Projecting power from Britain and Japan to the rimland, the US should make use of the latter as an intermediate region and buffer against the USSR – an idea that matched the containment policy of the Truman administration even better than Mackinder's Heartland Theory did.

Spykman's methodology is almost identical to the one applied by Mackinder. He began his analyses with the location of a state, reasoning that 'it is the geographic location of a country and its relations to centers of military power that define its problem[s] of security' (1942: 447). Topography was essential for him. Location, transport infrastructure and the accessibility of resources were to Spykman (1938b) indicators for the continental or maritime orientation of a state.[4] The fact that he took into consideration transport infrastructure and trade orientation reveals that for him Classical Geopolitics was not strictly limited to physiogeographical conditions. Many of its proponents referred to what one may call manmade structures in geographical space. Of course, these structures were seen as determined by nature; reading Spykman's book *America's Strategy in World Politics* (1942), however, one can hardly miss the dominance of economic geography over physical geography.

Sticking to the principles of Classical Geopolitics, Spykman regarded the ability of mankind to overcome natural conditions as very limited: 'Since the Red Sea parted for Moses and the sun obligingly paused for Joshua, the human will has been unable to recapture the control over topography and climate exhibited by those forceful gentlemen' (1938a: 28). In this sense, he coined the better-known phrase 'ministers come and go, even dictators die, but mountain ranges stand unperturbed' (1942: 41). What these two paradigmatic statements mean is that Geopolitics is not about the ebb and flow of politics. Its concern, rather, is the constant geographical conditions that exist as independent variables. From the viewpoint of Geopolitics, geographical conditions set a general frame for politics and, hence, explain long-term patterns of behaviour in international relations. There is variation within this often narrow frame, fluctuations which have to be explained by nongeographical factors. This is why Mackinder adapted his Heartland Theory several times and why it is not identical to the Rimland Theory.

In this sense, Spykman (1938a) qualified the relevance of topography. It is crucial for the coherence of a state. Mountains, which form a natural barrier, and navigable rivers, which serve as lines of communication and transport, demonstrate this. Yet, technological progress – for example the invention of steamboats – changes the interaction of mankind with nature. It may turn a natural barrier into a means of transport. In other words, Spykman's work was guided by the assumption that geographical conditions need to be seen within their specific context if they are to explain social phenomena. Understanding that specific context, wherein geographical factors are crucial, requires the inclusion of nongeographical factors because they reveal how geographical conditions guide economics and politics.

Spykman not only derived the aforementioned general patterns of world politics from geographical factors, he also showed how location and physical geography influence the expansion of states. Geography sometimes provides favourable

---

4   Later, Meining (1956) combined the question of a continental or maritime orientation with the Rimland Theory, suggesting that rimland states were either inward-looking towards the heartland or outward-looking towards the maritime world.

conditions for building lines of communication and transport, for example along navigable rivers. Making use of these geographical opportunities is rational, so is expansion into areas that possess vast natural resources. Some strategies of expansion – for instance circumferential control of large bodies of water – are sensible and geographically induced too (Spykman and Rollins 1939b). Briefly, the expansion of states follows what Spykman and Rollins called the 'ease of movement' (1939a: 392). Spykman (1938a, 1938b) accordingly pointed out that the topography of ancient Greece made most Greek city-states become maritime powers and hegemons in the eastern Mediterranean because, after having gained the control of their small valley, they would build ships for further expansion. This geography-induced approach brought about a strategic advantage over rival powers. More generally, landlocked states, island states and states that possess land and sea borders pursue different foreign policy strategies – most apparent in the realm of national defence – because of these geographical factors (1938b). From an analytical perspective, geographical conditions hence become a signpost to international politics. If one understands the political implications of geographical conditions, one will be able to explain and predict the forms that international relations will take.

Fairgrieve's Geopolitics
Mackinder and Spkyman are the best-known proponents of Classical Geopolitics, also because the Heartland Theory and the Rimland Theory could easily be applied to international politics in the twentieth century. James Fairgrieve is, meanwhile, less famous. His main work *Geography and World Power* (1917), first published in 1915, does, however, represent a good example of geopolitical thinking. Fairgrieve sought to explain the course of history by its geographical conditions. He distinguished between the 'drama of world history' – meaning economic and political developments – and the 'stage of world history' – that is, geography or nature. The red line that characterises his argumentation is that the stage determines the drama. It is crucial to recognise that he did not have in mind a direct causal relationship between economic and political developments on the one side and nature on the other when he wrote about the stage controlling the drama. Geographical factors do not necessarily spur human action, because they cannot force people to act in the same way that one person can make another do something. Human beings are, hence, not compelled to do anything just because of nature's mere existence.

However, Fairgrieve showed that nature does affect the development of societies. First of all, human action is only possible within the limits set by nature – if there had not been any coal in England the country would not have industrialised so early. What is more, nature provides certain opportunities – thus making certain courses of action probable. The presence of coal did not control the English in the sense that it forced them to industrialise their country. It, rather, provided an opportunity – and because the English chose to do what had to be considered rational in their geographical context, they consequently advanced from a preindustrial to an industrial society.[5]

Aside from *Geography and World Power*, Fairgrieve did not publish any major scientific works. He did, however, co-author six textbooks for schoolchildren. They were also guided by the assumption that knowledge about location and physical geography enables us to explain social phenomena. For instance, he argued that the location of essential resources, such as water, explained where permanent settlements are to be found, unless technological progress had allowed for the construction of pipelines and reservoirs. Even then, physical geography still matters because reservoirs are built wherever geomorphology dictates is suitable terrain (Fairgrieve and Young 1956). There is a certain geodeterminism in this reasoning. Geographical factors guide history by making some courses of action rational and hence more likely to occur than others: 'men's acts are conditioned by their surroundings', as Fairgrieve put it (1917: 22). He did not, though, call into question whether human action necessarily follows what is rational according to geographical conditions. Together with Young (1956), he pointed out, for example, that the railway line from London to Bradford entered the latter city's main station in the mid-twentieth century coming from the north, even though London is located south of Bradford. The authors claimed this was due to the presence of a chain of hills south of Bradford that made a direct connection very difficult to achieve.

Fairgrieve incorporated intervening variables into his reasoning. Following the narration he developed in *Geography and World Power* (1917), geographical factors have to be seen in interaction with human capabilities and needs. The guiding impact of geographical conditions on history is, therefore, not static. For instance, trade between Europe and the Far East was diverted to the sea lanes around Africa, and the previously important Arab intermediaries lost their economic relevance to Europe in the sixteenth century. The reason for this was technological progress in shipbuilding and navigation. This means that many geographical conditions are only important within a specific technological – hence temporal – frame: the US rose to the level of a world power in the nineteenth century because coal constituted the essential basis of national power within the technological framework of the Industrial Revolution. Before the Industrial Revolution, the coal of the US did not matter. What is more, Fairgrieve took into consideration manmade geography. Together with Young (1956), he argued that the English city of Birmingham received water from reservoirs in Wales not only because precipitation in some parts of that country is higher and its landscape offers better geomorphological conditions for the building of reservoirs. The pollution caused by industries in Birmingham in the first half of the twentieth century also made it unsafe to drink local water.

---

5   Barrows (1922) therefore suggested speaking of a human adjustment to nature, instead of nature's control over mankind.

All adherents of Classical Geopolitics share the assumption that humans do what is rational according to their geographical surroundings. Fairgrieve (1917) went further than Mackinder and Spykman in this regard. He argued, for example, that the topography of Italy induced both the very idea and the practice of constructing roads in order to facilitate travel in the time of the Roman Empire. It is plausible to argue that the Romans built roads because the topography of Italy provided conditions favourable to this mode of transport. Yet, Fairgrieve also reasoned that geographical conditions directly accounted for the course of history 'by reacting on the mind [of human beings] and causing it to choose courses of action' (1917: 66). He found that it was 'natural that people who inhabited the Nile Valley should have learned how energy might be saved by means of irrigation', because geography provided a setting with fertile soil and abundant water (1917: 31).

It definitely makes sense to argue that geography provided certain opportunities in these cases, ones that made particular developments quite likely to occur. One should, however, be cautious about drawing conclusions about the human mind. This line of reasoning led Fairgrieve to the odd notion of a geographically formed mentality amongst particular peoples, which is a recurrent theme in *Geography and World Power*. Phoenician traders, for instance, 'learned to be brave [because of their] constant voyaging over wild seas', and were therefore a freedom-loving people who were able to withstand the aggression of others (1917: 49). Fairgrieve considered people from the Eurasian steppes, meanwhile, to be courageous and willing to put collective needs ahead of individual ones, because geographical stimuli enforced such characteristics on them – without these traits they would not have survived in the harsh climate of the steppes. Here, geographical determinism takes on a social Darwinist tinge.

There are several ways to tackle Fairgrieve's reasoning on how geographical conditions seemingly shape the human mind and way of thinking. First, the approach that I seek to develop here, Realist Geopolitics, is less ambitious than Fairgrieve's version of Geopolitics was. It is not meant to explain anything related to the human mind and way of thinking. Second, most geographers lack the necessary methodological and theoretical knowledge to study how the human mind reacts to material stimuli. Geographers are not psychologists. Third, Fairgrieve's reasoning on the human mind and mentality is not fully compatible with his own conceptual statements. Certain courses of action – the ones that fit with the geographical setting – are more probable than others. The geographical setting does, however, not sufficiently explain social phenomena on its own. Fairgrieve accordingly recognised that nature controls 'history more or less directly by making one course more possible than another' (1917: 53).

Towards Realist Geopolitics

Ontology, epistemology and the constructivist agenda
As shown in the preceding sections, Classical Geopolitics is based on a very particular epistemology. Its ontology differs from that of today's mainstream

Political Geography too. Spykman claimed to study the most enduring factors in the foreign policy of states. Mackinder and Fairgrieve were convinced that they could explain the history of mankind by geographical context. These claims reveal two things. First, adherents of Classical Geopolitics considered themselves able to explain the very fundaments of international relations. Second, they thought that they could do this objectively, from a Cartesian point of view. What interested scholars of Classical Geopolitics, therefore, were geographical factors – specifically, the way that they exist 'out there'.

Present-day Political Geography, on the other hand, is dominated by the conviction that geographical factors do not (only) matter in the way that they exist out there. What (also) matters with regard to geographical factors is, rather, the way that they exist in our minds. Early post-Mackinder geographers already called for the incorporation of a subjective perspective into the analysis of the impact of nature on mankind (Kristof 1960). Moderate adherents of current constructivist approaches argue that perceptions, interpretations and representations interact with a de facto existing reality. They account jointly for human action (Lacoste 1993). Taylor and Flint (2000) accordingly propose the concept of 'geopolitical codes', which constitute 'the operating code of a government's foreign policy that evaluates places beyond its boundaries' (2000: 371). Such geopolitical codes furthermore include the identification of partners, enemies and threats as well as the elaboration of strategies and their justification.

From this perspective, practical geopolitics is the way that 'elites make sense of the world in order to respond [to] or create events in [a way to] their state's advantage' (Taylor 1993: 36). Agnew and Corbridge (1995) pursue a comparable but much broader approach. They conceptualise 'geopolitical orders' as systems of governance that include a definition of actors and principles of interaction, arguing that geopolitical research should be about how key actors divide geographical space and ascribe values to distinct territories because these values are the fundament of geopolitical practice. Adding another example, Lacoste (1993) studies violent conflicts from the perspective of 'representations of space' – in other words, the stories told about particular areas. As a phenomenon, they constitute each side's claim to a disputed area. As an analytical means, they capture how the warring parties see and depict their territorial claim and their rivalry. Combining constructivist and materialist perspectives, Lacoste seeks to explain how material geography has throughout history been transformed into representations of space.

Some constructivists go much further, claiming that geopolitical concepts, theories and practices result from subjective understandings of physical reality, which include the projection of cultural and political assumptions. Geopolitical concepts, theories and practices cannot be understood without taking into consideration their author's spatiotemporal context (Ó Tuathail 1996, 1999; Ó Tuathail and Dalby 1998). Doing this leads to the *re*construction of Geopolitics and shifts the analytical focus from a structural to an actor-specific level. Ó Tuathail (1992), for instance, shows how much the Heartland Theory reflects Mackinder's own political socialisation into the ethos of late Victorian Britain.[6] Going beyond mere reconstruction, many constructivists see academic Geopolitics as a tool for legitimising certain policies instead of scientifically analysing them (Lacoste 1976; Ó Tuathail and Agnew 1992). Negating the existence of one reality – or at least of our ability to grasp this one reality in an intersubjective way – they are convinced that the adherents of Geopolitics are actually creating the reality that they claim to be analysing objectively (Ó Tuathail 1996).

The discourse analyses carried out by constructivists thus aim at the *de*construction of geopolitical concepts, theories and practices in order to reveal a presumed ideological content – meaning the interests and power structures underlying them. For instance, Agnew (1983) reveals that US exceptionalism is a socially constructed story about the US and its role in the world. It justifies and even induces certain policies. Yet, many adherents of Critical Geopolitics see nothing except for ideology in Geopolitics. Dalby describes it as 'an ideological exercise which [...] pits geographically defined political organisations against one another' (1990: 39). He does not investigate whether it was the intention of Mackinder, Spykman and others to advance ideologies, as his statements suggests. What is more, adherents of Critical Geopolitics long to play an emancipatory role, supporting the people (and states) supposedly oppressed by those who dominate the geopolitical discourse. Still, they implicitly promote alternative geopolitical interpretations in the process of deconstruction. This is inevitable; it is also contradictory to the fundaments of Critical Geopolitics.

In response to the critique advanced by constructivists, Deudney (1997, 1999) reasons that geography possesses a materiality – or a physical reality – that cannot be explained as a mere social construct. The opportunities and constraints that Fairgrieve, Mackinder and Spykman addressed are due to location and physical geography. They do not originate in the perceptions and interpretations of powerful politicians or of these scholars – they exist independently from them. Those who reject that geographical conditions exist regardless of social constructs ignore the most fundamental frame for human action. As Gray puts it, 'geography [...] is inescapable' (1999: 163). Polemically but fittingly, he adds that social constructs are 'ever apt to be trumped by what needs recognition as "objective geography". [...] Thinking warm thoughts of home could not protect thinly-clad German soldiers in Russia [in January 1943] against frostbite' (1999: 164). Rational action must, therefore, refer to objectively given geographical conditions. Disregarding objectively given geographical conditions sometimes leads to catastrophe.

Deudney (1997) uses the term 'natural–social science' for theories that are based on these considerations. For him, Geopolitics is a set of functionalist–materialist theories about how nature shapes social outcomes: variations in nature cause variations in social outcomes. Kristof accordingly defines Geopolitics as 'politics

---

6   This reconstruction of the Heartland Theory is not wholly new: a long time before constructivism emerged, Weigert (1949) stressed how much Mackinder's thinking had been influenced by him being a citizen of the British Empire.

geographically interpreted or analysed for its geographical content' (1960: 34, 36). It generates geographical explanations for political phenomena. Geographical factors serve as the independent variable and politics as the dependent one.

Hypotheses about the impact of geographical factors on regional powers
Analysing geopolitics from a natural–social scientific viewpoint does not negate that social outcomes are influenced by nonmaterial factors. Still, Realist Geopolitics limits the analysis to the frame that material structures in geographical space create for economics and politics. The idea behind this approach is that these structures delimit a realm of options in economics and politics that can be realised. Those who take decisions related to economic and political matters may choose between various available options within this realm. Their choice is, however, limited by the fixed boundaries of that realm of feasibility. Geographical factors thus set these boundaries; they dictate what is feasible.

A simple example makes this clear: a South African car manufacturer does not have to use the port of Durban for shipping the cars that have been assembled in their plant in KwaZulu-Natal, they can also use the port of Maputo, in Mozambique. Material structures in geographical space – in this case transport infrastructure – give rise to these two options. Many other alternatives – for instance shipping via the port of Luanda, Angola – are not feasible because of adverse geographical conditions, an insufficient transport infrastructure to be precise. Examining material structures in geographical space thus helps to delimit the number of possible choices. Moreover, geographical factors indicate that Durban is usually a better choice than Maputo for various reasons, first of all distance. Choosing Durban instead of Maputo is not forced on the car manufacturer though. Such a course of action is only rendered more likely. Taking into consideration nongeographical factors, Maputo is sometimes a better choice than Durban – for instance if workers at the port of Durban are on strike. With regard to the port of Luanda, nongeographical factors are irrelevant. A strike in Durban cannot make the car manufacturer ship their cars via Luanda, because material structures in geographical space prevent them from pursuing such a course of action.

The idea that geographical conditions create a realm of feasibility that not only makes certain options possible and others impossible but also indicates which of the former are most likely to be taken up leads me to two hypotheses that will be tested for South Africa's regional relations:

H1 Location and physical geography set a frame that guides economics and politics. The patterns of expansion of regional powers – meaning the directions in which they focus their crossborder influence – result from location and physical geography.

H2 Manmade material structures in geographical space that cannot be altered in the short term – like railway lines – guide economics and politics in a way similar to how naturally given structures – such as mountain ranges – do.

Of course, one also has to consider intervening variables when analysing the interplay of geographical conditions and social outcomes. Sprout and Sprout (1965) accordingly distinguish between 'environmental determinism' and 'free-will environmentalism'. Adherents of the latter recognise that nature influences human action but also that the latter is deliberate, meaning that irrational action – which disregards natural conditions – may occur. Spykman (1938b) provided an example for free-will environmentalism: Britain's decision to focus on maritime power in the eighteenth and nineteenth centuries was successful because the physiogeographical conditions of its coastlines favoured such a strategy. France's efforts to build a navy along it northern coast were, contrariwise, hampered by an unfavourable topography. Geographical conditions eventually trumped the ill-suited strategy of the French. Classical Geopolitics is unable, however, to explain why this strategy even occurred in the first place. Moreover, one may plausibly argue that the French would actually have been successful in their naval build-up if they had possessed better means to overcome the unfavourable topography of their northern coastline.

Reflecting these crucial notions, I recognise that geographical limits may be overcome, that courses of action that are ill-adapted to the geographical conditions at hand may be chosen – provided that those who make this decision possess sufficient capacities to successfully withstand the pressure that is exerted by geographical conditions in the face of their choice. With regard to regional powers, this means that their economics and politics are tied to a geographical frame – but they will be able to overcome the limitations set by this frame, at least partly, if they possess and use relevant capacities. I cover such courses of action – or, put another way, the idea that regional powers shape geography in a potentially irrational way – with a third hypothesis:

H3 The sphere of influence of a regional power reflects geographical conditions, meaning that the range of its influence is delimited by geographical forces. Geographical limitations will be partly overcome if the regional power invests disproportionately in the expansion of its influence.

Contemporary Physiocratic Approaches

Geography and strategic studies
Even though few geographers pursue realist geopolitical research today, thinking in the tradition of Classical Geopolitics remains popular in strategic studies – being usually undertaken by policy advisers. The defining criterion for the policy-oriented branch of Geopolitics is the spatialisation of politics, meaning that political strategies are derived from spatial configurations of power – or, at least, they are related to them. Physical geography plays a marginal role in such approaches. Sometimes, it is completely neglected. Geopolitical policy advice is moreover semiscientific; relatively plausible argumentations lack a sophisticated

methodology, as well as the hypotheses that would structure independent, intervening and dependent variables.

During the Cold War, Secretary of State Henry Kissinger and National Security Adviser Zbigniew Brzezinski were the most prominent representatives of geopolitical policy advice. Kissinger reintroduced the term geopolitics into the wider debate on international relations. He conceptualised the discipline as being a method of analysis that could be directed against policies based on idealism or ideology. Practical geopolitics for Kissinger (1979) was the pursuit of national interests in a world functioning according to the principles of a necessary balance of power. Brzezinski (1986) shared this understanding of world politics. In contrast to adherents of Classical Geopolitics, he believed that the confrontation between the USSR, the leading continental power, and the US, the leading maritime power, resulted from nongeographical factors. In his post-Cold War publications, meanwhile, Brzezinski (1997) has since instead come to see world politics as being based on the strategic characteristics of supremely important regions, such as Central Asia and the Middle East.

The most prominent present-day scholar who stands in the tradition of Brzezinski and Kissinger is Robert Kaplan, who is closer in ethos to Classical Geopolitics. For example, he wrote in an article published in the *Wall Street Journal* on 7 September 2012 that China possesses such tremendous power potentialities because it combines the advantages of a continental and a maritime power; the People's Republic benefits from its long and temperate coastline with plenty of natural harbours close to the main shipping lanes of the Pacific Ocean. It also controls the vast resources of its heartlandic hinterland. The objective of Kaplan's most recent book, *The Revenge of Geography* (2012), is to show that geography – understood as physical reality – matters, and how so. He reasons, for instance, that the permanent threat of invasion – resulting from the location between powerful empires and the absence of natural borders – accounts for the long history of exceptionally oppressive dictatorships in Iraq because only strong dictators – from the Babylonian era to the Saddam Hussein years – were able to defend the country.

On the level of day-to-day policy advice, Geopolitics goes hand-in-hand with political-scientific realism. Thinking geopolitically means recognising 'the most blunt, uncomfortable, and deterministic of truths: those of geography', as Kaplan puts it (2012: 28). Yet, geographical factors do not impose a specific foreign policy strategy on state leaders. They only determine which strategies are sound. Consequently Kaplan calls for decision makers to concentrate on geographical realities, so as to advance appropriate policies.

Except for Kaplan and Cohen, whose work I address below, there are only two noteworthy scholars who have recently sought to apply the logic of Classical Geopolitics to present-day social phenomena. Gray (1988, 1991) connects foreign policy strategies to geographical factors, arguing that geography offers constraints and opportunities vis-à-vis every state's foreign policy choices. The interaction of states with these constraints and opportunities impacts geopolitical orientations, or 'strategic cultures'. In Gray's words, 'the political behavior of a country is the reflection of that country's history; and that country's history is in great part (though certainly not entirely) the product of its geographical setting' (1988: 43). Hence, we can understand chosen strategies vis-à-vis defence and foreign policy by analysing the interaction between the states in question and their geographical surroundings, because geographical factors account for strategic cultures. Geographical conditions do not dictate strategic cultures but the geographical setting constitutes a stage – though not a script – that suggests the plot and influences the characters of the play. In other words, there are intervening variables in play – sadly, though, Gray (1996) does not elaborate on them.

The other noteworthy present-day scholar who stands in the tradition of Classical Geopolitics is Jakub Grygiel. For him (2006), Geopolitics is about the externality of a state, an objective reality that each one faces. Depending upon which technologies predominate, certain resources – and, hence, certain places – become more important than others, as exemplified by the shift from coal- to oil-fired engines in the early twentieth century and the resulting key strategic role of sites of oil extraction from that point on. The foreign policy choices that statesmen make in response to this technology-dependent relevance of geographical conditions are what Grygiel defines as 'geostrategies'. From an analytical perspective, the most important feature of Grygiel's approach is that the three levels – geographical conditions, their technology-dependent relevance and geostrategy – are interrelated but nevertheless do not determine one another. The relevance of geographical conditions varies with technological progress. Ideological motives may interfere with geostrategies. Keeping a fundamental geopolitical position, Grygiel argues that only those geostrategies that are aligned with geographical conditions are rational. If strategies are not adapted to them, they will most likely fail and even put the survival of the state in question at risk. Sometimes, though, geographical conditions do not allow adequate geostrategies to be adopted. Grygiel explains the decline of the city-state of Venice in the Late Middle Ages as a consequence of such a mismatch.

Geography and anthropological studies
Two books written by the US anthropologist and geographer Jared Diamond elaborate on how physiogeographical factors can explain the long-term trajectories of societies. In *Collapse* (2005), Diamond analyses the decline of societies as a consequence of environmental damage. For instance, both natural climate change and self-inflicted environmental damage caused the Norse civilisation in Greenland to cease to exist in the fifteenth century. Having cut down almost all available trees, they were deprived of timber for construction. They also lost the ability to process agricultural products and iron ore because of a lack of firewood. Soil erosion became intense given the absence of protection from trees. The Norse could, thus, not run their farms anymore. Yet, there is more to the collapse of the Norse civilisation in Greenland than environmental change. Whilst the Norse did not adapt to the changing environment, the Inuit learnt to cope with it. They

built igloos instead of wooden houses, heated their homes by burning seal and whale blubber instead of timber and stretched sealskins over their kayaks instead of cutting down trees to build boats. The seal and whale hunting tactics of the Inuit were more efficient than those of the Norse. This means that there is an intervening social variable in the causal relation of environmental damage and societal decline: the capability of societies to adapt to environmental change.

From an epistemological perspective, *Collapse* is marked by its calling on a mixture of natural and social factors to explain why some societies coped with environmental damage whilst others did not. Diamond reasons that not only the degree of environmental damage but also the place-specific fragility and resilience of the environment, as well as natural climate change, have to be analysed. He also takes into consideration a society's relations with its neighbours and the impact of economic, political and social institutions as well as cultural values on chosen responses to environmental damage.

His approach is holistic. Environmental damage is conceptualised as a nonsocial force that requires a social reaction. Regarding the aforementioned case of the Norse in Greenland, Diamond describes Norse society as economically and organisationally weakened when it had to react to environmental damage. Trade with Europe was declining because the Crusaders had made African and Indian ivory accessible, causing severe competition for Greenland's main export good. Furthermore, a plague epidemic reduced the population of Norway by half in the mid-fourteenth century. As a consequence, the Greenland Norse's links to Europe were almost completely severed. The last bishop on Greenland, an essential authority figure in Norse society, died around 1378. He was not replaced by a new bishop sent from Norway. Diamond suggests that the Norse chiefs and remaining church officials were eventually unable to maintain public order given the increasing pressure put on them by environmental scarcity. This case exemplifies how environmental factors only reveal the ultimate reasons for the failure of civilisations – that is, the long-term factors behind a society's slow decline. Proximate reasons, which give the final blow to a weakened society, are beyond Diamond's conceptual framework.

In *Guns, Germs, and Steel* (2003), Diamond seeks to explain why some societies have developed faster than others, or, more precisely, why Europeans – being economically, militarily and politically superior to peoples from other continents – would conquer practically the entire world from the fifteenth century onwards. Spanish conquistador Francisco Pizarro and 168 soldiers were, accordingly, able to capture Atahualpa, the emperor of the Inca, beat Inca armies of tens of thousands of warriors in five consecutive battles and suppress two later rebellions because they possessed guns, horses and superior body armour. The Spanish invaded the lands of the Inca in the first place because innovations in navigation had enabled the former to cross the Atlantic. The Inca did not possess the means to expand in such a way. Again, Diamond seeks to explain the long-term causes behind these proximate reasons. His core point is thus that 'history followed different courses for different peoples because of differences among peoples' environments' (2003: 25).

In other words, nature explains history. Diamond identifies three major natural factors that have shaped human history. First, the various continents are marked by tremendous differences in the animal species and wild plants that are available for domestication. Peoples living in areas with favourable conditions in this regard could produce a surplus of food and feed nonfood-producing specialists – artisans, politicians and soldiers.

Second, since people usually learn from each other when they meet, by exchanging technologies for example, overcoming physiogeographical barriers to movement are essential for progress in civilisation. The most important point that Diamond makes about geographical obstacles to movement is that Africa and the Americas are marked by a long north-to-south extension, whereas Eurasia is dominated by an east-to-west axis. For domesticated animals and crops to spread over a continent, a predominant east-to-west axis is favourable. Its presence indicates that much of the same continent possesses roughly comparable climatic conditions, such as length of days and seasonality. Because of roughly comparable climatic conditions in between, domesticated animals and crops spread, for example, from the Fertile Crescent to Europe and India – whereas the areas of early food production in the Andes and Mesoamerica did not manage to connect up with each other.

Third, size matters in terms of territory and population. Large continents tend to possess a more substantial population size – meaning more potential inventors, more competing societies and more interaction. Population growth induced by these factors also exerts significant pressure on societies to organise in a more rational way, starting an autocatalytic cycle of progress in which population growth and civilisational advances reinforce each other. Coming back to the issue of the Inca and the Spanish, Diamond reveals that the peoples of the Americas made essential civilisational strides later than their European counterparts did, or even never at all, because of the former's less favourable geographical surroundings.

Geography and economic studies
Several publications by Jeffrey Sachs and his colleagues (1998, 1999, 2000) – most importantly John Gallup, Andrew Mellinger and Andrew Warner – are based on the same core idea that is found in Diamond's research: environmental or geographical conditions are essential for the performance of societies. Correlating differences in income and income growth on the national level with location and physical geography, they find that almost all tropical countries are financially poor. Prosperity is concentrated instead in areas of mid to high latitude. Coastal countries do better than landlocked ones. Multiplying gross domestic product per capita with population density, they furthermore show that the coastal and temperate zones of the Northern Hemisphere possess the highest economic densities in the world: those parts of temperate East Asia, North America and Western Europe that lie within 100 kilometres of the coast only account for 3 per cent of the world's

inhabited land but for 13 per cent of the global population and for 32 per cent of the global gross domestic product vis-à-vis purchasing power parity.

Gallup, Sachs and Mellinger (1998) explain this correlation by arguing that the tropical climate reduces economic growth through the generation of low agricultural productivity and a high disease burden. Landlocked countries, meanwhile, suffer from high transport costs (Radelet and Sachs 1998). The striking contrast between coast and hinterland also applies to the subnational level and to the First World, as Rappaport and Sachs (2003) show for the US. In this sense, geographical factors dictate the economic fate of each country.

Another posited link between geographical conditions and the level of development is the presence or not of malaria. Countries with high rates of this disease achieve only 30 per cent of the income level of malaria-free countries. Factors such as geographical isolation, tropical location and colonial history are controlled for in this calculation. Countries that suffer from the prevalence of malaria also grow slower; again, this is calculated with intervening factors such as initial income level or life expectancy being controlled for. The most important argument that Gallup and Sachs (2000) advance in this regard is that ecological conditions account for the distribution and intensity of malaria. They rule out as an explanation poor hygiene and inadequate medical services, which are due instead to poverty and thus explain why poor countries also suffer from diseases such as cholera and diarrhoea. Moreover, malaria control under supervised conditions has failed in Africa – which also suggests that malaria would not be eradicated even if African countries were richer. Since physical geography accounts for malaria, which in turn reduces economic and income growth, it is thus the former that is the ultimate cause of poor economic performance.

Methodologically, the value of the publications by Gallup, Sachs and Mellinger lies in their verification of a macrocorrelation – that geographical conditions account for economic performance – by the analysis of various microcorrelations. The latter reflect the argumentation that Gallup, Sachs and Mellinger provide in order to explain their macrocorrelation; geographical conditions in certain instances hamper economic development because of the climatic conditions that hinder agriculture and favour certain diseases, with being landlocked also constituting a negative influence. Proving the veracity of the microcorrelations summarised above makes plausible the macrocorrelation: if the spread of malaria only results from the climate of the tropics and if malaria-infested countries suffer from below-average economic growth rates, it is indeed quite convincing to argue that unfavourable geographical conditions hamper economic development.

Still, Sachs and his colleagues acknowledge that the impact of geographical factors is also conditioned by political choices. For instance, politicians can decide to upgrade their state's transport infrastructure and facilitate greater crossborder movement. Assessing the growth prospects for sub-Saharan Africa, Sachs and Warner (1997a), accordingly, make reference not only to access to the sea and the tropical climate but also to economic policies and market liberalisation. Given that geographical factors play a major role in economic processes, it is clearly essential not to neglect them.

In other publications, Sachs and Warner (1997b, 1999, 2001) reveal the negative effects of seemingly favourable geographical conditions – resource abundance to be precise. A high percentage of primary commodities going to the export market correlates with below-average economic growth rates – there is virtually no overlap between the group of resource-rich countries and the group of high-growth ones. Assuming that one accepts the argument that resource abundance has a negative impact on economic growth, Venezuela's gross domestic product per capita would have been 14 per cent higher in 1990 as compared to 1965 if it had not possessed any natural resources. The challenging part of showing that resource abundance causes poor economic performance is filling in the gap that exists between the independent and the dependent variable – that is, proving that the observed correlation constitutes a causal relation. Sachs and Warner present various likely explanations for the poor performance of resource-rich economies, meaning that they split the macrocorrelation into microcorrelations; resource-rich countries are prone to develop inefficient state bureaucracies and suffer from other features of bad governance such as corruption and rent-seeking behaviour by elites. They usually abstain from market-oriented policies, relying instead on state-centred developmentalism. The shocks in global primary commodity prices strongly affect resource-rich countries, in particular because they tend to concentrate on one primary commodity. Sachs and Warner then provide statistical evidence that strengthens the credibility of these explanations.

There is, however, a major intervening variable in the causal relationship between resource abundance and economic performance. The nontraded sector – that is, goods that are bound to one place and cannot be exported – benefits from resource booms because positive surges in wealth make people spend more on nontraded goods, in both relative and absolute terms. Sachs and Warner (1999) reason that resource booms will trigger economic growth if the nontraded sector is marked by increasing returns to scale, which result from intermediate goods being produced with decreasing average costs. The more a sector that uses intermediate goods grows, the more the average production costs of those intermediate goods decrease and the more competitive the entire sector thus becomes. This is why England, Germany and the US – countries that all experienced resource booms in the nineteenth century – industrialised. Advances in transport and refrigeration know-how led to higher productivity and better terms of trade for primary commodities. However, if the traded sector is marked by increasing returns, the boom will draw capital out of the increasing returns sector and slow down the entire economy. In the early twentieth century, productivity grew rapidly in manufacturing – in doing so favouring those countries that possessed human capital rather than natural resources. This is why the Latin American resource boom, which drew capital out of the traded sector, accounted for the region's economic stagnation (Sachs 1999).

Geography and security studies I:
Resource scarcity as a root cause of violent conflict
In some contributions to security studies, geographical factors constitute a key independent variable. Homer-Dixon and his research team (1991, 1994, 1999) argue that environmental scarcity is a significant security risk because it negatively affects agricultural production, causes a general economic decline, leads to population displacements and weakens a society's institutions. The two essential aspects in the causal chain leading from environmental scarcity to violent conflict are scarcity-driven pressures and the capacity of societies to adapt to changing circumstances. A shortage of water, for instance, may lead to declining agricultural production and, hence, put societies under pressure to adapt – meaning that in order to survive they will have to use dwindling resources more efficiently or alternatively find substitutes for them. A plausible assumption made by Homer-Dixon and his colleagues is that greater environmental scarcity reduces the ability of the concerned societies to respond. If adaptation fails, violent conflicts will probably subsequently occur.

However, the idea that the causal links existing between environmental scarcity and violence are 'tight or deterministic' is rejected (1991: 78). Environmental scarcity, as the ultimate cause, and violent conflict, as the potential result, must be connected by an intervening variable that captures processes of decision making. For example, facing desertification, the elders of a nomadic tribe have to choose between various different options: they may move to a more humid area, change their habits of consumption and agricultural production or attack other tribes in order to steal their cattle. What needs to be shown is how specific features of environmental scarcity – such as a sudden drought that occurs as part of a long-term process of desertification – influence decision-making processes. Alternatively, one may reason about the individual steps that connect environmental scarcity to violent conflict. It is apparent that numerous intervening variables render convincing reasoning about such causal chains difficult. As will be shown in Chapter 2.3, there are other obstacles to proving causal relations exist between environmental scarcity as the independent variable and violent conflict as the dependent one. Homer-Dixon and his colleagues nonetheless succeed in showing that many violent conflicts can be traced back to environmental scarcity as a necessary but insufficient precondition.

The German Advisory Council on Global Change (1996) carries out research on similar issues. Its members propose taking a 'syndrome approach', in order to capture how global environmental change is caused by human interference with the natural environment. The syndromes are grouped into three categories: the inadequate use of natural resources; human–environment problems resulting from unsustainable development; and, environmental degradation caused by the inadequate disposal of waste. The council identifies nine human- and physiogeographical spheres that can be used to measure the severity of the syndromes, and also proposes a vast range of indicators for them – for instance measuring the extent of the depletion of the ozone layer for the state of the atmosphere and the level of consumption of energy and raw materials for the economic sphere. The precise identification of dependent and independent variables is not an objective of the council. Its experts seek to capture the linkages between all factors that contribute to a certain phenomenon or syndrome so that they can predict whether and how the concerned societies will be able to prevent, fix and adapt to it. The capacities of societies to react to environmental change and disasters play a crucial role in mitigating the extent of their vulnerability – marginalised people in poor countries are usually the most vulnerable.

Furthermore, the council (1998, 2007) ascribes a core role to governance, because it accounts for the ability of a society both to elaborate sound strategic responses and to carry them out. It recognises that humans rate the risks resultant from environmental change differently. Organisational structures and the degree of international connectivity are mentioned as other intervening variables. A key objective for the council is to find out under which economic, political and social circumstances environmental degradation and disasters lead to violence. Being aware of any environmental changes is considered essential for policy advice, because they indicate who is under threat – and how greatly so. Thus, the council pleads for the mapping of global environmental change as a first step and the assessing of its location-specific severity as a second one. An analysis of the capacities of the concerned social groups, societies and/or states to react constitutes a desired third step.

Shifting the focus to interstate relations, Michael Klare argues that present-day world politics is shaped by a shortage of resources and especially of those related to the generation of electrical energy. His more recent publications, *Blood and Oil* (2004) and *Rising Powers, Shrinking Planet* (2009), are about the scramble for oil. In his earlier *Resource Wars* (2002), he also addresses international conflicts fought over water and civil wars started over minerals and timber. Yet, for him oil differs from other resources because it is essential to the entire US economy. The strategic relevance of oil is comparably high in most other countries around the world, which explains why statist energy policies are currently en vogue. Energy security alters the international system in so far as national power in the twenty-first century is determined by the vastness of a country's oil resources, and also by its ability to generate other sources of wealth in order to purchase oil. The competition over oil – or, more broadly, vital energy resources – constitutes 'the governing principle behind the disposition and use of military power' (2002: 213–14) – as best exemplified by the emerging Sino–American confrontation in Central Asia, the East and South China Seas and the Persian Gulf. Klare concludes that the nature and frequency of future warfare will depend upon three interrelated factors: the political environment in which decisions on resource issues are taken; the supply and demand of resources; and, the spatial characteristics of resources and especially oil.

In order to understand international relations one must, therefore, know about geographical conditions – specifically, the geographical characteristics of the oil industry. The canals and straits through which the major share of the globally traded oil passes are crucial. So are the lay of oil pipelines as well as the probable disturbances to them, which range from difficult terrain to armed conflicts. Economic control and political power matter too; the scramble for energy resources is a competition between giant private and state-owned companies, which each try to secure their own share of global resources. As this combination of natural and manmade variables shows, Klare is no orthodox geodeterminist. Nonetheless, the presence of valuable resources constitutes his prime indicator for the probability of violent conflict breaking out. The general premise of his work is that resource scarcity is a stress factor. Economic cooperation and political negotiations may sometimes settle conflicts, but if a certain resource is considered vital by two or more opponents then the risk of an escalation of violence will be quite high.

Geography and security studies II:
Resource abundance as a root cause of violent conflict
In a striking contrast to the aforementioned research, Collier and Hoeffler (1998, 2002) reason that the abundance of resources provides potential rebels with the means to finance their uprising, through systems of de facto taxation. Resource abundance is, hence, a root cause of violent conflict. Collier and Hoeffler do not consider natural resources to be the exclusive means by which rebels can finance their uprising, though. Diasporas, for instance, may serve the same purpose. Other intervening variables such as the availability of potential soldiers and of weapons also need to be taken into consideration. Concentrating on the natural environment, Collier and Hoeffler incorporate geomorphology, vegetation and the spatial concentration of the population into their statistical model – arguing that mountains and forests protect rebels from the security forces of the government. A high degree of population dispersal is expected to make it much more difficult for the government to control a particular area, too.

In a separate publication, Collier (2006) provides further correlation analyses: countries that did not export primary commodities in large quantities rarely experienced civil war during the last four decades of the twentieth century. He also reveals intervening variables: a high degree of population dispersal correlates with civil wars occurring; countries that have recently experienced civil wars are likely to suffer from a recurrence of violence; the longer peace prevails, the better the chances are of avoiding another war; large diasporas constitute a destabilising factor; poor performance in education correlates with civil war; countries that are marked by above-average rates of population growth are more prone to domestic violent conflicts; and, if one ethnic or religious group constitutes 45 to 90 per cent of the total population, the risk of civil war will increase significantly. Collier does prove that the aforementioned phenomena correlate with civil war. However, he provides only a limited number of arguments that make plausible these causal relations. Sometimes, what Collier presents as the independent variable rather appears to be the dependent one. It makes more sense, for example, to argue that civil war accounts for a low level of education instead of ascribing, as he does, the outbreak of civil war to poor education standards.

Nonetheless, the research by Collier and Hoeffler is exceptional and helpful insofar as it reduces the independent variables significantly. Economists like these two see violent conflicts as something akin to organised crime, being phenomena that can be better understood by examining the specific local circumstances that make them possible. From this perspective, three causal explanations are feasible. First, one may argue that violent conflicts are driven by greed, meaning that the aggressors seek to do well out of war. Second, it appears somewhat plausible that violent conflicts reflect the aggressors' lust for power. However, in this case, such conflicts will only occur if they are economically viable. Third, violent conflicts can be seen as based on grievances. Again, however, they will only occur if they are economically feasible. Comparing these explanations, it should be noted that it is not essential to find out which one applies to any specific violent conflict. Economic sustainability is a necessary condition for all of them. Relevant research can, therefore, exclude considerations of the motive(s) of the belligerents. One should, hence, understand the research by Collier and Hoeffler as being about the conditions of violent conflicts, and not the causes. In this vein, environmental conditions make violent conflicts possible; they do not, however, necessarily cause them.

Refining the arguments advanced by Collier and Hoeffler, Le Billon (2004) points out that not all primary commodities are lootable. Whilst there is empirical evidence that secondary diamonds – that is, those found in rivers – increase the probability of civil war occurring, primary diamonds – which by necessity have to be mined from underground – contrariwise decrease the risk of civil war onset. Governments can easily control those few mines from wherein primary diamonds are extracted. Working underground requires sophisticated machines and know-how, assets that rebels do not possess. In order to capture systematically how the geographical aspects of resource location shape violent conflicts, Le Billon proposes a four-field matrix that distinguishes between 'diffuse' and 'point' resources – meaning dispersed and concentrated resources respectively – and between 'distant' and 'proximate' resources – that is, resources far away from and close to centres of power respectively.[7]

Combining these two criteria, he argues that diffuse and distant resources make warlordism – which is structurally compatible with rebel movements – likely. Alluvial diamonds or timber in peripheral parts of a country provide the opponents of the government with fall-back options. The diffuse nature of these resources implies that various different armed groups can potentially exploit them; there is no need for centralised control. Diffuse and proximate resources are associated with mass rebellions. Le Billon does not elaborate on this category any further but elsewhere refers to violent conflicts over croplands and freshwater as examples (2001b). Point and distant resources tend to trigger secessions, as in the case of South Sudan. The exploitation of point resources requires a substantial level of administration and control – oil cannot simply be picked up off the ground in

---

7   Le Billon (2001a) earlier applied this concept to the civil and proxy war in Angola.

the same way that alluvial diamonds can and loosely-connected traffickers cannot smuggle it across national borders either. Controlling the national centre of power is, however, not necessary because of its distance from the resources. Point and proximate resources favour coup d'états. In Congo-Brazzaville, for instance, several factions amongst the country's élite tried to control the capital city and the nearby oilfields in the mid-1990s. Given their geographical proximity, only the control over the centre of power would provide control over the resources in question – assets which could not be exploited without the presence of a certain degree of state-like coherence.

An empirical study carried out by Ross (2003) on 15 violent conflicts supports these ideas. Ross presents evidence that barely lootable resources, oil for example, coincide with separatism. Highly lootable resources correlate with nonseparatist conflicts. There is also a tendency for rebels to benefit more from lootable resources. Moreover, Ross finds that the presence of natural resources prolongs violent conflicts; lootable resources doing so to a greater extent than unlootable ones do. Obstructable resources – meaning resources whose extraction and transport can be blocked – increase the duration and intensity of violent conflicts. A large-N analysis by Fearon (2004) confirms that civil wars that involve contraband goods – cocaine and diamonds for instance – last much longer than those that do not involve such goods do.

Conclusions for a revitalisation of Classical Geopolitics
As the previous sections have shown, the most famous proponents of Classical Geopolitics have made reference to location and physical geography in order to explain social phenomena. They recognise that there are intervening, nongeographical variables – but consider them to be of only minor relevance. Many researchers today also address geographical factors as independent variables. The physiocratic approaches surveyed here do not, however, constitute a homogenous physiocratic theory. They range from semiscientific policy advice to highly elaborated research, incorporating therein different qualitative and quantitative methodologies. Moreover, those researchers presently shaping physiocratic debates are not themselves geographers. Realist approaches are alien to present-day Political Geography. The constructivist approaches that currently predominate in Political Geography fail to capture the most fundamental likely causal factors for many phenomena: material structures in geographical space. In order to revitalise realist approaches in Political Geography, several elements from present-day physiocratic research and from my discussion of Classical Geopolitics will have to be henceforth taken on board:

- Geographical factors are very suitable explanations for the general patterns and long-term processes in many of the phenomena that social scientists address. They are much less useful explanations for case-specific particularities and short-term developments. By combining geographical and nongeographical variables, one can geographically frame individual cases – for example the foreign policy strategy of a regional power – and reveal the general patterns behind their particular features and the short-term processes therein.

- In order to show both that geographical factors matter and how so, it is helpful to trace processes or to establish causal mechanisms – specifically by using qualitative research methods. These approaches should, furthermore, be combined with quantitative methods, in order to split the macrocorrelation of a geographical cause and a social effect into different microcorrelations – and thus make plausible the notion that there is a chain of microcorrelations that informs the assumed macrocorrelation. In this way, one can also further examine the interplay of geographical and nongeographical factors.

- Realist Geopolitics has to acknowledge equifinality, meaning that the causal mechanisms and processes it captures are, probably, only one of the available paths to the outcome. For the paths addressed by Realist Geopolitics, it makes sense to conceptualise geographical factors as necessary but insufficient conditions for social phenomena – as summarised in this subchapter, contemporary adherents of physiocratic thinking almost always bear in mind that the impact of geographical conditions on a social phenomenon is influenced by nongeographical factors.

- Geographical conditions should not be seen as an irreversible fate, but rather as a set of opportunities and constraints that must be taken into consideration if decision makers are to elaborate sound policies. Hence, opportunities provided by geography will be foregone if humans fail to take the right decisions – that is, if they act irrationally from a geopolitical perspective. Any constraints will (partly) be overcome if human actors possess sufficient material capacities to do so.

These key thoughts are encompassed by the three hypotheses developed earlier in this subchapter. Before proceeding to test them in the context of Southern Africa, I will first elaborate on data sources and on methodologies in the subchapter that now follows.

2.3 Applying Realist Geopolitics:
The Functionalist Approach and its Methodological Realisation

Analysing Geopolitics

Centripetal forces and the functionality of political units
Whilst Classical Geopolitics has a strong narrative tendency, the political geographers of the post-Mackinder generation sought to analyse the relationship between political power and geography in a conceptually guided way. For this purpose, they studied the 'centripetal forces' that bind together the different

components of a political unit – the provinces of a state for example. The forces that tear a political unit apart, meanwhile, were termed the 'centrifugal' ones (Cohen 1963; Hartshorne 1950). The concept of centrifugal and centripetal forces indicates that early post-Mackinder Geopolitics was holistic in its ethos, meaning that it captured all factors somehow related to the phenomenon under consideration. For Richard Hartshorne, its most important proponent, Geography was chorography. Adapting the approach that Whittlesey (1922, 1933, 1934) had used in his studies on Andorra and Cuba, Hartshorne (1935a, 1935b, 1954) defined Political Geography as the study of the variation in political phenomena from one place to another. He wanted to find out how the surface of the Earth, politically unstructured in its essence, had become organised into various kinds of sustainable political units – meaning units that are durable and furthermore possess the necessary material assets and output for realising their key functions. The variations between spaces organised as political units, he argued, had to be examined in the context of both the manmade and natural features that differ from place to place.

Trying to explain the sustainability of political units, Hartshorne (1960) argued that such a unit would split into several independent ones or merge with another one if economic, military and/or political functionality were not givens. In his 1960 article 'Political Geography in the Modern World', published in the *Journal of Conflict Resolution*, he put forward four defining features of functional or sustainable political units. First, every unit is spatially limited. The extent of its spatial reach results from unique geographical, historical and political conditions. If these conditions change – as they did, for instance, in the era of decolonisation – there will be an adjustment of its spatial dimensions. From an ideational point of view, the limitation of a political unit depends upon its *raison d'être* (explained in more detail below).

Second, a political unit will not be sustainable if it is not subdivided down into smaller constituent parts. Even in authoritarian and centralist systems, the subunits become local fields for the integration of political forces that demand some degree of autonomy. In contrast to political units, subunits do not necessarily compete with other subunits. The criteria for viable subunits are, hence, less strict than those for viable units are: handicapped subunits receive subsidies from the unit level and are sustained in this way.

Third, all subunits must be bound together by an agreed standard of what is desirable vis-à-vis societal organisation. Hartshorne (1954, 1960) termed this standard 'homogeneity'. Although mostly associated with cultural and social values, homogeneity also depends upon overcoming spatiomaterial disparities – for instance the different levels of economic development that mark the various provinces of a state. Homogeneity, both in an ideationalist and in a materialist understanding, is based on 'uniformity' – and states must consequently achieve at least a minimum degree of ideational and material uniformity if they are to maintain their functionality.

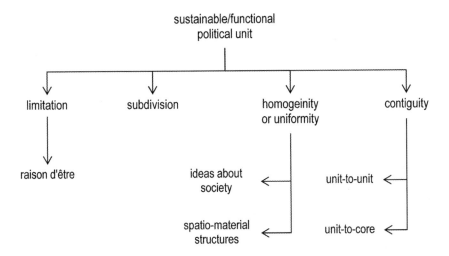

Figure 2.1   Features of functional/sustainable political units

Source: Author's own compilation, based on Hartshorne (1954, 1960).

The fourth and most important feature of functionality or sustainability is 'contiguity'. This addresses the degree to which the subunits of a political unit are tied together by centripetal forces. If all subunits are sufficiently bound together, the whole political unit will attain the productive capacities needed for fulfilling its functions and will successfully interact with other such units. 'Horizontal contiguity', meanwhile, denotes the degree of interconnectivity between the subunits; 'vertical contiguity' is about subunits being dependent upon the centralised economic and political functions of a core. Figure 2.1 summarises the features of functional or sustainable political units.

As noted, contiguity matters more than the other three criteria do. If every subunit is strongly tied to each of its neighbours, the whole will be efficiently integrated. Hartshorne (1950, 1954) complemented the concept of contiguity with that of 'coherence'. Contiguity describes connections at the subunit level – either of neighbouring units or between a central unit and peripheral ones. Coherence, on the other hand, addresses the direct integration of every subunit into the whole – covering province–state instead of province–province relations for example. If either coherence or contiguity is low, subunits will form links with areas lying beyond the borders of the whole. Alternatively, isolated subunits might opt for secession, depending upon the viability of them making such a move. On the international level, alliances – whose adherents form a contiguous system of states, or a political unit – can be analysed on the basis of the concepts of coherence and contiguity. With regard to states exerting power beyond their own borders, one can apply the concepts of coherence and contiguity as a way to capture the extent of their ability to exert control over foreign locations.

From societal functions to the raison d'être *of political units*

Physical barriers and systems of communication and transport are all sensible indicators for contiguity. The former tear a unit apart; the latter pull its subunits together. They exert a strong impact on societal functions such as migration and trade. In Hartshorne's words, 'a basic requirement [for contiguity is] physical routes and facilities of communication and transport among the several regions and between each region and [...] the capital' (1960: 59). Whilst manmade geography is depicted as the key factor here, physical geography also still matters because 'modern technology has made it possible to overcome almost all physical barriers, but [...] the cost of construction is a prohibitive factor' (1960: 59). Spykman (1938a) also stressed each state's need for contiguity. He recognised it in the presence of efficient conduits of communication and transport, and the absence of counterbalancing forces – such as physiogeographical obstacles to movement.

Hartshorne (1950), however, argued that societal functions indicate whether any efforts will be undertaken to overcome physical geography. Thus, it is these functions that should be the focus of geopolitical research. The honing in on them in post-Mackinder Geopolitics is what distinguishes it from its classical predecessors, whose adherents considered societal functions given factors lying beyond the scope of their analysis. Hartshorne reasoned that one was 'not ready to begin the study of farm geography until [after having] analyzed the farmer's purpose – the idea under which his piece of land is organized' (1950: 111). Scholars of Classical Geopolitics would ascertain the way a farm is used from its soils and the availability of water, assuming that the farmer acts rationally in following a path prescribed by nature. Yet, in the world of post-Mackinder Geopolitics, one must also know the grand visions that businesspersons and politicians pursue, before then examining how these imaginings interact with material structures in geographical space.

As Jones (1954) showed, ideas about geographical space have direct consequences for material processes: the prohibition of alcohol in the US, being a political decision based on certain norms applied to a spatially limited area (people living in the US should not drink alcohol), caused the legal trade in alcohol to cease and different forms of illicit commerce to arise. These new types of trade then shaped the economic and political geography of the US. Based on this example, Jones suggested the study of how the differences in the strength of fields created by political forces – the 'political action area' – influences the movement of goods, people and ideas – in other words, the effects of the spatially and temporally fluctuating efficiency of law enforcement vis-à-vis the illegal trade in alcohol, and its trade routes. In other words, Jones's analysis started with political ideas and decisions and ended at the material reality of economics and politics. He thus implicitly negated the hypothesis that geographical forces beyond human control condition the transformation of ideas into political action areas.

The phenomena that specifically aroused his interest were the slight changes in the course of history, the comings and goings of politicians – something that Spykman had wanted to keep out of Geopolitics. These ideational factors can also be seen as the (partial) realisation of grand visions. Gottmann (1951) and Hartshorne (1954) both labelled these grand visions the '*raison d'être*' of a political unit. They provide a unifying concept, one that can ideationally bind together all subunits. Political units that are marked by an identical *raison d'être* – that is, a shared concept of who they are and what they want – should be expected to merge. Being a political idea, a *raison d'être* is the starting point for the making of geopolitics. Political ideas lead to political decisions and political action. The latter often has material expressions in geographical space – indeed, it forms geographical space. Jones (1954) applied this reasoning to the formation of the state of Israel: Zionism as a political idea led to the Balfour Declaration. Based on this political decision, politically relevant action occurred in the form of the Third Aliyah and Jewish settlements in the British mandated territory of Palestine. The settlements (the political field) later became the fundament of a political action area, the State of Israel.

Hartshorne (1950) therefore suggested that one should first determine the area to which a *raison d'être* applies, then differentiate it into subareas of varying coherence as regards the *raison d'être*, examine how such differences affect the entire unit and finally compare the region delineated via the *raison d'être* with areas already existing as political entities. Location and physical geography do not feature in this analytical sequence. For Hartshorne, natural–social scientific approaches had by now come to a dead end: '[they] offer no possibility of [a] progressive advance' (1966: 63). In both Classical Geopolitics and Realist Geopolitics, the just mentioned course of analysis is not possible. If one wants to stick to a natural–social scientific approach, one has to analyse political action areas as conditioned or shaped by material structures in geographical space. The *raison d'être* of a political unit should be examined as the outcome of a geographically – meaning materially – driven process, and not as its starting point.

The functionalist approach from a materialist perspective
Adherents of the functionalist approach remained much more embedded in materialist thinking than the previous section suggests. Hartshorne's holistic approach relied on natural and social factors, which should explain the areal differentiation of Earth. It appears that the question of whether a certain phenomenon is due to natural or social causes was not an essential one for him. He cared, rather, about the interrelationship of all factors that account for areal differentiation. In his earlier publications, he stressed that he was not only interested in the ideas behind political units, their *raison d'être*, but also in their dependence upon physical geography (1935a, 1935b). Even in his later publications, he argued, for example, that a river might be the essential factor that pulls several subunits together, creating contiguity (1954).

How important location, physical geography and manmade geography remained in post-Mackinder Geopolitics is revealed by the analytical scheme that Hartshorne (1954) proposed for the examination of politics from a geographical perspective. Geographers should first analyse the 'morphology' of a political unit. Morphology comprises the size and shape of the unit, its internal nodes and subdivisions, the lines of communication and transport present as well as the features that have been chosen or established to demarcate borders. Scholars of Classical Geopolitics would agree that these factors are relevant independent variables, although they would have seen the ones that are manmade as being conditioned by those that are naturally given.

Second, the internal dynamics of political units – meaning the shifting relationships between centres and subcentres – have to be studied. Observations ought to be made regarding the congruence of politically delimited units with cultural, socioeconomic and natural areas. This reveals whether there is 'territorial harmony'. Third, every political unit is located in amongst other units. The basic idea behind analysing the location of a political unit with regard to other units can be traced back to Classical Geopolitics: location matters for international relations. Fourth, inter-unit relations cannot be divulged exclusively from location (and physical geography). This is where Hartshorne went beyond Classical Geopolitics. He argued that inter-unit relations possessed a logic based on economics and politics, for example in their trade strategies and international alliances. These nongeographical factors, which adherents of Classical Geopolitics would have related to location and physical geography, became independent variables in Hartshorne's approach. Figure 2.2 gives an overview of the analytical scheme just described.

One should understand the functionalist approach that Hartshorne developed as being about the material expression of idealist forces. In his article 'The Functional Approach in Political Geography',[8] published in 1950 in the *Annals of the Association of American Geographers*, he thus suggested studying borders specifically with regard to their effects on and adjustment to crossborder flows. He did not reconstruct and deconstruct narratives and practices about borders in order to reveal the ideology or power–knowledge structures behind them, as present-day scholars of Critical Geopolitics would do. In another publication, Hartshorne (1959) listed the determining factors of economic development: energy-related resources; raw materials; labour; transport facilities; markets for finished products; financial capital; entrepreneurship; and, capital goods. First of all, this list reflects the holistic nature of Hartshornian Geography. Furthermore, some of the categories give emphasis to the relevance of physical geography in their underlying logic.

Following Hartshorne (1959), energy resources are essential because economic advancement requires the generation of mechanical power. Coal, oil, gas, uranium and the potential for using renewable energies indicate whether a country can prosper, although a lack of domestic resources can also be compensated for with imports. The same reasoning applies to other resources that are not directly related to energy generation. Economic advancement will not occur without an adequate

---

8   Hartshorne's terminology – that is, calling the approach functional instead of functionalist – appears inaccurate, because being functional implies that the approach possesses a specific function or purpose.

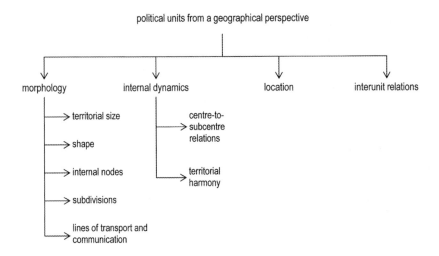

Figure 2.2   Scheme for a geographical analysis of political phenomena
Source: Author's own compilation, based on Hartshorne (1950, 1954).

number of labourers who are sufficiently qualified to work in new, innovative sectors. Domestic shortages can be compensated for by in-migration. Hence, transport systems – navigable rivers and railway lines for example – are essential to the accessing from abroad not only of energy-related resources and raw materials but also labour. Related to this, financial or surplus capital is usually generated by advanced economies. It flows partly into less advanced economies, where it is used to acquire material assets in the form of inputs to industrial production.

Cohen's categories for geopolitical analysis
Hartshorne's concepts remain rather descriptive due to his aforementioned holistic understanding of geography. Refining these concepts, Saul Cohen advanced analytical categories for geopolitical analysis that I have myself since adapted to the needs of Realist Geopolitics. For Cohen (1957, 1963), places and movement – with the latter binding together the former – were the objects of scientific interest. In order to learn more about these two aspects, he began his analyses by investigating location and physical geography. This starting point concurs with that of traditional approaches. Kelly (1997), whose work on shatterbelts is an important tie-in to Cohen's geopolitical theory, built his entire analysis of South America on the location of that continent's states, their climatic conditions and their levels of resource endowment. Cohen went further than this, insofar as he linked location and physical geography to transport infrastructure, economic capabilities and the spatial distribution of the population. He examined core areas of population and economic activity, and the connections between them, contextualising these phenomena in terms of location and physical geography.

The location and structure of core areas of population and economic activity are revealing with regard to the basic economic and foreign policy orientations of a given state: having its core areas of population and economic activity on the East and West Coasts, the US, for example, is a maritime or outward-oriented power. The major agglomerations of the former USSR (predominantly Russia) are far away from the world's major oceans. Hence, Russia concentrates economically and politically on domestic affairs instead. It is, thus, a continental or inward-oriented power (Cohen 1963). Politics is not a primary factor for the geopolitical orientation of states from this perspective. Hartshorne (1935b) accordingly argued that Bolivia was not so much separated from the Pacific Ocean because it lost its coastal territory to Chile in the War of the Pacific of 1879 to 1884 but because the Andes constitute a natural barrier between Bolivia and the coast. What is more, the area between Bolivia's largest cities and the Pacific Ocean is sparsely populated, not marked by major economic activity and lacks transport infrastructure.

Cohen's (2009) distinction between an 'ecumene', 'effective territory' and 'empty area' allows me to incorporate information on core areas of population and economic activity into Realist Geopolitics. An ecumene is a centre of population and economic activity. It possesses a sophisticated communication and transport infrastructure. Effective territory, meanwhile, holds the potential to one day become part of an ecumene because of its advantageous location and physical geography. Such territory is usually found at the edge of the ecumene or in-between different ecumenes. An empty area, on the other hand, does not possess the potential for significant future development because its location and physical geography are too disadvantageous.[9]

In order to incorporate ecumenes, effective territories and empty areas into Realist Geopolitics, geographical factors must be seen as more than just the circumstances that have been provided by nature. They also comprise manmade structures in geographical space, which constitute material realities that are hard to overcome. If one considers the combination of location, physical geography, transport infrastructure and socioeconomic aspects to be essential to geopolitical analysis, the impact of geographical factors on mankind will be less permanent than was assumed by adherents of Classical Geopolitics.

For example, the US did not expand into the Caribbean in the early nineteenth century because at that time Florida was sparsely populated and its swamps constituted a physical barrier. This changed when Florida benefitted from the implementation of major infrastructure projects and from agglomerations being developed there. From the late nineteenth century until today, Florida has served as a bridge to Cuba and other Caribbean islands. Its location and geographical

---

9   These key terms and the attached indicators can be traced back to Derwent Whittlesey's book *The Earth and the State* (1944). Whittlesey took into consideration population density, transport infrastructure, trade links and the location of resources in his work, and concentrated specifically on laws as indicators of geopolitical processes occurring.

characteristics, including both natural and manmade features, explain US influence in the Caribbean (Cohen 1963). Alongside seeing the expansion of states as being based on the three aforementioned factors, Cohen also went beyond natural–social science in his consideration of the economic, political and social forces that either pull the Caribbean towards the US or push it away. In this vein, its trade with the US is a centripetal force, whereas racism in the latter is a centrifugal force. For Cohen, Geopolitics is not exclusively about how political processes are affected by geographical factors, it deals also with the formation of geography by politics. As noted, nongeographical factors can only partly be incorporated into a materialist or realist version of Geopolitics.

Applying the functionalist approach to regional powers
Making use of the functionalist approach for a realist geopolitical study of regional powers means elaborating on the geographical centrifugal and centripetal forces that explain the nature of their international relations. Doing this also helps to delineate their spheres of influence, because centrifugal and centripetal forces that arise from location, physical geography and manmade structures in geographical space account for the contiguity and coherence of political units – including in a region that is dominated by a regional power. In addition to generating further empirical knowledge about South Africa's relations with other states in Africa and thus being an important contribution to research on regional powers, such an investigation will also reveal more generally that geographical factors matter for international relations – and how so.

Following the concepts introduced in the preceding sections of this subchapter, an apposite approach to regional powers is one that starts with the assessment of the effects of location and physical geography on the functionality of a region that is bound together by a regional power. Physical geography will be broken down into three constituent aspects for this purpose: climate, geology and topography (or geomorphology). Conducting a survey of the regional climate will provide some general conclusions about local agricultural conditions. This may, for example, reveal that the regional power in question needs certain inputs – such as water – from its neighbours. Examining the dispersal of mineral resources across the region in question will indicate the industrial potential of the regional power, as well as its capacity to incorporate its neighbourhood into industrial commodity chains. Generally speaking, climate and geology tell us what the regional power can provide to the economies of its neighbouring countries, and also what it needs from them. Considering localities will reveal where the regional power is likely to enter into relevant interactions with other countries. Distance and common borders are the most apparent determinants in this context because they increase the costs of trade between the regional power and its neighbours. Geomorphology shows whether the regional power can easily access these places of interest. Oceans, mountain ranges and vast rivers constitute natural barriers that limit the capacity of a regional power to project its influence and, thence, delineate its envisaged region.

Realist Geopolitics is not only about location and physical geography. Based on the functionalist approach cast in the mould of Cohen and Hartshorne, two additional categories of factors that explain international relations from a geopolitical perspective need to be addressed. They both cover manmade geography. First, transport infrastructure constitutes the main centripetal force that helps regional powers to overcome locational and physiogeographical obstacles to the spatial expansion of their influence. A survey of regional transport infrastructures will reveal which places – identified as relevant because of their climate or geology – are accessible to regional powers. Second, the distribution of core areas of population and economic activity also has to be examined. They are part of manmade geography, just as transport infrastructure is. The agglomerations in regional powers can be expected to serve as regional cores, binding the regional periphery to them. In a slightly broader context, scrutinising the regional distribution of ecumenes, effective territories and empty areas will indicate the directions in which regional powers project their influence.

Methodological Realisation

Questions for the empirical study
As just explained, my analysis is about discovering centripetal and centrifugal forces with the help of four categories that capture material structures in geographical space. I start with location and physical geography, and then take a close look at transport infrastructure and socioeconomic aspects. Hence, I address two categories of naturally given forces and two categories of manmade ones. I first deduce from locational and physiogeographical factors what regional relations should theoretically look like. This constitutes a classical geopolitical perspective. Then, I examine existing and envisaged railway lines, roads and harbours as well as the structural, socioeconomic aspects of South Africa and its neighbouring countries in order to reveal how manmade geography combines with location and physical geography. In positing what Realist Geopolitics expects with regard to regional relations, I address the following key questions:

- Where is South Africa located? What expectations can be drawn from its relative location to other African countries?
- Where does physical geography provide conditions favourable to the movement of people and goods? Where do natural barriers limit such movement?
- Where are key resources – ranging from oil, gas and minerals to crops and water – located? Which resources are of particular interest to South Africa?
- Where are the regional core areas of population and economic activity located? How are they linked with each other?
- What means of transporting people and goods have been put in place? What, if any, future transport infrastructure projects are envisaged?

As summarised in Chapter 2.1, regional powers are defined as those states that lead their region and that are thus highly influential on the regional level. Whilst location, natural resources, transport infrastructure and socioeconomic assets (as well as their interconnectivity) certainly do not constitute a complete list of the bases of national power, they nonetheless still represent important features that enable a state to act as a regional power – in particular because they combine power as an asset (control over natural resources, for example) with power as control over networks (economic links and transport infrastructure within the region, for example). In other words, the geopolitical analysis of South Africa following the aforementioned categories aligns with the key characteristics of regional powerhood.

In order to test whether the aforementioned geographical conditions and economic and political outcomes are interrelated, I compare the implications of location, physiogeographical factors, transport infrastructure and socioeconomic aspects with de facto existing regional economic and political relations. With this in mind, I thus analyse the expansion of firms from South Africa into the region and, furthermore, elaborate on their impact there. I delineate South Africa's regional economic impact quantitatively, referring to its share of the imports and exports of African countries. An overview of the paradigms informing South Africa's foreign policy frames my analysis of the Southern African Customs Union (SACU), the Southern African Development Community (SADC) and of South African security policy (in both Central and Southern Africa). I also examine South Africa's relevance to the foreign and economic policy strategies chosen by its fellow SADC members. These issues are addressed by answering the following questions:

- What role(s) do South African businesses play for and in neighbouring countries? What are the regional patterns of trade and investment?
- What role(s) does South Africa play for its neighbours in economic terms? How is its role as a regional power reflected in the regional organisations that exist, as well as in the chosen political strategies of other states in the region?
- Do geographical factors matter to South Africa's security policy in the SADC area? If so, how do they interact with nongeographical factors?

If these additional questions were to go unanswered, my study would ultimately only provide policy advice based on an assessment of material structures in geographical space. It would indicate what should be done following the presumption that geographical conditions are essential to the success of economic and political strategies. By answering these additional questions, I am thus also able to test whether Realist Geopolitics is indeed a valid theory. This soundness will be confirmed if the economic and political role played by South Africa in and for its neighbourhood concurs with what the survey of geographical conditions predicts will be true on the ground. Answering the additional questions furthermore serves to reinforce the link between my geopolitical approach and political-scientific research on regional powers. I examine the de facto influence of a regional power in terms of economics, regional integration, security policy and the relevance ascribed to it by its neighbouring states.

Sources of information and operationalisation
of the dependent and independent variables

I have obtained much of the data used for the empirical part of this study – especially with regard to locational and physiogeographical factors – from monographs written on Southern African regional geography. At least for phenomena that occurred before the late 2000s, I refer to the various other scientific publications that also address them. Regional newspapers that are available online have been a helpful source of more recent information. Aside from all these sources, I also draw on the *Africa Yearbook*, the *World Factbook*, reports by the Economist Intelligence Unit and on business information taken from the web portal *Who Owns Whom*. Regional and international organisations such as the Development Bank of Southern Africa (DBSA), the Southern African Power Pool and the World Bank also provide qualitative and quantitative data that I have thus incorporated into my empirical analysis.

South African ministries have published various strategy papers that cover South African–African relations. SACU and SADC have uploaded their key documents on their websites. Similar information is, however, not available for other regional states, either because such documents are not publically available or they simply do not exist. Interviews conducted by me with diplomats from the SADC region have been used to learn about the political strategies of their respective governments and South Africa's role therein. Other information gaps have been closed by interviews with diplomats from the regional states, officials from South African ministries and staff of key businesses – South Africa's state-owned electricity provider Eskom, the national transport company Transnet and mining giant AngloGold Ashanti for instance. Interviews with leading economists and political scientists from South Africa, who are often involved in policy advice, add further input and also serve as a means of crosschecking data obtained from newspaper articles and nonacademic interviews.

As noted, my empirical analysis begins with South Africa's absolute and relative location. For the purposes of my particular study, to measure the absolute and relative location of a country in quantitative terms would not be helpful. Instead, I describe South Africa's location on the global stage and its location in relation to other African countries in order to arrive at conclusions concerning its economic and political relations on the regional level. With regard to physiogeographical factors, I make use of: temperature, rainfall and evaporation; variability of rainfall; the regional distribution of soils; geomorphological structures, as far as they exert an impact on transport; and, the location and quantity of natural resources. Seemingly, a significant amount of quantitative data can be utilised in this part of my study. Combining such data with qualitative assessments from existing literature and interviews provides a sound picture of what physical geography implies with regard to South Africa's relations with its neighbouring countries.

Concerning transport infrastructure, I use data on the costs and quantities involved in the regional transport of goods by rail, ship and truck. A comparison of the volume of goods handled at regional harbours combined with a rather qualitative assessment of their connections to the hinterland by rail and road forms an essential indicator of the relevance and spatial reach of South Africa. Moreover, I refer to political-scientific literature from the 1980s and early 1990s in order to place regional transport infrastructure in its historical context, because the region's contemporary transport system is largely reflective of decisions that were taken either in the colonial era or during the years of struggle against the apartheid regime. Socioeconomic aspects, meanwhile, are covered by a variety of different indicators. They range from the location of core areas of population and economic activity, and their interconnections, to patterns of crossborder migration to the transnational ties that interlink the key sectors of the economies of South Africa and its neighbouring countries.

In order to capture the outcome – meaning the existing economic and political relations of South Africa with its neighbouring countries – I provide mostly qualitative assessments thereof. Whilst it is easy to tell who is a member of SACU and SADC, analysing South Africa's regional security policy is more challenging in this particular context. It requires explaining the role of geographical factors in it – meaning that I have to assess the relevance of geographical factors analysed in the first empirical chapters to particular security operations. Scrutinising policy paradigms and political strategies, I investigate both what role the region plays for South Africa and simultaneously that country for its neighbouring states. When it comes to economics, my analysis is made complicated by an overlap of socioeconomic structures in geographical space, part of my conditions, and economic ties, part of the outcome. With regard to that outcome, I attempt to explain the regional economic expansion of South Africa by referring to the geographical factors previously analysed. I concentrate herein on patterns of trade and investment. I also show where geographically South African firms are currently active.

QCA: Configurations; sufficient and necessary conditions
My empirical research is based on a medium number of cases: about a dozen countries, all members of SADC (plus the Comoros), with relatively close economic and/or political ties with South Africa. For these countries, I predict the impact of different geographical factors on their economic and political relations with South Africa. This makes my analysis a comparative study. Given that the objective is to test the validity of Realist Geopolitics as a theory, I not only compare the relations of the SADC member countries with South Africa empirically but also strive to generate general knowledge – that is, knowledge that transcends the parameters of my own cases. QCA is the most suitable methodology for such an endeavour. It constitutes a middle course between quantitative, mean variable-oriented, and

qualitative, mean case-based, approaches. Whilst standard quantitative studies lose the connection to the particularities of their cases, qualitative studies do not offer up the possibility of making generalisations. They explain their few cases ex post, and sometimes contain predictions for the future that are limited only to these cases. QCA thus allows me to derive general knowledge from case-based knowledge. It is, as Charles C. Ragin writes in *The Comparative Method* (1987), useful for modest generalisation, and adequate for summarising and exploring data as well as for generating and testing theories – which is the overarching purpose of my study.

The starting point of QCA is to see cases as configurations of aligned conditions[10] – namely the geographical factors identified above. All possible configurations of the conditions are shown in a truth table in order to find out, by using Boolean algebra, which ones lead to the outcome. Analysing configurations hence means revealing different paths to the outcome. In the case of my study, geomorphological conditions that favour transport may occur together with a structural compatibility vis-à-vis agricultural production, and consequently lead to dense trade between South Africa and its neighbouring countries. The same outcome can also result from resources existing in one regional state that are of high value to South African industry. Comparing such combinations of conditions, QCA allows me to ascertain how relevant each condition is. This way, I can make sense of the observed cases, for instance by setting up a typology (Ragin 2006). A condition (hereafter X) or a combination of conditions will be *sufficient* for an outcome (hereafter Y) if X always leads to Y. This means that there are no cases in which X is given but Y does not occur: $X \rightarrow Y$. One can, however, not conclude that the absence of X comes along with the absence of Y because an outcome may have various causes. X will be *necessary* for Y if there is no Y without X. Cases that do not reach Y but possess X may exist: $X \leftarrow Y$ (Berg-Schlosser et al. 2009; Dion 1998; Ragin 1998). Combining necessary and sufficient conditions, one arrives at the conditions or combinations of conditions that are *necessary and sufficient*. This means that there are no cases that possess X but do not reach Y (X is sufficient) nor are there cases that reach Y without possessing X (X is necessary): $X \leftrightarrow Y$ (Dion 1998; Ragin 2000).

This understanding of necessary and sufficient conditions is essential to Realist Geopolitics, which omits nongeographical factors at the beginning of every analysis. Yet, nongeographical factors certainly play a role in the relationships that I analyse here. I do not argue that geographical factors deterministically lead to anything. Other conditions have to come along, but I am interested in the geographical conditions that are, as I seek to show, a necessary part of a larger

---

10   In QCA, the term 'condition' is used for what may erroneously be called an 'independent variable'. The conditions in QCA are not independent variables because each condition is analysed in combination with – meaning regarding its dependence upon – other conditions (Rihoux and De Meur 2009). In contrast to independent variables, conditions cannot simply be added. They have to combine together in order to cause the outcome.

causality – a combination of conditions – that represents one path to the outcome(s) I observe. In order to show that geographical factors are necessary, though probably insufficient on their own, I refer to the concept of INUS causality (Mackie 1974). For example, two countries do not necessarily trade with each other just because they are connected by a transport infrastructure. Yet, two countries will not be able to trade if they are not connected by such a transport infrastructure. Strong corporate relations taken together with a good transport infrastructure are, most likely, sufficient for trade. Strong corporate relations are not necessary though. Trade may alternatively occur because geographical factors are favourable and politicians advance a project of regional integration. In other words, I seek to prove that geographical factors are at least an *insufficient* but *necessary* part of an *unnecessary* but *sufficient* combination of conditions (hence the acronym INUS) that account for the economic and political phenomena of South African regional powerhood.

QCA: Truth tables and minimalising configurations
Truth tables are the central tool used in QCA to summarise data and test theories. Table 2.1, which is a model truth table, shows hypothetical values for three conditions (A, B and C), their convergences (AB, AC and BC) and the outcome (Y) in all possible combinations (combinations 1 to 8). A hypothetical number of observed cases are added. Before filling in a truth table, one has to choose between the crisp or fuzzy set variant of QCA. Crisp set QCA only requires ascribing a value of 0 or 1 to every condition, therein revealing whether it is fulfilled or not. Fuzzy set QCA, on the other hand, works with continuous values, ranging from 0.0 to 1.0. By using the latter type of values, one is able to further incorporate the degree to which a condition or an outcome is fulfilled. If the purpose of the QCA is only to identify necessary and sufficient conditions, the crisp set variant is more adequate because the question of necessary and sufficient conditions is a simple matter of aggregation and logic (as shown below). Identifying necessary and sufficient conditions is much more difficult in the fuzzy set variant, given that all cases belong to the outcome to differing degrees. I thus apply a crisp set QCA in the empirical part of this study, as the aim therein is to identify the necessary and sufficient conditions for an observed outcome.

Depending upon the complexity of the truth table, key results can often be directly observed. In Table 2.1, one notes that only B is a necessary condition for Y because neither A nor C always occurs when Y is reached: B ← Y. Neither A nor B nor C is sufficient for Y. There are always cases in which A, B or C occurs but Y is not reached. Looking at all possible convergences of the conditions, one sees that BC, which occurs in combinations 4 and 8, always leads to Y. BC is sufficient for Y: BC → Y. For a complete QCA, one has to analyse whether the absence of A, B or C – expressed by lower case instead of capital letters – is necessary or sufficient for Y. All possible combinations of the complementary values, their convergences, and their convergences with A, B and C have to be examined. For my study, such complexity can be avoided because there is no reason to assume that economic and political linkages are caused by the absence of the very geographical features that I expect to favour them. I examine the complementary values here only in order to show how QCA helps to reduce complexity so that general conclusions can be drawn. For the hypothetical data of Table 2.1, an analysis of the complementary values and their combinations shows that neither a nor b nor c is sufficient for Y. Nor is a, b or c necessary for Y. Amongst all possible convergences, only aB is a sufficient condition for Y. In sum, either aB or BC is sufficient for Y: aB + BC → Y, which indicates that QCA is capable of identifying equifinality or multiple conjunctural causation – there are several ways to Y (Berg-Schlosser et al. 2009).

Table 2.1   Hypothetical values for a QCA

	Conditions						Outcome (Y)	Cases
	A	**B**	**C**	**AB**	**AC**	**BC**		
Combination 1	0	0	0	0	0	0	0	10
Combination 2	0	0	1	0	0	0	0	15
Combination 3	0	1	0	0	0	0	1	5
Combination 4	0	1	1	0	0	1	1	25
Combination 5	1	0	0	0	0	0	0	20
Combination 6	1	0	1	0	1	0	0	20
Combination 7	1	1	0	1	0	0	0	5
Combination 8	1	1	1	1	1	1	1 (assumed)	0

Source: Author's own compilation.

In a disaggregated manner, the sufficient conditions for Y – that is, combinations 3, 4 and 8 – can be expressed as aBc + aBC + ABC → Y. This formula is crude insofar as it brings together all combinations that lead to Y. One may simplify it mathematically to (ac + aC + AC) B → Y, which implies that B is highly relevant for Y. Alternatively, looking separately at the first part of the formula, aBc + aBC, one sees that aB is sufficient regardless of C. The crude formula can be simplified into aB + ABC → Y. Two disaggregated 'primitive expressions' are transformed into one 'prime implicant' (Ragin 1987). Similarly, the latter part of the crude formula, aBC + ABC, indicates that A does not matter. The crude formula may, therefore, be transformed into aBc + BC → Y as well. Cutting out conditions this way – 'minimisation' in Boolean terms – will only work if the combinations differ in one condition, not in two or more (Ragin 1987). Comparing the first and the second way of finding sufficient conditions causes confusion, because the final statements are not identical at first glance. Thinking of the combinations as circles in a Venn Diagram, which shows all possible logical relations between a finite number of sets, helps to overcome the confusion: the small circle aBc is a part of the large circle aB; BC contains ABC. Hence, the formula aB + BC → Y is a simplified version of the two other ones.

QCA: Coverage and consistency
Bringing in a hypothetical number of cases for each possible combination shown in Table 2.1 allows combinations that are only theoretically relevant to be excluded. The easiest way to do this is to compare the number of cases for combinations 3, 4 and 8, which all lead to Y. Combination 8 appears to be a theoretical way to achieve Y. It does not occur in reality – or, at least, in my sample. Filling in the table, I have assumed that a positive configuration of all conditions leads to the outcome. Moreover, Combination 4 is the most important one because it occurs five times more often than Combination 3 does.

In order to test the quality of a sufficient combination of conditions in a more elaborate way, one can calculate its 'coverage'. This denotes the share of cases covered by the concerned condition of all cases that lead to Y. It indicates how relevant this condition is as an explanation (Ragin 2006). The coverage of the formula deduced above, aB + BC → Y, is 100 per cent. All cases that lead to Y are explained by it. Coverage becomes interesting whenever there is a formula that appears sound but one or two combinations contradict it. If the contradicting combinations relate to only a few cases, the coverage will still be close to 100 per cent, which means that it should be seriously considered. Accepting coverage below 100 per cent often leads to simplified formulae. For the data in Table 2.1, one can simplify the rather complex formula aB + BC → Y to B → Y. Strictly speaking, this is an incorrect formula because B occurs in Combination 7, which does not lead to Y. The coverage of B → Y remains, however, 100 per cent because all 30 cases – those from combinations 3 and 4 – are explained by this formula. The formula C → Y, which also simplifies the initial formula, has a lower coverage however – it only explains 25 out of 30 cases, or 83.3 per cent of them.

The second indicator of the quality of an explanation is its 'consistency', denoting all combinations in which the concerned condition occurs. It does not indicate how relevant but rather how accurate an explanation is. Complex formulae can be simplified provided that consistency remains high. Whilst B → Y is perfect regarding its coverage, it lacks consistency: B not only occurs in combinations 3 and 4 but also in combinations 7 and 8. Combination 8 is irrelevant but Combination 7 has five cases and does not lead to Y. The consistency of B → Y is 30 (the number of cases explained by B) divided by 35 (the total number of cases in which B occurs), which makes 85.7 per cent. The consistency of my second simplified formula, C → Y, is lower. C occurs in 60 cases and C → Y only explains 25 of them, which makes a consistency of 41.7 per cent. This example demonstrates that one should, contrary to the way in which it was just done here, check consistency first and coverage second – because even though C → Y has a good coverage, the formula is ultimately meaningless given that it is not consistent.

The explanations and calculations of consistency and coverage above refer to sufficient conditions. The consistency and coverage of necessary conditions are calculated by turning the formulae around. For testing the consistency of sufficient conditions, one has to ask whether the conditions are a subset of the outcome. For a condition to be necessary, the outcome has to be a subset of the condition. The coverage of necessary conditions is, accordingly, calculated in the same way that the consistency of sufficient conditions is (Ragin 2006).

The correlation–causal relation problem and Process Tracing
A frequent coincidence of geographical conditions and certain social outcomes – a correlation – does not necessarily mean that there is a causal relationship between them. To illustrate this, one can take up the challenge of explaining the scenario of two dominoes lying flat on the ground: if the first and the last domino of a chain of 50 dominoes lie flat on the ground with their tops pointing in the same direction there will be a correlation. There are various explanations other than a chain reaction for the two dominoes lying flat on the ground. Some of them are almost immediately obvious – someone may, for example, have simply placed the two dominoes flat on the ground. Other explanations are unlikely but possible – an earthquake for instance. Even if one assumes that there has been a chain reaction, meaning that the position of the two dominoes is related, it remains unknown which domino fell first because correlation is indifferent to the direction of causality. This problem cannot be solved convincingly by QCA, because QCA only reveals the combinations of conditions that lead to an outcome. It does not reveal anything about the actual mechanisms at work (Curchod 2002). The formulae derived from truth tables indicate simultaneous occurrences. They have to be interpreted with regard to causality. It is, therefore, imperative to try to understand the case-specific meaning of any QCA formula. The narratives behind the formula matter. Ragin (2000) argues that the success of a study based on QCA also depends upon the ability of the researcher to reason convincingly, so as to persuasively link theory to empirics.

Thus after having shown by QCA that there is a correlation between geographical conditions and economic and political outcomes, I will need to make plausible the suggestion that this correlation constitutes a causal relationship. Process Tracing is highly suitable for this purpose. It addresses the process between the two dominoes and helps to find out whether there was a chain reaction starting with the first domino that culminated in the last one lying flat on the ground. In order to verify the chain reaction hypothesis, one has to investigate the dominoes that are situated in between. The macrocorrelation of the first and last dominoes thus has to be broken down into the microcorrelations positioned in between (Roberts 1996). Examining these microcorrelations means gathering evidence that makes the reasoning on the macrocorrelation more plausible: if all dominoes between the first and the last one lie flat on the ground, and if their formation suggests that they all bumped against each other, it will be much more convincing to argue that the last domino lies flat on the ground because of the first one doing so.

Additionally, someone might have heard or seen the dominoes falling – which would count as 'hardening evidence'. One can alternatively increase the probability of the chain reaction hypothesis being valid by excluding other explanations such as human interference or an earthquake. In other words, Process Tracing means mapping the process from original cause to eventual effect (Checkel 2005). By filling in the knowledge gaps about what lies between initial cause and ultimate effect, Process Tracing thus shows the mechanism(s) at work (George and Bennett 2004). Process Tracing is similar to putting together the pieces of a puzzle. One has to assemble bits and pieces of evidence from various sources, and put them together so that they form a coherent picture that explains the phenomenon at hand. In contrast to putting together the pieces of a puzzle, the person undertaking Process Tracing comes across evidence that does not contribute to explaining the phenomenon at hand, across pieces that are not part of the puzzle. At the same time, some pieces of the puzzle are missing. The mixed and incomplete pieces of many different puzzles lie in front of him/her. In Process Tracing, one therefore includes the information that is able to contribute to the obtention of the full picture and leaves out anything that causes confusion (George and McKeown 1985) – doing so without falling into the trap of constructing a story that serves the purpose of proving what one would have originally like to have proved.

Examining the relationship between environmental scarcity and violent conflict, Homer-Dixon and his colleagues (1991, 1994) try to solve the problem of the direction of causality by arguing that the former results from a naturally given ecosystem vulnerability. Environmental damage is sometimes so severe that it cannot be reversed and hence constitutes an exogenous variable. In order to capture this situation lying beyond human control, the operationalisation of environmental conditions has to remain independent from the social outcomes. Environmental scarcity can be operationalised by decreasing precipitation but not by diminishing access to water – because the latter may, for example, result from the destruction of wells by armed groups.

Similar to Homer-Dixon and his colleagues, I argue that the locational and physiogeographical phenomena that I address here are beyond human control: South Africa will always be located at the southern edge of the African continent. The East African Rift Valley will not turn into a plateau (at least not within a timespan relevant to mankind). Even many manmade material structures in geographical space cannot be significantly altered in the short term. Railway lines and major roads best connect the different countries of Southern Africa to South Africa, with Angola being an important exception. As such, existing transport corridors have not changed much since the colonial era.

Whilst Homer-Dixon and his colleagues convincingly resolve the problem of the direction of causal relations, their answer to the more fundamental question of whether the correlations they observe are even causal relations at all is less sophisticated. They plausibly reason in various case studies that specific correlations are, in fact, causal relations. They explain that human action in specific places and times, and under specific conditions, is driven by environmental scarcity. The case-specific argumentation offered captures the processes and steps in between that lead from environmental scarcity to violent conflict. Strictly speaking, this methodological approach only leads to more or less plausible causal relations. Its rather low generalisation capacity does not matter much for my own study though. What I try to show here is that geographical factors are relevant for the international relations of regional powers – that is, they matter in some cases. I do not claim, however, that geographical factors explain every single phenomenon that we observe and will ever observe in international relations. I do not argue that they alone are a sufficient explanation either. For such moderate purposes, Process Tracing is suitable – whilst QCA widens the potential for subsequent generalisation.

Adapting Process Tracing to Realist Geopolitics

According to George and Bennett (2004), Process Tracing has to be based on well-developed theories if the complexity of potentially relevant factors is to be reduced in a reasonable way. They argue that this methodology advances rather than tests theories, which it achieves by deepening our knowledge of causal mechanisms. My understanding of Process Tracing contrariwise concurs with Homer-Dixon's observation that those who apply it often rely on rules of thumb in order to generate hypotheses on macro- and microcorrelations. This inevitably includes a preselection of possible causes, effects and intervening factors. Given that one cannot be certain about interactions, feedbacks and nonlinear relations, Homer-Dixon (1996) admits that case selections for Process Tracing do not fulfil strict scientific criteria.

Reducing complexity with the help of rules of the thumb is legitimate for the purposes of my study. I seek to prove that geographical factors play an important role in the economics and politics of regional powers. Homer-Dixon and his colleagues, who try to show that environmental scarcity causes violent conflict, are not interested in the whole variety of factors that shape the latter. Similarly, I do not analyse systematically all intervening, nongeographical factors in South Africa's regional relations. Homer-Dixon and his colleagues describe sets of conditions under which violent conflict occurs and recognise that nonenvironmental conditions are necessary to fully understand this phenomenon. Their research question is, however, whether environmental change has a significant impact on society, and if so how it leads to violence. My scientific interest in the study presented here is identical: I acknowledge that nongeographical factors are important but I am only interested in them insofar as they complement geographical factors, therein forming a sufficient combination of conditions. The emphasis hereby shifts from explaining the current incidence of the outcome to understanding the conditional role of geographical factors in it.

In other words, I focus on showing that geographical conditions are necessary components – probably even the most important ones – of some paths to the observed outcomes. The analyses of climate change as a security threat carried out by the German Advisory Council on Global Change (2007) are similarly structured. The council's experts start with a form of environmental degradation, for example floods, and then reason about how intervening factors such as weak statehood turn this environmental phenomenon into a sociopolitical crisis. Tracing relevant processes, they have divulged how environmental degradation is not a determining cause of sociopolitical crisis but rather an insufficient and necessary component of combinations of conditions that are sufficient but unnecessary for it.

This means that environmental degradation plays an important role as a security threat. It is not, however, the only one. Nor does it necessarily lead to crises. Certain nonenvironmental conditions have to be fulfilled in order for such an outcome to be reached. The paradigm of Diamond's (2005) aforementioned book on the decline of societies is identical. He does not maintain that damage caused to the environment necessarily leads to the collapse of societies. Rather, Diamond seeks to show that environmental damage plays a role alongside other factors. Examining the impact of geographical factors on the economics and politics of regional powers from this perspective of INUS causality, I have adapted the basic questions posited in the research carried out by Homer-Dixon and his colleagues (1996) as a way to test the validity of Realist Geopolitics as an applicable theory:

- Do geographical factors influence the regional economics and politics of South Africa?
- If yes, do geographical factors influence the regional economics and politics of South Africa significantly?
- If yes, how exactly – in other words, in combination with which other factors – do geographical factors influence the regional economics and politics of South Africa?

Answering these questions involves specifying both geographical conditions and economic and political outcomes so that I am able to tell, ultimately, which geographical factors shape which economic and political dynamics. In the following chapters, I first address the geographical conditions that I expect to influence South Africa's regional relations and second elaborate on the economic and political outcomes that they – working together with nongeographical factors – generate.

Chapter 3
Location and Physical Geography
in Southern Africa

In chapters 3–6, I apply Realist Geopolitics to South Africa and its regional economic and political relations. I first provide information on location and naturally given geographical conditions, concentrating on those factors that may cause links to be formed between the different regional states and especially between themselves and South Africa. After elaborating on South Africa's location, I address climatic conditions, first as an overview for the whole of Central, East and Southern Africa, then for the individual regional countries. I also analyse geomorphological and geological conditions in such a two-step approach.

3.1 Location

South Africa is located at the southern edge of the African continent. It borders with Botswana, Mozambique, Namibia, Swaziland and Zimbabwe. Lesotho is virtually an island nation within South African territory. Taking only geographical location into consideration, Lesotho and Swaziland should strongly depend upon South Africa. Lesotho is just 300 kilometres away from those areas of South Africa that host half of all South African industrial activities and account for 79 per cent of the regional power's mining output (Nel and Illgner 2001). In the case of Swaziland, the possibility exists to reach the world's oceans by crossing Mozambican territory, although the transport infrastructure for this still needs to be upgraded. Assuming that the necessity of making shipments via South African territory leads to economic and political dependence upon that country, landlocked Botswana is also closely tied to South Africa. Zimbabwe is closer to the Mozambican coast. Mozambique and Namibia possess few sites suited to being deepwater harbours. Five continental members of SADC do not share borders with South Africa. Links from South Africa to Angola, the Democratic Republic of the Congo (hereafter DR Congo), Malawi, Tanzania and Zambia are complicated by the fact that there is in each case always at least one country lying in between.

Location moreover suggests that the island states of Southern Africa are poorly linked to the continental mainland. The Madagascan landmass broke away from the rest of Africa about 20 million years ago. On its western side, altitude increases slowly up to the Hauts Plateaux, which form a ragged landscape with mountains, valleys and alluvial plains. On the eastern side of the island, the terrain slopes sharply. The rivers on the west side create broad alluvial valleys, whereas those of the east cross a narrow sedimentary plain. They end in lagoons and sandbars. Because of higher sea levels in prehistoric times, rivers on the northwest coast feature large and deep estuaries that are advantageous for modern deepwater ports (Heseltine 1971). The fact that Madagascar's best location for harbours is the most distant point from South Africa pushes the island state even further away from the African continent.

The two main and few smaller islands that belong to the state of Mauritius are, meanwhile, even further away besides – approximately 3,000 kilometres so. They were all formed by volcanic eruptions, which began some 12 million years ago and ended about 100,000 years ago. Processes of erosion have shaped the landscape. The highest mountain of Mauritius rises only 828 metres above sea level (Toth 1995). The Comoros contrariwise reach a maximum altitude of 2,361 metres, although they are smaller than Mauritius in terms of their territorial span. The reason for this is that volcanic activity is still ongoing in the Comoros, which offsets the effects of erosion (Ercolano 1995). The Seychelles, however, were not formed by volcanic activity, but cut off from the Indian Plate approximately 65 million years ago (Tartter 1995). The Comoros and the Seychelles are roughly as far away from South Africa as northwest Madagascar is.

Concerning continental Southern Africa, South Africa is favourably positioned for trade with Europe, the Far East and North America because it is situated on both the Atlantic Ocean and the Indian Ocean. It is the only African country with shores on both – a fact that was crucial to great power politics in the age of imperialism; the Portuguese met with fierce resistance from the British when they sought to connect by rail – or even to merge – their two colonies, today's Angola and Mozambique. The Germans tried and failed to link Namibia and Tanzania via the Zambezi River. Later, a major goal of the proxy wars backed by South Africa's apartheid regime was to sabotage the railway lines that connected the landlocked Frontline States to the coasts. Until this day, the intention behind regional economic integration and economic growth strategies in the SADC region remains to a large extent the connecting of the hinterland to the world's oceans, as I explain in more detail later in this chapter. This means that providing access to the seas – which South Africa can do much better than other countries in the region because of its own location – is a source of power. South Africa possesses centrality and, hence, power, because it links its neighbourhood with the cores of the global economy. Being located at the edge of the African continent, South Africa's economic and political relations should, moreover, reflect a mix of continental and maritime strategies, as already indicated by its role as a hinge between the regional economies and their overseas trading partners.

3.2 Climate

The climate of Africa is shaped by the annual shifting of the Intertropical Convergence Zone (ITCZ) between the Tropic of Cancer and the Tropic of

Capricorn, wherein 75 per cent of the African continent is located. In the ITCZ, air moves upwards because of it being heated by zenithal solar radiation. It cools down in the process of rising, causing significant precipitation. In the subtropics, the air masses from the ITCZ – now dry because they have lost their humidity in the process of rising in the tropics – move downwards. The subtropics are, therefore, arid, at least in winter. The air masses return to the ITCZ along the ground as trade winds, absorbing water whenever they pass over ocean surfaces, which leads to even higher precipitation in the tropics. The equatorial area of the Congo Basin receives high precipitation almost all year long: more than 1,500 millimetres. Further north and further south, summers are rainy and winters dry. The greater the distance to the equator, the shorter the rainy season – various forms of savannahs line up parallel to latitudes with deserts present. There, rainfall decreases to less than 250 millimetres per year, which means a permanent shortage of water. Because of the shift of the ITCZ, all climatic zones beyond the inner tropics are marked by a strong seasonality of rainfall – that is, a sharp contrast in water volume between rainy and dry seasons. Only the extreme southwest of the continent, the Cape region, is influenced by the Westerlies in winter and thus forms a so-called 'Mediterranean climate' – with hot and arid summers but temperate and humid winters.

The climatic change that comes with latitude is overlain by an enormous difference between the eastern and western sides of Southern Africa. Along the Atlantic Ocean, trade winds that head from land to sea cause aridity. Aridity is also due to the effects of the cold Benguela Current. Deserts predominate. On the coast of the Indian Ocean, meanwhile, trade winds coming in from sea to land account for high levels of precipitation. The humid climate reaches far south into Mozambique and KwaZulu-Natal. Africa's highland plateaux are another exception to these latitude-oriented climatic regions. They form heating surfaces in summer, creating rising air movements and attracting the Easterlies in a process that resembles the one taking simultaneously place in the ITCZ. The upwards air movement and the Easterlies cause high levels of precipitation. Map 3.1 provides an overview of the climate of Africa south of the equator.

Similar to rainfall, temperature in Africa is, first and foremost, marked by its difference at the equator to at the poles. In the inner tropics, the monthly average temperature remains at about 25°C all year long. The day-to-night amplitude varies by up to 10°C. North and south of the equator, temperature differences between summer and winter matter more than the daily amplitude does. The warmest month in Livingston, Zambia (18° south latitude) is October with 26°C, just before the rainy season begins and clouds scatter and reflect solar radiation. In June and July, average temperatures fall to 16°C. In Kimberley, South Africa (27° south latitude), the average temperature is 10°C in June and July but 25°C in December and January. There are exceptions to this south–north pattern. Since temperature declines by about 0.65°C per 100 metres of elevation, the annual

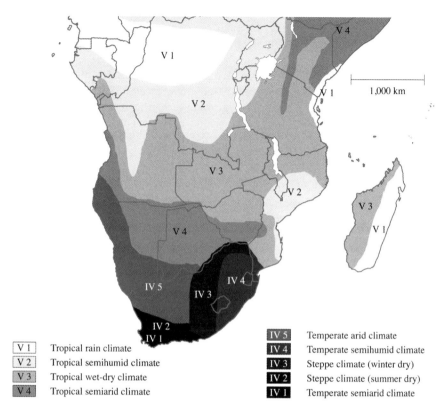

V 1	Tropical rain climate		IV 5	Temperate arid climate
V 2	Tropical semihumid climate		IV 4	Temperate semihumid climate
V 3	Tropical wet-dry climate		IV 3	Steppe climate (winter dry)
V 4	Tropical semiarid climate		IV 2	Steppe climate (summer dry)
			IV 1	Temperate semiarid climate

Map 3.1   Climate of Africa south of the equator

Source: Author's own draft, based on Jarret (1979) and Stock (1995).

average temperature of Kigali, Rwanda (2° south latitude, 1,497 metres NHN)[1] is 20°C, whereas the one of Mombasa, Kenya (4° south latitude, 55 metres NHN) is 26°C. Moreover, the annual amplitude decreases with increasing proximity to oceans. It is about 7°C in Port Elizabeth, South Africa (34° south latitude) – notably much less than in Kimberley.

Precipitation, together with temperature and parent rock material, accounts for soil formation – which is essential to agriculture. Permanent chemical weathering in the humid tropics leads to oxisols – also known as laterite soils – and to ultisols, or red clay soils. Their layer of humus is thin. They are neither able to absorb many fertilisers nor are they rich in minerals. With declining precipitation, entisols and inceptisols become predominant; the former in Angola and northeast Namibia, the latter in Tanzania. Compared to oxisols and ultisols, entisols and inceptisols

---

1   NHN stands for *Normalhöhennull*, meaning standard elevation zero. The equivalent of sea level, it is used to measure height.

are quite fertile. Entisols consist of nothing but an A horizon.[2] Fluvents are their most fertile subcategory: they occur in river valleys and deltas. Inceptisols, meanwhile, are older. They lack any accumulations of aluminium, clay, iron and organic material. The arid subtropics – that is, most parts of Namibia and the Northern Cape – are marked by aridisols. These soils suffer from a severe lack of organic material and run a high risk of salinisation occurring. Strictly speaking, the surface of the Kalahari Desert consists of shifting sands, not soils. The area close to Cape Town and a wide strip running from the coast of the Eastern Cape and KwaZulu-Natal to Zimbabwe are both marked by alfisols. They also occur in northern Mozambique. Alfisols are rich in clay, aluminium and iron – being, therefore, very fertile. The vertisols of Gauteng are even more fertile because of their thick A horizons – which directly connect up with the C horizon – and also due to their high share of montmorillonite. In some high mountain regions, very fertile andisols benefit from the fresh minerals that they receive from volcanic ash. Map 3.2 provides an overview of the major soil types found in Africa south of the equator.

Climate in Southern Africa is not, however, as constant as this overview might suggest. There is a strong natural variability, especially regarding rainfall in semiarid areas. The entire region is marked by a 20-year cycle of increasing and decreasing precipitation (Tyson 1986, 1991). These shifts impede agricultural practices and cause losses in production whenever the climate changes from relatively wet to relatively dry. Tyson (1981) would argue already 30 years ago that these natural shifts in climate, in combination with a growing human population, made the collapse of dry farming systems in some parts of Southern Africa and consequential irreversible desertification likely eventualities. The natural shifts in climate also hamper the generation of electricity by hydropower stations.

Another factor in the variability of rainfall in Southern Africa is El Niño, a natural phenomenon that occurs every two to eight years – it starts with a reversal of the Humboldt Current and affects the entire Southern Hemisphere. In El Niño years, the risk of drought in Southern Africa increases by 120 per cent (Thompson et al. 2003). Research from the mid-1990s suggests that more than 60 per cent of the variance in Zimbabwe's maize production is due to this phenomenon (Cane, Eshel and Buckland 1994). For the entire region, El Niño is believed to cause a 20 to 50 per cent drop in the yields of groundnuts, maize, millet and sorghum. The difference in maize yields between the extreme years of El Niño and the extreme years of La Niña (meaning very wet years) amounts to the volume that is theoretically needed to feed 15 million people (Stige et al. 2006). This does not, however, mean that La Niña is an overall beneficial phenomenon. Heavy rainfalls may cause severe damage to crop farming. It is important to note that the natural variability of rainfall does not affect all parts of the SADC region equally: the frequency of droughts is rather low in the DR Congo and northeast Angola, whilst

---

2   A horizons or topsoils are the mineral horizon on the surface, in which humified organic matter is mixed with mineral material.

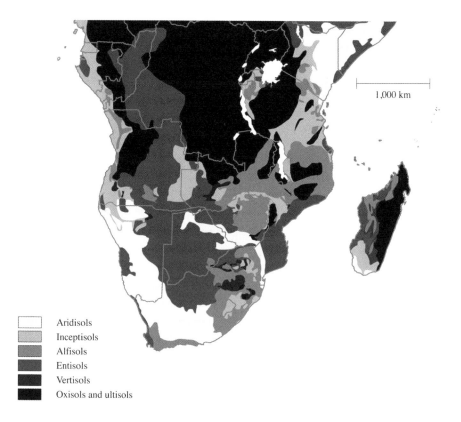

	Aridisols
	Inceptisols
	Alfisols
	Entisols
	Vertisols
	Oxisols and ultisols

Map 3.2   Soils in Africa south of the equator

Note: Since andisols only occupy very small areas, they are not included herein.
Source: Author's own draft, based on Jarret (1979) and Stock (1995).

it increases heading southwest in reaching its peak at the strip between 20° and 25° south latitude (Usman and Reason 2004).

The intraregional contrast of abundance and scarcity of water is reinforced by manmade climate change. Between 1960 and 2003, the annual average temperature in South Africa increased by 0.21°C per decade. Hot days became more frequent. The number of cold days declined meanwhile (Kruger and Shongwe 2004). Total rainfall and the number of days with heavy rainfall decreased in Southern Africa in the years from 1961 to 2000, but the amount of rainfall on days or in periods of heavy rainfall increased (New et al. 2006). In other words, the rainy season became shorter and more intense. This severely hampers agriculture, because temporal shortages of water have become increasingly likely.

Since the early 1970s, droughts have occurred more often in the aforementioned dry corridor lying between 20° and 25° south latitude. In the DR Congo, northern Angola and northern Zambia, precipitation caused by the ITCZ has, contrariwise, become more intense. The coast of the Western Cape has been receiving more rainfall too (Usman and Reason 2004). The frequency of El Niño/La Niña has increased, causing more droughts and more floods (Dollar and Goudie 2000). In the coming decades, rainfall is expected to decrease by 40 per cent in the western part of Southern Africa. Winter rainfall throughout the entire region will probably decline by 30 per cent, whereas summer rainfall in the Drakensberg area will increase (International Panel on Climate Change 2007). In the east, there will be almost no more rainy days in winter but more in summer, meaning that there will be a sharper distinction between the dry and rainy seasons. Temperatures may rise by 4–6°C during the next 30–50 years. The western interior especially will heat up (Dollar and Goudie 2000; Tadross, Jack and Hewitson 2005). In East Africa, malaria will most likely proliferate because of higher temperatures and higher summer rainfall (Hay 2002).

This tremendous fallout from climate change is having consequences, above all, for agriculture. Alarmist scenarios predict a total decline of crop yields in South Africa by between 9–90 per cent until the year 2100. The decreasing amount of land used for cultivating maize suggests that some areas of South Africa have already become too hot for maize, which is particularly problematic because half of all the maize produced in the SADC region is grown in South Africa. Some parts of the Free State and the Western Cape are no longer suitable for growing wheat. Sorghum cultivation has moved from the Western to the Eastern Cape, which is wetter (Benhin 2006). In the first half of the twenty-first century, climatic conditions in Southern Africa are likely to change to an extent greater than at any other time during the recorded history of mankind concludes Tyson (1991). Leading South African businesspersons consequently argued in an article featured in the *Mail & Guardian* on 18 March 2012 that their country's agricultural and industrial output is now threatened by the likelihood of an imminent water crisis in the Vaal catchment area. The former deputy director of South Africa's Department of Water Affairs, Mike Muller, warned in another article in the *Mail & Guardian* (19 February 2011) that metropolitan areas are heading for a water crisis by 2020 at the latest.

3.3 Country-specific Analysis: Climate

South Africa

South Africa's climate is diverse. KwaZulu-Natal resembles the tropics with its average temperature of 20°C and annual precipitation of 1,000 millimetres, concentrated in seven to eight humid months in summer. Even pineapples and sugar can be grown there. The eastern interior, the Highveld, receives 500 to 1,000 millimetres of rain, also mostly in summer. It is predominantly humid because of lower air temperatures. As noted, the most fertile soils of Southern Africa are found there. Further west, precipitation decreases to less than 450 millimetres per year. The sparser vegetation of different types of steppes demonstrates how aridity increases with distance from the coast, and from east to west. Livestock farming – first cattle, then sheep – becomes predominant.

In the Western Cape, precipitation varies locally for topographical reasons. The Great Karroo, which lies between the Highveld and the Cape Ranges, is one of the driest parts of South Africa. Cape Town receives an annual precipitation of 523 millimetres – a typical volume for a Mediterranean-like climate. In total, only 10 per cent of the country receives an annual precipitation of more than 750 millimetres. Fifty per cent of all rainfall is used for agriculture (Benhin 2006). Potential annual evaporation is high: slightly less than 1,500 millimetres in KwaZulu-Natal and up to 3,000 millimetres in the Northern and Western Cape (Christopher 1982).

In the eastern interior – where Gauteng, the major centre of economic activity and population, is located – the flow conditions of rivers are irregular. Large rivers do not occur. As noted, climate change has increased overall shortages of water. The UN already today considers South Africa a water-scarce country. By 2025, South Africa is expected to be amongst the world's most water-scarce countries (Benhin 2006). Nonetheless, precipitation in the Drakensberg high mountain area is sufficient to create permanent rivers that mostly flow into the Atlantic Ocean. These rivers are used to generate hydropower in medium-level quantities. The two largest nonpumped storage hydropower stations of South Africa are located on the Orange River. A power station at the Gariep Dam, 150 kilometres southwest of Bloemfontein, can generate up to 360 megawatts. Another power station stands at the Vanderkloof Dam, 130 kilometres further downstream. It has a capacity of 240 MW. All hydropower stations in South Africa together can generate 2,000 MW. According to an article published in *Engineering News* on 11 April 2008, some consultants estimate that another 5,000 to 7,000 MW of hydropower are possible. Others argue, as summarised in another article that appeared in the same magazine on 5 June 2009, that no further generation potential exists given that the country has already become water-scarce.

Another climatic problem of South Africa is the high variability of rainfall. What matters in this regard is not so much the aforementioned 20-year cycle of drier and rainier periods but rather annual variability. Medium variation is lowest in the coastal areas, excluding the extreme northwest, and in Gauteng, being less than 20 per cent there. It reaches 20–30 per cent along the borders with Mozambique and Zimbabwe. In the central interior and the northwest, medium variation increases in semicircles ranging from 20–30 per cent in Bloemfontein to 40–50 per cent near Upington. Moreover, the regionally dominant 20-year cycle is overlain by subnational cycles. They last 16–20 years in the northeast, 10–12 years near the coast between Cape Town and Port Elizabeth and two to three years in the central and western interiors (Tyson 1986) – the latter are thus most vulnerable to droughts.

Angola

Angola falls almost entirely under the influence of the ITCZ in summer. Rainfall is consequently high there, with 1,000 to 1,500 millimetres per year in northern and central Angola (except for the coastal strip). Most of it falls in the months from September to May. In the south, the rainy season only lasts from December to March. Angola's southern coastal area forms a desert, with an annual precipitation volume of around 10 millimetres. The southern interior is semiarid: 493 millimetres of rain per year fall in Ondjiva. Nonetheless, high transpiration means that only the Kwanza River Valley and the central uplands are truly humid. Temperature declines with elevation, which increases heading inland from the coast.

Angola's agriculture reflects these general climatic patterns, meaning that the country has the capacity to grow a wide variety of agricultural products. Yet, the variability of rainfall increases from the northeast to the south. It remains rather low, with 15 per cent at the border with the DR Congo but reaching 30–50 per cent in the southeast and 100 per cent in the mid- and southwest (Kuder 1971). Because of the relatively high level of precipitation, the generation of hydropower is possible – particularly in the centre and north of the country. Hydropower stations in southern Angola – such as the envisaged Epupa and existing Ruacana Stations on the Cunene River – are unreliable because of the high variability of rainfall in the area. Nevertheless, revitalising hydropower stations throughout the entire country and building new small-scale ones is the cornerstone of Angola's present energy policy according to an article that appeared in the *Jornal de Angola* on 27 April 2011.

Botswana

The pattern of increasing aridity heading northwest marks not only South Africa but also Botswana. Whilst the northeast part of the country is influenced by the ITCZ in summer and receives 650 millimetres of rain per year, the rest lies under the almost continuous influence of subtropical anticyclones – which cause aridity. In the southwest, only 250 millimetres of rain fall per year. The southeast, meanwhile, is semiarid, with an annual precipitation of 550 millimetres. The variability of rainfall increases from 25 per cent on the border with Zambia to 80 per cent in the extreme southwest (Klimm et al. 1994). Annual evapotranspiration would reach 2,000 millimetres here if there were sufficient precipitation. Around 80 per cent of Botswana's human and animal population are dependent upon groundwater (Mpotokwane, Shaw and Segodi 1993). The only region of Botswana that is marked by a periodic surplus of water, the Okavango Delta, carries considerable potential to serve as a basis for regional cooperation through the Okavango River Basin Commission – founded in 1994 by Angola, Botswana and Namibia. On the national level, water carriers are being planned to connect the Okavango Delta to the Orapa Diamond Mine. Even pipelines running from the Okavango River to Gaborone and Francistown have been considered (Mpotokwane, Shaw and Segodi

1993). Such an extensive diversion of water would, however, require gaining approval for this from neighbouring countries.

The DR Congo

Large parts of the DR Congo lie almost permanently under the influence of the ITCZ. The inner tropics are humid all year long. Annual rainfall there amounts to between 2,000–2,500 millimetres. Two to five arid months interrupt the rainy season in the northern and southern parts of the country. There, the annual rainfall of 1,200–1,600 millimetres is concentrated in the summer months. Due to high temperatures and high insolation, most of it evaporates quickly. The vegetation changes from rainforest to savannah. The variability of rainfall increases and constitutes an impediment to agriculture. Poor oxi- and ultisols also hamper agriculture in the inner and outer tropics. Temperatures fall with increasing altitude in the eastern DR Congo and change significantly from daytime to nighttime. The climatic conditions of the eastern mountains, in combination with fertile andisols near volcanoes, proved favourable to the spread of a European-style agriculture in the colonial era – especially livestock farming, which still marks the eastern DR Congo. Cocoa, coffee and tea are also grown there.

Because of high rainfall, the DR Congo – unlike most other African countries – does not ever run short of water. The vast network of rivers present serves as a transport system and holds enormous potential for hydropower generation. At the lower reaches of the Congo River between Kinshasa and Matadi, which are separated by a horizontal distance of 350 kilometres and a vertical distance of 270 metres, an average of 40,000 cubic metres of water flow per second (Stock 1995). The theoretical hydropower capacity of all SADC members excluding the DR Congo is 48,000 MW. The DR Congo has a generation potential of 100,000 MW, of which less than 2 per cent is currently being created (Maupin 2015). At the envisaged Grand Inga Dam, 44,000 MW could be generated, mostly for export to Southern Africa, at least according to an article that was published in *Engineering News* on 5 June 2009. Until recently, the completion of the Grand Inga Project was envisaged as happening by the 2020s. Its realisation has, however, proven to be difficult for political reasons. The two existing power stations situated on the Inga Dam presently generate a total of 1,775 MW. At Lac Nzilo, close to the DR Congo–Zambia border, there is a 108 MW station. The 246 MW Nseke Station near Mbandaka is currently being upgraded. Another article in *Engineering News*, published on 4 July 2008, suggests that Congolese hydropower plants may not only provide electricity but also have triggered local industrialisation – for example in the form of an aluminium smelting project by BHP Billiton.

Yet, the dense river network of the DR Congo also has negative implications. It constitutes a serious obstacle to movement. Its swamps and moving sandbanks are natural barriers to large-scale expansion. Providing reliable transportation by boat and the construction of a durable transport infrastructure becomes expensive because of floods and changing riverbeds. *Mining Weekly* reported on 8 July 2011 that the transport of mining products in Katanga Province – for instance on the N39 highway from Likasi to Kolwezi – was almost impossible, and certainly not reliable during the rainy season.

Lesotho

Although Lesotho lies at a much higher altitude than the neighbouring Free State, not all parts of the mountain kingdom receive more rainfall: the annual average of Maseru is just 699 millimetres. Only the high-mountain regions are clearly above these levels, receiving 1,000–1,400 millimetres. This explains why Lesotho accounts for 50 per cent of the flow stream of the Orange River, even though the country constitutes a mere 5 per cent of the catchment area of that river. This rich endowment with water is the basis for the Lesotho Highlands Water Project (LHWP), whose catchment areas receive 1,905 millimetres of rainfall per year (Nel and Illgner 2001). Temperatures in Lesotho, meanwhile, are marked by a high degree of amplitude. Maxima of more than 30°C in summer and minima of slightly more than 0°C mark the lowlands. In the highlands, frost is common in winter – thus being a problem for crop farming.

Malawi

Malawi's Shire River Valley is marked by average temperatures of over 24°C. Annual precipitation is less than 800 millimetres. Small rivers fall dry in winter. They thus do not reach the valley, but instead end up in swamps. In the upper valley, maize and peanuts are grown; the lower part is suitable for the cultivation of cotton. Higher precipitation and the presence of vertisols, giving some of the most fertile soils in Africa, increase the potential for agriculture being practiced in the areas around Lake Malawi: cotton is grown in the south; coffee, peanuts and tea in the north. The lake itself provides an enormous reservoir of drinking water and fish. Due to its elevation, average temperatures here decline to between 18 and 23°C, and even fall below the former level in winter on the plateaux surrounding Lake Malawi.

Whilst the lee side plateaux are dry, the southern plateaux receive significant rainfall: 1,000–1,850 millimetres per year, mostly in summer. Cash crops – in particular tea and tobacco – are grown there. On the plateaux above the Great Escarpment, average temperatures decline to between 15 and 18°C. Precipitation is generally higher there than in most other parts of Malawi: 1,600 millimetres per year. There is extensive small-scale variation in local climates and vegetation there. Agriculture in Malawi benefits from climatic differentiation, but suffers from an annual variability of rainfall that ranges from 20–25 per cent on the plateaux east of Lake Malawi and in the Shire River Valley to slightly more than 25 per cent on the southern plateaux, along the eastern coastal plain of the lake and in the extreme north (Lienau 1981).

Mozambique

The climate of central and northern Mozambique is shaped by the monsoons that occur between October and March. They account for 90 per cent of the annual precipitation in this part of the country: on average 1,000 millimetres. The winter months are extremely dry. Because of incidents of heavy rain during the monsoon season, floods are frequent along the rivers and consequently the fertile fluvents cannot be used the whole year round. Southern Mozambique lies under the influence of anticyclones most of the year. Precipitation decreases from 900 millimetres near the coast to 300 millimetres in the interior. Dry savannahs predominate in the latter. The annual variability of rainfall across the country is between 20 and 40 per cent, with its maxima south of the Zambezi River. The dry south depends upon its upstream neighbours South Africa and Zimbabwe to guarantee its water supply. Vertisols in the interior and entisols near the coast offer better conditions for agriculture than the oxi- and ultisols of the north, but also suffer from evaporation-induced high concentrations of salt (Kuder 1975). Given these natural conditions, Mozambique's agricultural potential is ultimately rather limited.

Compared to the countries situated on the western side of the SADC region, Mozambique is in a favourable position for the generation of hydropower because the Zambezi River passes through its lands. The power station at Cahora Bassa is, after the one at Lesotho's Katse Dam, the second largest in the whole of Southern Africa. Cahora Bassa has a capacity of 2,025 MW, most of which has continued to be sold to South Africa ever since the restoration of a transmission line to Johannesburg in the 1990s. The Zambezi River holds tremendous potential to provide electricity for mining and smelting in central Mozambique. Some speculate that it could be used to generate up to 50,000 MW (Schröder 2005). Although physical geography is a necessary condition for Mozambican–South African cooperation on electricity, it does not fully explain Cahora Bassa's existence. The power station was also built because the apartheid regime supported Portuguese colonial rule in exchange for electricity (Middlemas 1987). The post-independence proxy war then halted the continuous generation of electricity, which only resumed in 1998. Until today, electricity from Cahora Bassa has to be transmitted to Maputo via South Africa.

Namibia

Because the effects of the ITCZ become diminished the greater the distance from the equator, and given that the Westerlies barely reach beyond the Western Cape, rainfall in Namibia decreases from 600 millimetres per year on the border with Angola to 150 millimetres per year in Keetmanshoop. The coastal strip is even drier, with less than 100 millimetres of rainfall per year – not only because of predominant offshore trade winds but also due to the cold Benguela Current. The latter causes offshore rainfall of the rare onshore trade winds that reach Namibia. As a national average, 83 per cent of the rainfall evaporates shortly after precipitation occurs. Another 14 per cent is absorbed by plants. Only 3 per cent reaches rivers and/or becomes groundwater. Physical weathering predominates because of aridity. There is not much vegetation and soils are poor. Due to evaporation, hard crusts occur in all parts of the country. Even in the semiarid north, no more than 26 per cent of the soil is suitable for crop cultivation (Chimhowu et al. 1993).

The variability of rainfall further hampers agriculture. In western and southern Namibia, the deviation from the long-term mean reaches 50–70 per cent; around Windhoek, it is 30–40 per cent (Klimm et al. 1994). Rain-fed agriculture – with barley, beans, maize and sorghum being the main products – is only possible in the very north and in the slightly elevated area of Grootfontein and Tsumeb. Extensive livestock farming marks the central and southern interior. Namibia's rivers only temporarily contain water, except for the Cunene River at the northern and the Orange River at the southern border – they are dependent upon rainfall in Angola and South Africa respectively. This temporary lack of water is also a problem for its supply to Namibian households as well as to the country's mining and processing sectors, for instance the uranium mines and fishing industry in Walvis Bay – where, according to an article published in *The Namibian* on 23 July 2009, expensive desalination is now being considered.

Swaziland

Swaziland is, compared to the neighbouring provinces of Mozambique, quite rainy. As Swaziland's mountains virtually catch the clouds that come in from the Indian Ocean, higher elevation causes greater precipitation: 1,250 millimetres per year on the Swazi Highveld, 900 millimetres on the Midveld and 700 millimetres on the Lowveld. Whilst citrus fruits, maize and pineapples are grown semisubsistently on the Midveld, Swaziland's key export good – sugar cane – is typical for the Lowveld. Cotton is grown there as well. The Highveld can hardly be used for agricultural purposes because of its steep slopes, poor soils and frost. Commercial forestry, including the processing of timber, is undertaken there. High precipitation, combined with Swaziland's landform, makes the country suitable for hydropower generation. Yet, Swaziland only produces 15–20 per cent of the electricity that it consumes – mostly from three rather small hydropower stations that each have a capacity of between 10–20 MW. On 24 February 2009, *Engineering News* reported that the Ngwempisi Hydropower Cascading Scheme – likely to be realised in cooperation with Eskom – had as its aim the generation of an additional 120 MW.

Tanzania

The interior uplands of Tanzania are humid in the south, the west and near Mount Kilimanjaro. Average annual rainfall there is 800–1,200 millimetres. The rainy season lasts from November until April. Andisols from volcanic minerals increase agricultural potential there. Because of lower elevation, the coastal savannah is hot. Dar es Salaam's average annual temperature is 26°C (58 metres NHN), whereas Dodoma's is only 23°C (1,120 metres NHN). High temperatures increase evaporation and make Tanzania's coast rather dry; the exception is the rainy season from March to May, during which moist Easterlies bring rain. The northern savannah on the border with Kenya is even drier, with less than 600 millimetres of annual rainfall.

Tanzania's main agricultural regions produce a variety of crops. In Mtwara Province, cashew nuts, cassava, maize and sorghum are grown. The southern highlands are dominated by maize and rice as food crops, and coffee, tea and tobacco as cash crops. The slopes of Mount Kilimanjaro, Mount Meru and the Usambara Range are used for the traditional agroforestry of cash crops such as bananas, coffee and tea. In the drier parts of the country, especially the northern central plateau, cattle grazing predominates. Similar to with the rivers in many other Southern African countries, those in Tanzania are also quite suited to hydropower stations. The landscape configuration is favourable in this regard. The lack of water in the dry season, however, complicates the process of generating electricity by hydropower. Tanzania's hydropower stations are, therefore, currently rather small. The largest one, Kidatu Power Station, reaches a capacity of 204 MW. Altogether, hydropower stations generate 60 per cent of Tanzania's electricity. Their relevance is increased by the fact that the dams built for them also supply the surrounding areas with much-needed water.

Zambia

Zambia is as diverse as the entire SADC region itself with regard to agroclimatic conditions. The north – both in its eastern and western parts – receives more than 1,000 millimetres of rain per year. Most of it falls between October and April. Temperatures are moderate due to elevation: between 18 and 23°C on average. Evaporation is, therefore, not as high as in other parts of the country, which allows cassava and maize to be cultivated there. The variability of rainfall is only 15–25 per cent. In the extreme northwest and the central northeast, precipitation is more than 1,200 millimetres – thus enabling the cultivation there of coffee and tea. In the Luangwa Valley and the Zambezi Valley, precipitation of less than 800 millimetres per year and a high degree of evaporation limit agriculture to the growing of millet and sorghum. In central, eastern and southern Zambia, 800–1,000 millimetres of rain falls per year. Cotton, maize and tobacco are harvested between November and March. In the extreme south, precipitation remains below 800 millimetres and sometimes varies by more than 30 per cent from one year to another. The cultivation of maize is no longer possible there. Crops have thus been replaced by livestock instead (Drescher 1998; Schultz 1983).

One should, however, not form the impression that only the very south of Zambia is water-scarce. Eighty-eight per cent of precipitation evaporates throughout the entire country. Eighty per cent of the water that flows through the country's rivers does so in the rainy season. Many of them fall dry in winter (Schultz 1983). In spite of their temporary aridity, large rivers provide good conditions for hydropower stations. At the Kafue Gorge Dam, there is a 900 MW power station. The *Lusaka Times* reported on 7 January 2010 that another one at almost the exact same location would be built by 2017, with a capacity of 600 MW. Also on the Kafue River, at the already-existing Itezhi–Tezhi Dam, a 120 MW power station is scheduled to become operational in the near future according to an article in *The Post* on 11 February 2011. The Kariba North Power Station has recently upgraded its capacity from 600 to 720 MW. A new 360 MW station nearby is being constructed by Sinohydro, financed by a loan from the DBSA.

Zimbabwe

Zimbabwe experiences a dry season of six to eight months. Almost all rain falls in the summer when the interior part of Southern Africa serves as a heating surface that makes air move upwards locally, thereby attracting moist Easterlies. The average temperatures of Zimbabwe's Highveld are moderate, being between 15–20°C. Rainfall reaches about 800 millimetres per year, a volume that increases moving eastwards. The Highveld is the country's best farming region. Cotton, maize, tobacco, vegetables and wheat are grown intensively there. Tobacco has been Zimbabwe's key cash crop since colonial times. On the Midveld, rainfall decreases to 600 millimetres per annum. It becomes highly variable. Soils are less fertile. Drought resistant crops – such as cotton, sorghum and soya beans – are cultivated on mostly communal land. In the south and west, rainfall decreases even further. Only extensive agriculture is possible here. The valleys of the Lowveld are marked by average temperatures far above 20°C. Intensive farming is impossible, also because the Limpopo and Save Rivers become muddy pools that are joined by a trickle of brown water at the end of the dry season.

The upper Zambezi contrariwise holds considerable potential for hydropower generation. The Kariba South Power Station can produce up to 750 MW. When it reaches its full capacity, it provides 60–70 per cent of the electricity consumed nationwide. Until 2008, about 25–35 per cent of domestic demand used to be met by electricity imported from South Africa. The remaining 5 per cent was generated thermally. As *The Herald* reported on 26 April 2010, the Zimbabwean government recently signed a USD 400 million deal with the Chinese company Sinohydro to expand Kariba South's output by an additional 250–360 MW.

3.4 Geomorphology and Geology

The African continent can be divided into Low Africa (average altitude: 300 metres), which ranges from the southern slope of the Atlas Mountains to the Congo Basin, and High Africa (average altitude: 1,200 metres), which begins in the Ethiopian Highlands and then reaches southwards to the Cape Mountains. High

Africa is marked by plateau landscapes, vast basins and the Great Escarpment. The interior plateaux and the Great Escarpment is a tectonic bulge from the Cretaceous Era of 145.5–65.5 million years ago. This bulge is more intense on its margins, which explains the bowl-like shape of Southern Africa. The Great Escarpment forms its very edge along a fractured zone. It separates the interior of the continent from the coastal plains. The rivers that pass through it – many on the eastern but few on the western side, for climatic reasons – contain rapids and waterfalls. Transport is further hampered by the fluviatile formations of the coastal landscape: river mouths are deltaic. Coastal waters tend to be shallow near the shore. Because of longshore drifts, Africa's coasts have few bays but many sandbars. Mangroves and shallow inshore waters occur frequently. Lagoons and swamps often abut the coasts. Only the coast of South Africa provides steep cliffs with at least some bays that can be used as harbours. In short, most of Southern Africa – and especially the interior plateaux – is cut off from the rest of the world by geomorphological structures. Figure 3.1 shows an elevation profile for the overland route from Durban to Johannesburg, which demonstrates the impediment to transport posed by the Great Escarpment.

Africa comprises, moreover, only few high-mountain regions. South of the Sahara Desert, there are the Ethiopian Highlands, the massifs of Mount Kenya and Mount Kilimanjaro, the Drakensberg (also shown in Figure 3.1) and the Cape Mountains. Only the latter two ranges have the typical appearance of high-mountain regions – that is, a steep, rugged rock surface without vegetation. That there are so few high-mountain regions in Africa is due to the geological and geomorphological history of the continent. Its Precambrian basement complex – Africa's primary geological feature, whose oldest parts were formed 3.7–2.6 billion years ago – has been vastly eroded and planed down. On top of the basement complex, there are younger sediments that form modestly waved plateau landscapes. Cuestas and tectonic ridges occasionally alter the landscape, which is otherwise marked by monotonous peneplains and inselberge. Deep valleys in permanently dry parts of the continent's interior – such as the Fish River Canyon in southern Namibia – are the legacy of rainier eras tens of thousands of years ago, when rivers eroded their basins but then fell dry because of natural climate change.

Today, few permanent rivers occur in the deep valleys situated on the plateaux. They pass through arid regions such as the Northern Cape and are dependent upon rainfall upstream. Small-scale variation in landscape, which is typical for younger continents, barely occurs in Africa because of long-term processes of weathering. This geomorphological structure makes transport on the interior plateaux very easy. All over the African continent, large basins occur between the plateaux. The Congo Basin's rainforests and extended rivers and the Kalahari Basin's steppes are characteristic traits of the region. The effects of these two basins on human movement are totally different. Whilst the Congo Basin is a severe physical barrier to it, the Kalahari provides good conditions for such transportation. The reason for this is not geomorphology but climate; as explained above, the climate of the inner tropics accounts for the dense vegetation and the vast river network of the Congo

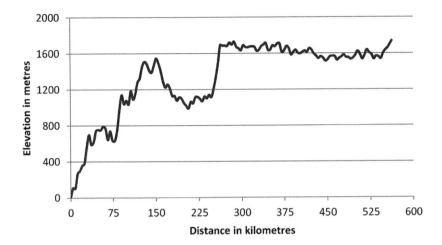

Figure 3.1   Elevation profile Durban to Johannesburg
Source: Draper and Scholvin (2012: 12).

Basin. The Kalahari, being influenced all year long by subtropical anticyclones, is neither fragmented by rivers nor does vegetation hamper human movement through it.

Only the temporarily flooded Okavango Delta poses a physical barrier to movement from the southwest to northeast. So do the Cunene and Zambezi Rivers north of the Kalahari Basin. In East Africa, tectonic activity – the drifting apart of the African Plate and the Somalia Plate – has formed faults and volcanic mountains during the last 35 million years, for instance Mount Kenya. The East African Rift Valley – where areas lying at sea level connect up with ones of an altitude of 2,000 metres on a horizontal distance of 40–60 kilometres – ranges from Eritrea to the mouth of the Zambezi River in Mozambique. The Great Lakes are its most visible feature. Lake Albert, Lake Edward, Lake Kivu and Lake Tanganyika are the western branch of the Rift Valley. In Lake Malawi, the western branch merges with the eastern one – which crosses the uplands of Kenya and Tanzania. The East African Rift Valley is a tremendous obstacle to human transport. It connects up with the Congo Basin and delimits Southern Africa from a geomorphological perspective. Figure 3.2 shows the elevation profile for the overland route from Dar es Salaam to Lusaka, which passes through the Great Escarpment in Tanzania and the East African Rift Valley in the Tanzanian–Zambian border region.

The longevity of the continental interior not only explains the distinct geomorphology of Africa; it also accounts for the abundance of mineral resources to be found there. The geologically oldest parts of Africa are known as 'cratons'. The Kaapvaal and Zimbabwe Cratons both date back 3.7–3 billion years, being a mixture of terranes and gneisses that are penetrated by granitic plutons. Further south, the Bushveld Complex is one of the richest systems of mineral deposits

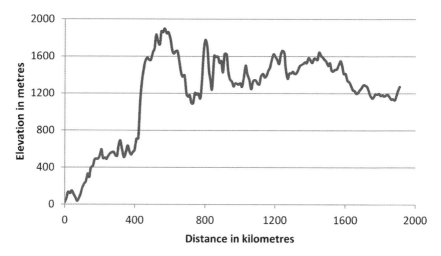

Figure 3.2   Elevation profile Dar es Salaam to Lusaka

Note: In comparing figures 3.1 and 3.2, it is important to keep in mind that their horizontal axes are different.

Source: Draper and Scholvin (2012: 12).

in the world. Being a 2-billion-year-old layered intrusion, it contains chrome, iron, nickel, platinum, titan and vanadium in an area of roughly 30,000 square kilometres lying between Polokwane and Pretoria. Zimbabwe's Great Dyke – a group of layered ultramafic intrusions that are 2.5 billion years old – spreads 550 kilometres from north to south, doing so in a Y-shape. It is rich in cobalt, copper, gold, nickel and platinum group metals. The other such areas in the region – that is, the Congo, Kalahari and Tanzania Cratons – also contain minerals, though not in such great diversity. Most noteworthy is the Congolese–Zambian Copperbelt. It extends for 200 kilometres from east to west, and is rich in copper and cobalt. The minerals therein were formed in the Precambrian Era, and then became concentrated due to tectonic activity that occurred about 500 million years ago (Eriksson 2000).

Besides the mineral deposits located in these ancient cratons, the Karroo System is rich in coal. It dates back 200–300 million years to the Carboniferous, Permian, Triassic and Jurassic Eras, and stretches through the Free State, KwaZulu-Natal and Mpumalanga (Petters 1991). About half of the coal deposits therein can be easily obtained by surface mining. Smaller fragments of the Karroo System are spread over Southern Africa. They are the only coal deposits in the region. As explained below, oil and natural gas are mostly found offshore. Angola's offshore oilfields close to Cabinda Province stand out because of the vast quantities of the fossil fuel that they hold. Other oilfields have also recently been discovered off the coasts of Mozambique and Namibia, as well as in Tanzania's Rift Valley. Natural gasfields occur in Botswana, and along the coast of Mozambique, southern Namibia and

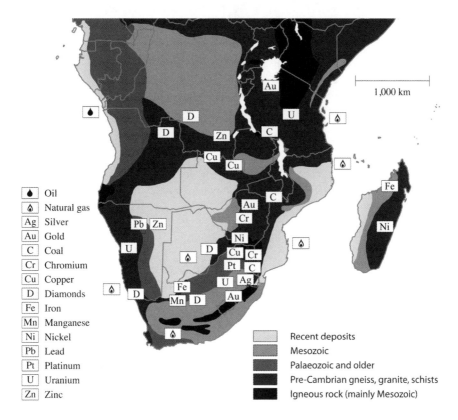

Oil
Natural gas
Ag Silver
Au Gold
C   Coal
Cr Chromium
Cu Copper
D   Diamonds
Fe Iron
Mn Manganese
Ni Nickel
Pb Lead
Pt Platinum
U   Uranium
Zn Zinc

Recent deposits
Mesozoic
Palaeozoic and older
Pre-Cambrian gneiss, granite, schists
Igneous rock (mainly Mesozoic)

Map 3.3   Geological features of Africa south of the equator
Source: Author's own draft, based on Jarret (1979) and Stock (1995).

Tanzania. The exploitation of shale gas is being discussed for the Karroo in South Africa (Fig and Scholvin 2015). Map 3.3 shows the aforementioned geological features of Africa south of the equator, and includes the most relevant mineral deposits that are present there.

3.5 Country-specific Analysis: Geomorphology and Geology

South Africa

South Africa consists of the Kalahari Basin, the surrounding plateaux, protruding cuestas and the coastal plains. The latter two are separated from the plateaux by the Great Escarpment. The Cape Mountains in the southwest – a complex structure of parallel ridges separated by long valleys – and the Drakensberg in the east are exceptions to the Precambrian orogeny and plain landscapes of the rest of Africa. The interior plateaux are shaped by smooth cuestas. Elevation rises steadily from 1,000 metres in the west of the Northern Cape to 1,500 metres in the Free State. South Africa's coasts mostly consist of lagoons and sand dunes in the northeast and west. In the south and southeast, rocky cliffs, strong ocean currents and heavy winds are impediments to maritime transport and ports. Bays exist where the Cape Mountains come close to the sea, but they are hardly protected from the strong Westerlies. The major lagoons along the eastern coast – Durban, Lake St Lucia and Richards Bay – are barricaded by sandbars. Nonetheless, these places provide better conditions for harbours than the coasts of the other countries of the region do.

In addition to the aforementioned Bushveld Complex, many different mineral resources are found in the northeast of South Africa. The Witwatersrand possesses deposits of gold, manganese and uranium. The world's largest-known gold placer is located there. The border region with Namibia is comprised of deposits of copper and zinc. With the exception of cobalt, which is instead predominantly found in the DR Congo and Zambia, South Africa possesses the majority and by far the largest diversity of the entire SADC region's mineral resources. The only key resources that the regional power does not possess in significant quantities are oil and natural gas. The feasibility of exploiting shale gas in the Karroo remains to be proven (Fig and Scholvin 2015). Historically, mining has served as a key foundation for the regional dominance of South Africa. The previous expansion northwards of white settlers – led by Cecil Rhodes, whose company De Beers had made a fortune from diamond mining around Kimberley – would not have happened if South Africa had not been so rich in mineral resources and if Rhodes and his partners had not expected to find more minerals up north.

What Fine and Rustomjee (1996) call the 'minerals–energy complex' stresses the continuing relevance of mining: it provides crucial inputs to the manufacturing sector and merges with manufacturing in large industrial conglomerates that benefit from economies of scale. The generation of electricity – up to 90 per cent of which is reliant on coal – and the chemicals industry – which transforms coal into liquids – are tied to these conglomerates as well. Fine and Rustomjee calculate that the minerals–energy complex contributed to between 20–30 per cent of South Africa's gross domestic product in the early 1990s. It accounted for about two-thirds of the country's exports. What is more, the country's financial sector serves as a 'conveyor belt', interlinking mining, manufacturing and other sectors related to production. Six capital axes practically controlled the entire South African economy in the early 1990s. The state is bound to the minerals–energy complex too. It invests in key industries such as chemicals and steel and provides the necessary transport infrastructure for mining and related activities. McDonald argues that the minerals–energy complex remains 'vertically and horizontally integrated into a composite set of related industrial […] activities', with links to the service sector, finance in particular (2009: 8). It finds one of its most significant expressions in the Energy Intensive User Group, which is a highly influential lobbying organisation whose members, such as AngloGold Ashanti,

Lonmin Platinum, SABMiller and Transnet, consume approximately 44 per cent of South Africa's electricity. Leading politicians of the African National Congress (ANC) sit on the boards or hold shares in mining companies, most prominently the party's vice-president, Cyril Ramaphosa.

Angola

Angola is largely located on the ancient African massif. East of the steep slopes and characteristic waterfalls of the Great Escarpment lie the Lunda Uplands and the Cassange Basin, the latter in the central north. Both are marked by a monotonous cuesta landscape and valleys. Angola's coastal plain is thin: only 15 kilometres wide in the narrowest parts. In the south, it is covered by dunes. Further north, cliffs mark the coastline. This means that Angola should possess a continental orientation, because most of its coastal strip is cut off from the rest of the country by the Great Escarpment – leading to poor conditions for economic activity and it being unfavourable to harbours. The hinterland is, contrariwise, not separated from the neighbouring states by any major physical barriers.

Diamonds are one of the two essential geological features of Angola. They are found in Lunda Norte Province between the Cassai and Dundo Rivers. The mining area extends south and west to the Cuango River and the Cassange Basin. Mining diamonds remains exclusively in the hands of the state-owned Empresa Nacional de Diamantes, which cooperates with De Beers. In Cuanza Norte and Huila Provinces exist deposits of iron ore. Manganese is found in the Alto Zambeze and Cassai Districts, situated in central Angola and in the coastal desert in the south respectively. Copper is mined and smelted near Maquela do Zombo, a town that has – as reported by the *Jornal de Angola* on 30 December 2010 – recently been connected to a hydropower station on the Capanda Dam.

Angola's second essential geological feature is oil. The former Portuguese colony possesses 99 per cent of Southern Africa's total oil resources. Most of them are located offshore in the exclave of Cabinda. Oil poses an exception to the geographically induced orientation inwards to the continent. It favours a maritime directionality because of its location near the coastline. Accordingly, Angola's two main customers are China and the US, which account for 45 and 23 per cent of Angola's oil sales respectively. Total exports amount to 1.8 million barrels per day (Energy Information Administration 2011b). Natural gas meanwhile – which occurs along with oil – is liquefied in northern Angola and shipped to Europe and North America.

Botswana

Coming from Gauteng, the average altitude of Botswana slowly descends to 1,000 metres. Monotonous basins and smooth ridges characterise the landscape. Eighty per cent of Botswana's surface belongs to the Kalahari Basin, which is filled with sandy sediments. Geomorphology is favourable to transport. The Okavango Delta in the northwest, which is temporarily flooded after the rainy season in southern Angola, poses the only natural barrier to movement. Many bridges in the Okavango Delta are too narrow and not stable enough for vehicles carrying large and heavy loads. An article in the *Namibian Sun* on 7 October 2010 pointed out that such problems hampered use of the Trans-Caprivi Highway and made transport from Namibia to Zambia via South Africa necessary in some cases. Whilst Namibia has at least built a major bridge across the Zambezi River near Katima Mulilo, lorries that pass through Botswana on their way from Durban to the Copperbelt and vice versa need to cross the river by ferry near Kazungula (Curtis 2009).

In the east of the country, the Precambrian crystalline basement reaches the surface. Minerals such as copper, gold and nickel are found there. Diamonds, the most important mining product of Botswana, are extracted within 200 kilometres of Francistown and Gaborone. The Opara Mine is the second largest diamond mine in the world (Newman 2011). The state-owned Debswana Diamond Company is a 50:50 joint venture with De Beers. Because of the abundance of diamonds and favourable working relations with De Beers, Botswana has turned from one of the poorest countries in the world at the time of its independence into a middle-income country. Botswana is also rich in coal, which is mined near Morupule. The coal-fired Morupule (A) Power Station has an installed capacity of 132 MW and provides 80 per cent of all the electricity currently generated in Botswana. Because Botswana is a net importer of electricity from South Africa, the government recently launched a project for a new 600 MW coal-fired power station: Morupule (B). The *Botswana Gazette* reported on 27 July 2010 that Morapule (B) would be supplied with coal from a nearby colliery. Botswana's estimated 212 billion tonnes of coal reserves are expected to be of such a high quality that the country may in the foreseeable turn into a regional energy hub and/or major exporter of coal. Railway lines would, though, have to be built from Botswana to Walvis Bay in Namibia, or to Techobanine in Mozambique to facilitate this. By injecting carbon dioxide into gasfields, natural gas may be exploited as well – thereby reducing Botswana's carbon footprint, as an article in *Mining Weekly* on 15 July 2011 suggested.

The DR Congo

Millions of years of chemical weathering have formed the plain landscape of the Congo Basin – which reaches an elevation of 400 metres – and of the surrounding plateaux lying at an elevation of 700 to 1,800 metres. The dense vegetation and river network of the Congo Basin hampers transport much more than the frequent changes from plateaux to closed depressions do. In the east of the DR Congo, there are active volcanoes. They belong to the western branch of the East African Rift Valley and form a considerable barrier to human transport. Provided sufficient infrastructure is built, the Great Lakes will be a centripetal force – easing transport from the eastern DR Congo, via Tanzania, to the Indian Ocean.

The DR Congo's geology – the Precambrian crystalline basement and younger magmatic intrusions in the eastern mountains – explains the abundance of diamonds and various other minerals found there, especially cobalt and copper. In 2011, Katanga Province was responsible for 5 per cent of the world's copper production, roughly 800,000 tonnes. The author of an article published in *Mining Weekly* on 11 November 2010 correctly predicted an increase to more than 1 million tonnes in 2012 because of the investor-friendly policies of the Congolese government. BHP Billiton is a key investor in copper mining in Katanga Province. The South African giant runs projects on the basis of licences held by it and Congolese partners. Bauxite and phosphate are also mined. Coal – found in central and northeast Katanga Province – is of low quality (Smith, Merrill and Meditz 1994).

Sociopolitical instability in the DR Congo poses a severe obstacle to mining. *Mining Weekly* reported on 10 July 2009 that there were 25,000 unemployed miners in Katanga Province alone. Instead of making mining activities a primary source of state income, the DR Congo had to borrow money from the International Monetary Fund in order to be able to pay its employees. An inadequate transport infrastructure further complicates mining. According to an article published in *Mining Weekly* on 8 July 2011, it takes 29–32 days to reach South Africa's harbours coming from Katanga Province, 14–15 days via Harare to Beira, 27–28 days to Dar es Salaam and 16–18 days to Walvis Bay. Beyond these considerations of the difficulties of extracting minerals in the DR Congo, it is crucial to note that practically all resources except for oil are all located in the southeast and at the eastern edge of the country. These areas of the DR Congo are somewhat distant from the capital and, for physiogeographical reasons, are more easily linked to East and Southern Africa.

Lesotho

Lesotho consists of several valleys and mountain ranges. The former have an elevation of about 1,800 metres; the latter reach up slightly more than 3,000 metres. Because of the frequent changes in altitude and relatively high precipitation, the mountain kingdom possesses a tremendous potential to serve as a water provider to neighbouring South Africa. Lesotho's Katse Dam provides 30 cubic metres of water per second to the Free State and Gauteng. The Muela Power Station, linked to the dam by a 45 kilometre-long pipeline, can generate up to 80 MW. Lesotho's total potential for hydropower is considerably higher (Tabirih 1993). Because of its unfavourable landscape configuration, one which is typical of high-mountain regions, only 2.5 per cent of Lesotho's territory is used for cultivating crops. Agricultural overuse is particularly dangerous because of ongoing erosion. An estimated 39 million tonnes of soil are lost every year in the country. Deep gullies mark the lowlands. Bare hills are common in the highlands. The shortage of timber contributes to this problem, because it is an important commodity for the agricultural and construction sectors – and a source of energy (Tabirih 1993).

Malawi

The most remarkable geomorphological feature of Malawi is the Shire River Valley. It descends from an altitude of 474 metres at Lake Malawi to just 40 metres at the border with Mozambique. The valley provides almost ideal conditions for hydropower generation. Between Matope and Chikwawa, the elevation drops by 308 metres across a horizontal distance of 81 kilometres (Lienau 1981). Eskom helped to build a 128 MW station at the Kapichira Falls. *Engineering News* reported on 25 February 2011 that the China Gezuba Group Corporation had recently been named by Malawi's government as its partner in upgrading that hydropower station. According to Malawian government sources cited in the same magazine on 3 September 2010, the generation of an additional 770 MW on the rivers of the country is a realistic goal for the coming decades.

Besides its potential for hydropower generation, Malawi is poor in natural resources. Coal is found in the Shire Valley and in the north but tectonic dislocations hamper mining – Malawi is part of the eastern branch of the East African Rift Valley. Exploitable resources have become scarce. The Kaziwiziwi Coalfield was closed in 1990. Until then, it had provided 60 per cent of the coal consumed in Malawi (Mhone and Nguira 1993). *Engineering News* reported on 13 May 2011 that the Malawian company Benga Energy and Mining was conducting a feasibility study for a coal-fired power station near the northern coalfields.

Besides the Shire Valley and Lake Malawi, the country consists of large plateaux having an elevation of between 900 and 1,400 metres on both sides of the lake and valley. Only a few inselberge and dambos – that is, tub-shaped, seasonally flooded valleys with grassy vegetation – occur in these plain parts of the country. The borderline between the plateaux and the valley is drawn by the Great Escarpment wherever it forms cliffy and steep faults. Altitude differs by 3,500 metres across distances as short as a few kilometres. Eroded mountain areas of the Great Escarpment contrariwise pass smoothly into the valley. In sum, Malawi suffers from tremendous geomorphological obstacles to transport, both on a national scale as well as regarding its integration into the wider region.

Mozambique

About 45 per cent of Mozambique is lowland. Its elevation is less than 200 metres. In the north, the coastal strip is 60 kilometres wide. There, the coast is marked by cliffs up to 100 metres high and by intertidal mudflats. Coral islands are located at a distance of 5–20 kilometres from the shore – poor conditions for harbours. The delta region of the Zambezi River comprises mangroves and swamps of about 8,000 square kilometres, or 70 kilometres of coastline. Heading west, ones passes through rather smooth cuestas and two plateaux, reaching a mountain region of over 1,000 metres at the border between South Africa and Zimbabwe. Except for inselberge, the landscape of the plateaux is plain. This geomorphological setting constitutes the fundament for Mozambique's rivers, which are characterised by a low incline in the south and a high one in the centre and north. Because of their high incline, the rivers in the centre and north possess considerable potential for hydropower generation – floods are frequent, however, thus hampering both this activity and human transport.

With the exception of alluvial deposits – principally gold along the Chimezi, Inhamurra, Muza and Revue Rivers – mineral resources are only found in Tete Province, which belongs geologically to the Precambrian shield. Sediments along the Zambezi River there are rich in coal. They are part of the Karroo System. These coal reserves are of high quality and can be used in steel production. Moderate amounts of bauxite are located in the Moriangane Mountains. The coastal sands north and south of Quelimane contain heavy minerals. Tete Province has aroused the interest of overseas mining giants such as Rio Tinto from Australia and Vale from Brazil. The latter already exploits Moatize's anthracite coal, which is the single biggest such deposit in Africa. *Mining Weekly* reported on 29 June 2011 that the output was expected to increase to 22 million tonnes per year by 2014. In connection with this investment, a 300 MW thermal power station and a coal-to-diesel plant are envisaged. The latter will produce 300 million litres of diesel per year. According to another article, published in *Mining Weekly* on 20 May 2011, Vale is also continuing to search for oil and natural gas reserves in collaboration with the state-owned Empresa Nacional de Hidrocarbonetos. *Engineering News* reported on 20 January 2012 that PetroSA had signed a cooperation agreement with Mozambique's state-run Petróleos de Moçambique. The Pande and Temane Gasfields are already connected to Sasol's Secunda Plant near Johannesburg by an 865 kilometre-long pipeline, whose inauguration has since increased the share of natural gas in South Africa's primary energy supply market from 1.5 to 4 per cent (Norbrook 2012).

Namibia

The interior parts of Namibia are marked by denudation surfaces. In the north, inselberge occur. There are cuestas south of Windhoek but in general the landscape is plain. Namibia's interior is separated from the coastal strip by the Great Escarpment. A gap in the Great Escarpment north of Swakopmund, where elevation increases gently, is a unique feature of Southern Africa. It eases transport. The only natural harbours along Namibia's coast are Lüderitz and Walvis Bay. The rest of Namibia's coast consists of narrow sandy beaches, which make the construction of ports almost impossible. Coastal waters are shallow. Even 5 kilometres offshore, the water is still only 100–200 metres deep. Just like Angola, Namibia should accordingly be inwardly-oriented towards the continent.

Namibia is rich in mineral resources. Copper, lead, vanadium and zinc are found in Precambrian rock near Tsumeb. The local smelter processes ore imported from the Congolese–Zambian Copperbelt via the Trans-Caprivi Highway. On a regional scale, Tsumeb's metal smelter is a significant centripetal force because Namibia, the DR Congo and Zambia would barely be able to process mined copper on their own for a lack of economies of scale (Honorary Consul of Namibia, pers. comm., 9 December 2009). In southern Namibia, close to Rosh Pinah, lead and zinc were formed by volcanic activity in earlier times. The Skorpion Zinc Mine reaches an annual output of 150,000 tonnes, which are exported via Lüderitz. Uranium mining near Walvis Bay makes Namibia the world's fourth largest exporter of this mineral. Its contribution to the country's gross domestic product is expected to increase from 5.5 per cent in 2008 to 14.8 per cent in 2015 according to an article in the *Allgemeine Zeitung* on 23 August 2010.

Younger sediments near Aranos contain 370 million tonnes of coal, which has not yet been mined for economic reasons. Nonetheless, the *Namibia Economist* reported on 13 June 2008 that South African entrepreneurs had purchased mining rights to 10 farms in the area. Diamonds are mined as secondary deposits on- and offshore in the Namib Desert. Since the beginning of diamond mining in Namibia in 1908, De Beers has held a monopoly over their extraction. Near the mouth of the Orange River, natural gas has been found. Offshore gas- and oilfields may also exist along the coastline of northern Namibia. Processing of natural gas and oil depends upon cooperation with South Africa, because Namibia's domestic market is itself too small (Honorary Consul of Namibia, pers. comm., 9 December 2009). South Africa has already shown interest in purchasing Namibian natural gas. An offshore pipeline from the deepwater port of Saldanha to Lüderitz is planned (Daniel and Luchtman 2006).

Swaziland

Swaziland lies mostly within the mountain ranges that form the border between Mozambique and South Africa. The Highveld, which reaches an elevation of 1,000–1,200 metres, comprises 29 per cent of Swazi territory. It constitutes the western part of the country. The Midveld, at 600–1,000 metres, accounts for 26 per cent. Thirty-six per cent of Swaziland belongs to the Lowveld, which is located in the east. Its altitude is 300–600 metres (Mdluli 1993). Since Swaziland possesses an expected 1 billion tonnes of coal deposits, building a 120 MW coal-fired power station in the country has been considered, as *Engineering News* reported on 24 February 2009. The Maloma Coal Mine, owned by South African Xstrata, is the largest mine in the country. *Mining Weekly* reported on 20 January 2012 that South Africa's Transnet and Swaziland Rail had agreed to construct a railway line from Mpumalanga Province in South Africa through Swaziland to Richards Bay – the most important port for bulk cargo for both East and Southern Africa – in order to facilitate coal mining. This railway line is due to become operational in 2016, and will reach a maximum capacity of 15 million tonnes. Shipping 6 million tonnes of Swazi coal via Maputo is another possible alternative (Senior official of TradeMark Southern Africa, pers. comm., 2 March 2012).

Tanzania

Except for the coastal strip, which is 15–65 kilometres wide, Tanzania consists of uplands with some volcanic mountains. Rift valleys encircle and divide the uplands, which are structured by erosion and fault scarps. Lake Malawi, Lake Rukwa and Lake Tanganyika are part of the East African Rift Valley. The Rukwa Valley lies 700–800 metres lower than the adjoining northeastern plateau. The coastal area is marked by hilly countryside, splitting it into various plain sections of low elevation. Coral riffs are frequent. Because of tectonic processes, many rivers in Tanzania end up in lakes without reaching the Indian Ocean. They do not open the hinterland. The rivers that reach the Indian Ocean form deltas with alluvial soils favourable to agriculture but problematic for maritime transport. Tanzania's coast contains some bays suitable for harbours.

Lying between Lake Malawi and Lake Tanganyika are approximately 1.5 billion tonnes in coal deposits. According to an article published in *Tanzania Daily News* on 14 December 2009, coal-fired power stations are to be constructed with Chinese partners in the southwest of the country and may achieve a joint capacity of 1,000 MW. Given recent discoveries of 0.85–1.13 trillion cubic metres of gasfields, the Tanzanian government is now planning to also build gas-fired power stations and a pipeline from Dar es Salaam to Mombasa in Kenya, as *Engineering News* reported on 3 June 2011. Another pipeline will be built from Dar es Salaam to Mtwara, close to the Mozambican border (Senior research fellow at the German Institute of Global and Area Studies, pers. comm., 12 October 2012).

The Australian company Beach Energy is searching for oil in Tanzania's Rift Valley. A Canadian company plans to mine 1,900 tonnes of uranium oxide per year over a period of 14 years, which will make Tanzania Africa's third largest exporter of uranium. Yet, Tanzania has not developed its energy-related resources sufficiently. The existing hydropower stations do not generate enough electricity in the dry season. Power cuts are frequent. Gold is the only resource that has so far been extensively exploited: Tanzania is the fourth largest gold producer in Africa. The Geita Gold Mine near Lake Victoria, which reached an output of 350,000 ounces in 2010, is entirely owned by AngloGold Ashanti. *Mining Weekly* reported on 12 October 2010 that this mine accounted for 6 per cent of the total gold production of AngloGold Ashanti worldwide, and was expected in the near future to increase its output to 500,000 ounces. British–Tanzanian African Barrick Gold runs the three other large gold mines of the country, all located near Lake Victoria. Their joint annual output is 850,000 ounces. In total, gold mining generates annual export earnings of USD 2.2 billion (Economist Intelligence Unit 2012).

Zambia

Zambia lies on a crystalline bloc, delimited by the East African Rift Valley to the northeast, the Zambezi Valley to the southeast and the Upembe Rift Zone to the northwest. To the southwest, there is no clear physical barrier. The Nyaika

Mountains on the border with Malawi reach altitudes of 1,800–2,150 metres. In the south and southwest, plateaux decrease to 900 metres. The landscape of the rest of the country is marked by plateaux of an elevation between 1,000 and 1,500 metres. These plateaux are structured by dambos. Vast valleys, which exist due to geological ruptures, have an extension of 30–80 kilometres and are sometimes separated from the plateaux by steep escarpments.

As mentioned above, the Copperbelt along the central border with the DR Congo is rich in minerals – mostly copper, hence its name. From the beginning of the liberalisation of the mining sector in the 1980s until today, Anglo American has established itself as the dominant foreign company active in the Copperbelt (Larmer 2005). In Kabwe, central Zambia, lead and tin was mined from 1902 to 1994. Kabwe is now the most polluted place in the whole of Africa. In 2011, British Berkeley Mineral Resources acquired mining rights for the Kabwe area. In an interview published by *Mining Weekly* on 28 March 2011, the company's chairperson cited the good transport infrastructure – which connects Kabwe to ports on the Indian Ocean and to South Africa – as an essential reason for their decision to invest there. Younger sediments throughout the country contain other valuable resources, for example the fluvial Gwembe Coal Formation found along the Zambezi River.

Because of mining, the demand for electricity is high. Currently, Iranian Farab International and Chinese Sinohydro are involved in constructing hydropower stations at the Kafue Gorge Dam and at the Itezhi–Tezhi Dam respectively. At Kafue, 300 MW will be added to the already existing 900 MW; 120 MW are envisaged for Itezhi–Tezhi. Eskom is in charge of the planning of the Kalungwishi Hydropower Station, which will reach a capacity of 160–200 MW – as *Mining Weekly* reported on 9 February 2007.

Zimbabwe

Zimbabwe is also rich in mineral resources. Most of them, with the exception of coal, are found in metamorphosed greenstones along the Great Dyke. Small cooperatives are characteristic of Zimbabwe, for instance in chrome mining, because the ore deposits of the Great Dyke are fragmented. Some large corporations – for example Anglo American and the Impala Platinum Group – run mines along the Great Dyke. In addition to chrome and platinum, the major minerals extracted from the Great Dyke, gold is mined throughout the Highveld. Copper and silver are found near Chinhoyi and Mhangura. Copper can be extracted from younger rock at the northern and southern edges of the basement schists too. The Mashava–Zvishavane area contains deposits of asbestos. Large deposits of coal are located in the northern and southern Lowveld. They have traditionally served as sources of energy and, hence, as the basis for the country's mining sector (Whitaker 1983). Zimbabwe's largest power station, situated at Hwange, is coal-fired and reaches a maximum capacity of 920 MW. The state-owned electricity providers of Botswana and Namibia have been granted partner status by the Zimbabwean government so that they can help revitalise this power station, which will in future also supply consumers in those two countries as well – as *Engineering News* reported on 5 November 2009.

With regard to geomorphology, Zimbabwe can be divided into four regions. The Highveld, an elevated savannah region lying at an altitude of 1,200–1,500 metres, makes up a quarter of Zimbabwe's territory. It lies between Bulawayo and Harare. The Eastern Highland is a mountain range with an extension of 350 kilometres stretching from Mount Nyangani to the Chimanimani Mountains. The Midveld is a plateau at 600–1,200 metres northwest and southeast of the Highveld. The Lowveld contains the valleys of the Limpopo, Save and Zambezi Rivers. In contrast to the Highveld, the landscape of the Midveld is structured by rivers and rock ruptures. Its western offshoots on the border with Botswana are plain. Especially in the north, steep slopes of up to 1,000 metres mark the border with the Zambezi Valley. The valleys of the Save and the Zambezi also feature escarpments. The eastern highland poses another physical barrier to the northwest. In sum, transport through Zimbabwe faces some problems in the east and the north. In the rest of the country, movement is eased by a plain or waved plateaux landscape.

3.6 Overview and QCA

All in all, Southern Africa as the natural sphere of influence of the regional power South Africa can be said to be delineated quite well by physiogeographical factors. Oceans frame the region to the east, south and west. The East African Rift Valley forms the northeastern borderline. Only to the north does a sharp delineation not make sense: the northern border of Southern Africa is not a line, and should rather be understood as a border zone or boundary. The valley of the Limpopo River on the South Africa–Zimbabwe border and the valley of the Zambezi River on the Zambia–Zimbabwe border both feature escarpments. Angola and Namibia are separated by the Cunene River. In Angola, comparatively small valleys are more frequent than in Namibia. Vegetation gets denser. Even though these obstacles to movement slow it down and make it more expensive, they do not change in elevation like the Great Escarpment does. The Lunda Uplands – which constitute a significant watershed separating the Congo Basin from the Kalahari Basin – are hardly noticeable as a borderline in the local scenery. Moreover, they are not a climatic boundary. Tropical influences reach beyond them. Yet, as soon as one gets to the river system of the Congo Basin, human movement becomes almost impossible. The rainforest virtually swallows up transport infrastructure and constitutes a seemingly insurmountable barrier. In sum, the northern boundary of Southern Africa comprises the Angola–DR Congo border region, proceeds through Katanga Province in the latter and connects up with the East African Rift Valley at the Great Lakes.

Aside from this, the Great Escarpment and the characteristic features of the coastline – which hamper the construction of ports – cut the region off from global markets. South African–Southern African interaction is, contrariwise, eased by the interior plateaux, because they do not pose an obstacle to movement. Physical geography thus suggests the existence of close ties between the countries located in continental Southern Africa but poor links with those situated overseas. The economies of the regional states can be expected to be inward-looking. Since South Africa appears to possess relatively good physiogeographical conditions for linking the region to the world's oceans, the continental members of SADC should be expected to be bound to South Africa and its harbours when it comes to their extraregional trade practices. From a physiogeographical perspective, South Africa's harbours can also be expected to represent some form of bottleneck between the region and overseas trading partners.

A striking fact about the region delineated above is that its countries show a high degree of complementarity in terms of agricultural potential, water supply, available minerals and energy-related resources present.[3] Hartshorne's understanding of a functional political unit implies that complementarity in essential resources and economic capacities make a politically integrated region sustainable. If one subunit possesses what its fellow subunits lack, and vice versa, then exchange will occur and tie all subunits together. In other words, Hartshorne would argue that SADC is a quite successful project and example of regional integration because its member states are economically complementary and, taken together, self-sufficient. This self-sufficiency through complementarity allows SADC to realise key functions – the facilitation of overseas investment by upgrading regional infrastructure, for instance.

One can, at least partly, assert that South African regional powerhood is derived from physical geography. The abundance and variety of mineral resources in South Africa explain the rise of its minerals–energy complex, which has expanded into neighbouring countries and accounts for South Africa's economic predominance not only in Southern Africa but across the entire continent (Scholvin 2011). Turning that perspective around, physical geography not only explains why South Africa dominates the region, it also reveals why South Africa is also dependent upon its neighbouring countries: the regional powerhouse is accountable for 80 per cent of total water consumption in Southern Africa, but only possesses 10 per cent of

---

3   Not all of areas of complementarity can be addressed in depth here. I elaborate on regional cooperation on water and electricity in Chapter 5.1 and 5.2 respectively. With regard to agricultural complementarity, one may argue that some regional countries have to focus on certain types of agricultural production. In semiarid Botswana and Namibia, for example, extensive livestock farming predominates for climatic reasons. Both countries have to import grain. The smallest countries, and in particular Malawi and Swaziland, possess good conditions for the cultivation of a very limited number of cash crops. Only geographically favoured South Africa – and to a much lesser extent Angola, Tanzania, Zambia and Zimbabwe – produce a wide variety of crops. They may each supply what their neighbours need. Hence, the SADC region should be tied together by trade in agricultural products.

that resource. It thus has to look for water beyond its borders. This dependence will, moreover, increase in the course of this century because of ongoing climate change.

I apply QCA in order to reduce complexity regarding the impact of location and physical geography on South Africa's regional relations. In Table 3.1, I summarise the locational and physiogeographical conditions discussed above. The value 0 means that such interaction is not favoured, and is perhaps even hindered. The value 1 means that the concerned condition favours interaction with South Africa. The values for location reflect whether the countries listed share common borders with South Africa. Concerning climatic features, those countries that are rated 1 receive a relatively high amount of rainfall or contain large rivers that may, hence, provide much-needed water to South Africa (or electricity generated by hydropower). The four island states are excluded from this ranking because their hydropower potential and water resources are irrelevant to South Africa for obvious reasons. My QCA disguises the fact that Botswana, Namibia and Mozambique (Maputo area) all suffer from a shortage of water, and can be expected to long for regional cooperation on water just like South Africa does.

Table 3.1   Data on location and physical geography for the QCA

Case	Location	Physical geography		
		Climate	Minerals	Movement
Angola	0	1	1	1
Botswana	1	0	1	1
Comoros	0	–	0	0
DR Congo (except for Katanga Province)	0	1	0	0
DR Congo (Katanga Province alone)	0	1	1	1
Lesotho	1	1	0	1
Madagascar	0	–	0	0
Malawi	0	1	0	0
Mauritius	0	–	0	0
Mozambique (except for Maputo area)	0	1	1	0
Mozambique (Maputo area alone)	1	0	0	1
Namibia	1	0	1	1
Seychelles	0	–	0	0
Swaziland	1	1	1	1
Tanzania	0	0	1	0
Zambia	0	1	1	1
Zimbabwe	1	1	1	1

Source: Author's own compilation.

Regarding mineral resources, I rate all countries 1 that possess a significant amount that may either be used by South African industries or be exploited by South African companies. I also evaluate the regional countries regarding the aforementioned physical barriers that hinder transport between them and South Africa. A sensible rating requires considering the DR Congo's Katanga Province and Mozambique's Maputo area as individual cases separate from the rest of their countries because they are so different regarding their location and physical geography.

Chapter 4
Transport and Socioeconomic Aspects in Southern Africa

As the second step of applying Realist Geopolitics, I now present manmade geographical conditions that are likely to have an impact on South Africa's regional economic and political relations similar to the locational and physiogeographical conditions analysed in Chapter 3. Referring to Cohen's concepts, I divide the region into ecumenes, effective territories and empty areas, and show how central places are interlinked by transport infrastructures. After providing an according overview for the entire region, I go into detail regarding the individual member states of SADC.

4.1 Ecumenes, Effective Territories and Empty Areas

The physical geography of both East and Southern Africa is one reason for their concentrations of population and economic activity at higher altitudes. The climate of the plateaux – in terms of temperature and air humidity – is more pleasant to humans and more suitable for agriculture. Diseases, especially malaria, are seldom found there. Since colonial times, agriculture has been marked by a dual structure of low input, low output semisubsistence farming and high input, high output commercial farming. The latter predominates in the most fertile areas of the interior plateaux and usually produces one or two types of cash crop per country, such as tobacco in Zimbabwe for example. Crop diversification, which characterises South Africa's agricultural sector, is rare. Semisubsistence farming marks the less fertile, peripheral parts of the interior plateaux, valleys and coastal strip. Although the share of agriculture in total employment is declining, the SADC countries remain far above the First World average. It still creates most jobs in Malawi and Mozambique. This and the monocrop structure make the region dependent upon agriculture and vulnerable to related crises.

What is more, the distribution of minerals in the SADC region additionally favours economic activity on the plateaux. Gold mining in Zimbabwe, iron processing around the Great Lakes and various mining activities in the Congolese–Zambian Copperbelt can be traced back 2,000 years in the region's history. Europeans first became involved in mining in Southern Africa during the 1870 diamond rush in Kimberley. They began digging for gold along the Witwatersrand in the mid-1880s. In the 1920s, the Belgians and the British started mining in the Copperbelt. These areas then experienced industrialisation and a rapid build-up of railway lines. They still constitute the core zones of mining. This extraction is not limited to the interior plateaux though. The exploitation of offshore oilfields began in Cameroon, the two Congos and northern Angola in the 1950s (Stock 1995). Today, Angola is the primary oil exporter in Southern Africa. As mentioned, it produces about 1.85 million barrels per day – mostly exported to China – and is the second largest producer in Africa after Nigeria. The country possesses almost all regional oil resources. On the east coast, natural gas has recently been found in the territorial waters of Mozambique and Tanzania. *The Citizen* reported on 5 November 2011 that the search for oil was ongoing there, but had not led to any conclusive results yet. Sites of exploitation do certainly possess potential for economic growth beyond resource extraction, but have remained isolated until now. The peripheries of the highland plateaux, especially the rainy eastern side of Southern Africa, are secondary cores – or, using Cohen's terms, effective territories. They provide relatively good conditions for agriculture, but do not favour industrialisation.

Map 4.1 shows ecumenes and effective territories in the continental SADC region. South Africa's regional influence, which I expect to expand via proximate ecumenes and effective territories, should reach to Botswana, southern Mozambique and via Zimbabwe to the Congolese–Zambian Copperbelt. Angola, the DR Congo (beyond Katanga Province) and Tanzania are separated from South Africa by vast empty areas. I provide a much more detailed assessment of ecumenes, effective territories and empty areas, and their regional links, in the country-specific analysis that follows.

The western half of Southern Africa and the lowlands – both coastal and interior – are hardly favourable to economic development. They fall within Cohen's category of empty areas. The alluvial coastal plains in Mozambique provide relatively good opportunities for agriculture but lack mineral resources. The plateaux of Malawi, northern Mozambique and western and northeastern Zambia, which join with the Lunda Uplands, suffer from disadvantageous climatic conditions and the prevalence there of the tsetse fly. Such obstacles to human settlement and economic activity become even worse in the basins of the Limpopo and Zambezi Rivers. Hydropower offers opportunities for development there. The Karroo and most parts of Namibia lack sufficient precipitation for intensive agriculture. Fisheries on Namibia's coasts are, along with minerals, the only advantageous features of these sparsely populated regions. The Kalahari Basin does not even possess these benefits. There, livestock breeding is only possible in small areas marked by sufficient rainfall and the absence of the tsetse fly. As practically empty areas, the latter mentioned parts of Southern Africa are, however, crossed by intraregional transport corridors. The narrow western coastal strip of Southern Africa mostly falls into the category of empty areas but some places – specifically the harbours that link the region to the rest of the world – constitute patches of effective territory holding huge potential for economic development.

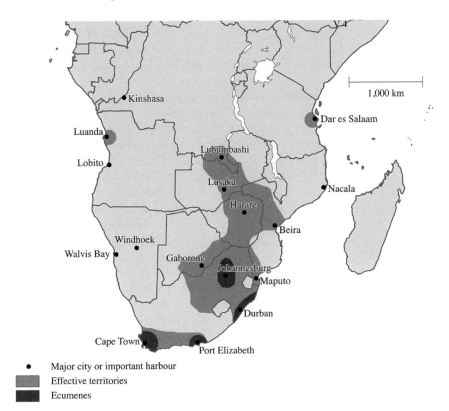

- • Major city or important harbour
- Effective territories
- Ecumenes

Map 4.1   Ecumenes and effective territories in the continental SADC region

Source: Author's own draft.

4.2 Central Places and Transport Infrastructure

I do not identify ecumenes, effective territories and empty areas exclusively from location and physical geography but also include in my analysis manmade material structures in geographical space. Nonetheless, it is striking how location and physical geography paved the ground on which colonial structures in East and Southern Africa were built, reinforcing what nature implied. In the colonial era, two types of place became subnational, national and even supranational cores. They still constitute the key locations to this day. First, inland mining towns – and, to a lesser degree, places situated near hydropower stations – have risen to become hubs of commercial and industrial activity. Metal smelters and chemical industries dominate the heavy industries typical of these towns. They are often linked to the food and textile industries.

Second, commercial and industrial activity is concentrated in coastal towns with international harbours. This concentration is due to the administrational and infrastructural functions that these places held during colonial rule, their central role in postcolonial import substitution and, today, in export-oriented development. Many of them feature export processing zones, which grant overseas investors significant tax exemptions amongst other advantages. The rapidly increasing regional and global interconnections of both East and Southern Africa have strengthened the role of harbours as economic hubs and gateways (Simon 2000). These two types of central places – harbours and major inland towns – usually constitute the start and end points for railway lines. Tarred roads interlink them. Urban infrastructure is fairly well developed there. On the national level, economic activity remains limited to the areas near transport corridors that interlink harbours, major inland towns and sites of resource extraction. Transport corridors are examined closely in Chapter 5.3. Map 4.2 shows the central places in the continental SADC region and the key transport infrastructure of it.

One city in the SADC region has risen to a regionally unique status: Johannesburg. When Hall wrote his book *The World Cities*, he advanced a definition that is still valid today: world cities are places where 'a quite disproportionate part of the world's most important business is conducted' (1966: 7). Johannesburg certainly fulfils this criterion. It is, at least in an African context, synonymous with driving capitalism. It constitutes South Africa's transport hub and hosts the most important science facilities of the continent. About 16 per cent of South Africa's gross domestic product is generated in Johannesburg. Especially tertiary sector activities – that is, accounting, advising, banking and insurance – are concentrated there. Twenty-three per cent of all formal employment in Johannesburg is in business and financial services (Rogerson 2004). The *Financial Times* ranks the Executive MBA programme of the Gordon Institute of Business Science in nearby Pretoria the sixtieth best worldwide. Other African universities do not even appear in the ranking.

As a business hub, Johannesburg exerts economic control functions that reach beyond the borders of South Africa. In a paper about South Africa as a 'gateway' to Africa, Peter Draper and I (2012) show that Johannesburg interlinks economic activities in Africa with the rest of the world, most importantly by serving as the key location for the regional headquarters of transnational companies that coordinate their African business from there. A very demonstrative feature of this role of Johannesburg is consultancy in mining: overseas mining companies that invest in Africa south of the equator usually cooperate with South African experts (Senior advisor at the US embassy in Pretoria, pers. comm., 27 August 2010), who then fill the airplanes departing from O.R. Tambo International Airport to places in the Congolese–Zambian Copperbelt or central and northern Mozambique (Mthembu-Salter 2012). Cape Town plays a similar but sector-specific role. Overseas companies active in oil and natural gas extraction along the Atlantic coast of sub-Saharan Africa operate from there. The Cape Oil and Gas Supply Initiative, which is driven by the metropolitan council of Cape Town and the

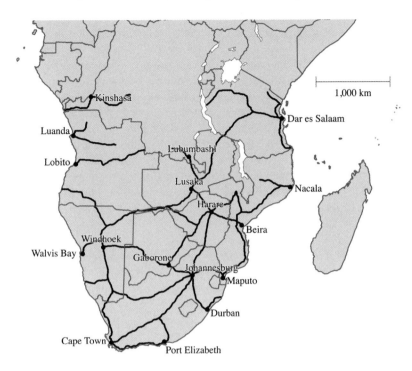

- Major city or important harbour
—— Major road or railway line (varying quality)

**Map 4.2   Central places and key transport infrastructure in
the continental SADC region**

Source: Author's own compilation.

provincial government of the Western Cape, aims at interlinking South African and
transnational companies. The Saldanha deepwater port is going to be upgraded so
that it can in future repair supertankers and handle large oil transhipments (Daniel
and Luchtman 2006).

Coming back to transport infrastructure, the regional railway lines, which are
the backbone of many of the transport corridors shown in Map 4.2, date back to
colonial times. Constituting a general pattern, the Germans and the Portuguese
sought to penetrate East and Southern Africa from the Atlantic Ocean to the Pacific
Ocean, whilst the British tried to connect the Cape to Cairo. Hence, railway lines
in Angola, Mozambique, Namibia and Tanzania go from east to west, whereas a
north-to-south axis predominates in the former British colonies. These railway
lines often reach beyond national borders. The patterns of those built in the
colonial era have much to do with geostrategy. It exemplifies the transformation
of political visions into political action areas. Imperialist strategies of expansion

not only aimed at better transport and more exploitation, they were also meant to connect occupied areas, to make military control easier this way and to cut rivals off from territory that had not yet been subjugated to imperialist rule.

However such geostrategies could only be realised within a frame provided by geography. For example, when the borderlines of the German colony of Southwest Africa were drawn, the Germans insisted on creating the Caprivi Strip because they wanted their colony to have access to the Zambezi River. They thought they could use it to cross the continent and reach the Indian Ocean. What the German politicians of the day did not know was that the Zambezi contains waterfalls that make it almost impossible to use as a means of transport. Hence, the German dream of connecting Namibia and Tanzania could not become a reality because it was in conflict with physical geography, and these colonialists did not possess the financial and technological capacities to overcome the barriers encountered along the Zambezi.

Given the failure of the Zambezi project, German-built railway lines remained limited to linking ports in Namibia and Tanzania to the respective hinterland: Lüderitz to Keetmanshoop, Swakopmund to Grootfontein and Windhoek, Tanga to Mount Kilimanjaro and Dar es Salaam to Kigoma. The railway lines built by the British and the Portuguese are far more important for the present situation on the ground because they are part of the transport corridors that link the landlocked regional countries to the world's oceans. As noted, the British sought to connect the Cape to Cairo. They envisaged a line of communication that would bring together the white agricultural settlements and mines of South Africa and the networks of the Congo, Nile and Zambezi rivers, which they considered essential for the surrounding territories from a commercial viewpoint. Plans and efforts to link the Cape to Cairo – at first only by a telegraph line, then also by rail – shaped Great Britain's Africa policy from the late nineteenth century right up until decolonisation began (Raphael 1973). In Southern Africa, the British linked the mines of Transvaal to harbours in the Cape Colony. In the early 1890s, they completed a railway line from the Johannesburg area via Bloemfontein to Cape Town, East London and Port Elizabeth. The port of Maputo, then called Lourenço Marques, provided an alternative gateway – one which was originally founded by the Boers so as to avoid dependence upon the British Empire. Furthermore, the British connected Bechuanaland and Rhodesia to the Cape Colony via Kimberly.

Also in the late nineteenth century, the Portuguese sought to merge their two colonies Angola and Mozambique by way of an inland corridor. In the mid-1880s, they settled the borders of Angola and Mozambique with the neighbouring German territories, thus delimiting the boundaries of this prospective corridor. The Portuguese then intensified their work on three railway lines, starting in Lobito, Luanda and Namibe, which was then called Moçâmedes. The so-called Benguela Corridor – which begins in Lobito – reached Dilolo on the border with the Belgian Congo in 1929. However, Cecil Rhodes's efforts to expand his influence to what is today Zambia along with massive pressure being exerted by the British government in London forced Portuguese King Carlos to renounce any claims beyond Angola and Mozambique – as expressed a few years earlier by cartographers in the famous 'mapa cor-de-rosa'. The final settlement, reached after a British ultimatum in 1891, not only ended Portuguese expansionism but also deprived Rhodes's African empire of its access to the sea. Portuguese-controlled Lourenço Marques became the main harbour for Transvaal; Beira served as the gateway for Rhodesia. Britain's Nyasaland Protectorate, which later became Malawi, was connected to Beira and to the port of Nacala in the north of Mozambique.

The second essential legacy of colonialism in Africa is landownership. Three general patterns of it can be distinguished in Southern Africa (Palmer 2000). In South Africa and Zimbabwe, white commercial farmers own(ed) vast quantities of fertile land; both countries have recently been trying to redistribute the white-owned land to black peasants. In 2000 – meaning before Zimbabwe's so-called 'fast-track land reform', white farmers owned 41 per cent of that country's agricultural land. In South Africa, the equivalent figure was 72 per cent at that time. Zimbabwe had by then already redistributed 23 per cent of its cultivated land since independence in 1980, as compared to the just 1 per cent of such land that had changed hands in South Africa since the country's first democratic elections in 1994 (Adams and Howell 2001). Zambia saw little white settlement during the colonial era. It now seeks to attract foreign investment for its agricultural sector, in particular white commercial farmers from South Africa who not only bring much needed capital but also knowhow regarding agricultural commodity chains (Senior officials at the Transvaal Landbou Unie, pers. comm., 20 October 2011). As the *Mail & Guardian* reported on 3 May 2011, this strategy stands in the context of a recent boom of white South African investment in farming in many other African countries – mostly in Mozambique, but also in the two Congos and even Sudan. Malawi, Mozambique and Namibia, meanwhile, were affected by white settlement only in some parts of their territory. They pursue mixed policies aimed at land reform and investment facilitation.

In the three countries where the need for land reform is most acute – namely Namibia, South Africa and Zimbabwe – governments not only try to make landless peasants benefit from the redistribution of land, they also support start-up black commercial farmers. Land redistribution suffers, however, from a discrepancy between the highly emotive goal of righting historical injustices on the one side and economically effective implementation on the other. In South Africa and beyond, black citizens appear to believe that owning land is an essential part of being politically independent (Mudge 2004). This may explain why, according to a 2009 survey, two-thirds of South Africa's nonwhite population think that land must be taken from white farmers and subsequently redistributed no matter what the consequences for the current owners and general national economic and political stability are (Atuahene 2011).

4.3 Country-specific Analysis: Transport and Socioeconomic Aspects

South Africa

The core zones of economic activity of Africa are located in South Africa. Gauteng's industry and service sector is comparable to the economic cores of Europe and North America. Cape Town and Durban also hold an above-average relevance in this regard. The gross domestic product per capita of these economically most advanced and densely populated parts of South Africa is far above the overall national average. The environmentally favoured east coast – where major harbours such as Durban and Richards Bay connect Gauteng to global markets – is a high-ranking but subordinate part of the core. In the northeast – and especially in Mpumalanga – coal mining dominates. Yet, many areas with an advantageous resource endowment lack an adequate transport infrastructure for their development. A closer look at what is summarised as industrial activities in Mpumalanga Province reveals that mining often only means resource extraction. Other vast areas of South Africa – most importantly the western part of the Northern Cape – run short of opportunities in agriculture and possess relatively few mining sites. Their gross domestic product per capita is at a typical Third World level.

The fact that South Africa is nonetheless highly developed as compared to its neighbouring countries can be explained by geographical factors. Because of the abundance of mineral resources in South Africa, an industrial sector could best develop there and then later spread into the wider region (Scholvin 2011). Yet, there are also nongeographical factors that need to be taken into consideration here. South Africa's industrialisation began during the First World War when its European suppliers could no longer export industrial goods in sufficient quantities. South African firms had a chance to establish themselves in an isolated market. Protectionism in the 1920s and the production of military equipment for the West after 1945 later laid the groundwork for a level of industrialisation that has never been reached by any other African country since (Manshard 1988).

At first glance, two political decisions seem to explain why South Africa went through a successful process of industrialisation: the government protected domestic companies from overseas competitors, and major Western powers considered South Africa a trustworthy partner and thus bought military equipment from it. From the perspective of Realist Geopolitics, I do not call into question the relevance of these political decisions. Nevertheless, I argue that they only led to industrialisation because geography first provided the opportunities for that. A wide variety of mineral resources is abundant in South Africa. The transport infrastructure connects the country relatively well to global markets. South African politicians took this opportunity, rather than creating it. Their strategic choice enabled their country to realise its geographical potential, which would have otherwise been foregone. Centripetal forces that result from South Africa's economic strength are numerous (Ahwireng-Obeng and McGowan 1998a):

- Not only because of its industrialisation but also due to commercial farming and, most importantly, the vast mining sector, South Africa has always attracted migrant labourers from neighbouring countries. As shown below, migrant labour to South Africa and the resulting remittances sent back home is most important for Lesotho, Malawi, Mozambique and Swaziland. It plays a considerable role for Botswana and Namibia but not for Angola, Tanzania, Zambia and the island states. Recent Zimbabwean migration to South Africa has been due to the political developments now unfolding in the former.
- Transport infrastructure in Southern Africa is interlinked and currently in a process of revitalisation. The Trans-Kalahari Highway, running from Gauteng via Botswana to the port of Walvis Bay, the Maputo Development Corridor, linking Gauteng to the port of Maputo, and the North–South Corridor from Durban via Gauteng to the Congolese–Zambian Copperbelt are just three of the most important such corridors that bind the countries of the region together. The DBSA is currently working on transport and development projects that are to one day connect all continental member countries of SADC together.
- South Africa needs natural gas, oil and water – the only important resources that the country does not currently possess in sufficient quantities. These needs account for regional cooperation, most prominently in the case of the LHWP. A close partnership between South Africa and oil-rich Angola makes sense but the South African government has only recently shown an interest in cultivating such an alliance. The regional power imports natural gas from Mozambique and may in future link up with Namibian gasfields.
- Regional cooperation on electricity may help South Africa to overcome its growing energy crisis. A transmission line 1,440 kilometres long from the Mozambican hydropower station at Cahora Bassa to Gauteng was built in colonial times. Large-scale projects such as the Grand Inga Dam in the DR Congo and their potential energy output are of considerable interest to Eskom, which presently supplies many of the other regional countries with electricity because of South Africa's coal-based power generation capacity.
- Further transnational links are created by South Africa's mining companies, which have expanded throughout sub-Saharan Africa. South Africa is the world's leading producer of chrome, diamonds, gold and platinum. South African companies possess relevant know-how. They mine coal in Nigeria, Zambia and Zimbabwe, diamonds in Angola, the DR Congo, Namibia and West Africa, and gold in both East and West Africa.
- A similar pattern of expansion vis-à-vis South African businesses occurs in the tertiary sector. South Africa's strong domestic market is the fundament for powerful service companies expanding out from that base across the entire African continent. South African-based financial service providers such as Absa Bank and Nedbank, retailers such as Pick n Pay and Shoprite, telecommunication firms such as MTN and Vodacom, and numerous small-

and medium-sized tourism companies have all gained dominant positions in Southern Africa, and in some cases beyond.

• There are also intergovernmental organisations that reflect South Africa's regional influence. The members of SACU, with the exception of Botswana, have pegged their currencies 1:1 to the South African rand. SADC guarantees regional free trade. The envisaged merger of the Common Market for East and Southern Africa (COMESA), the East African Community (EAC) and SADC may eventually lead to a free trade area stretching from the Cape to Cairo, which is certainly in the interests of the numerous South African service providers and retailers seeking market access all over the continent (Senior researcher at Trade and Industrial Policy Strategies, pers. comm., 16 October 2011).

Angola

After suffering from almost 30 years of civil war, Angola has lately realised an impressive level of economic development – one which relies almost exclusively on oil. Trickledown effects to the majority of the Angolan people are limited. In the early 1990s, oil was accountable for 90 per cent of official trade revenues. Its share has risen to stand at 95 per cent at present. Angola uses its wealth to project its power regionally. Angolan elite soldiers have thus secured weak governments in the DR Congo, Ivory Coast and, most recently, in the Central African Republic. Angolan ministers have frequently spoken of 'oil diplomacy' (Matondo 2005). Some experts – such as Alex Vines from Chatham House in an article in the *Mail & Guardian* on 23 September 2009 – argue that Angola sees itself as a 'regional superpower'. Given that South Africa does not possess any significant oil resources and meets 98 per cent of its needs by imports, it appears logical that the South African government would engage in the scramble for Africa's energy resources and obtain oil from Angola (Hudson 2007).

Cooperation between Angola and South Africa, which may help to upgrade infrastructure, is rational (Schubert 2010). Hence, at first glance, one would expect Angola to be closely integrated into regional economics. Its economic ties to South Africa are, however, less close than those of most other regional countries with the dominant power; Chinese banks, in fact, provide credits for rehabilitating Angola's infrastructure. China and the US purchase almost 70 per cent of all the oil exported by Angola (Energy Information Administration 2011b). As explained above, this does not contradict the argument that geographical factors matter but rather supports it – Angola's oil is located offshore and directly pumped into tankers. This method of transportation is not influenced by physical barriers and, thus, not bound to the region.

With regard to ecumenes, effective territories and empty areas in Angola, one can divide the country into two halves on either side of the 18th Meridian. The western half is marked by fertile soils. Most resources and human settlements are located there. The eastern half is characterised by traditional agriculture and diamond mining, a sparse population and poor transport infrastructure. On a smaller scale, the isolated spots of the colonial economy – where coffee, cotton, sugar and tobacco are grown and diamond, iron ore and oil are extracted – have remained a feature that marks Angola to this day. Three main railway lines built by the Portuguese link the interior with the ports in Lobito, Luanda and Namibe. The coastal towns dominate as administrational and economic centres. Corridors of development situated along the railway lines form Angola's ecumenes. The Luanda–Dondo–Malange corridor is the industrially most advanced part of the country. Luanda is the best developed port. The corridor that starts in Lobito, Angola's only potential deepwater harbour, used to connect Angola to the DR Congo, Zambia and Zimbabwe until the civil war began. The Namibe–Lubango– Cunene corridor provides links to northern Namibia, where it will eventually be connected to Walvis Bay and via the Trans-Kalahari Corridor to South Africa.

Even one decade after the end of the civil war, Angola is still split into three zones defined by the aforementioned corridors. Economic consultants from Namibia expect that it will take at least another decade for Angola's harbours to become well connected to their own country (Former research fellow at the Namibian Economic Policy Research Unit, pers. comm., 13 July 2010). With regard to South Africa's economic impact on Angola, the poor transport infrastructure boosts the centrifugal force exerted by the location of the latter; Angola is, in terms of distance and transportation times, not as close to South Africa as most other regional countries are. Furthermore, the area lying in between the cores of economic activity and population of Angola and South African territory are virtually empty. Nonetheless, Angola's booming economy is still attracting entrepreneurs from South Africa. Their penetration of Angola remains highly selective for reasons that hint at the limits of materialist geographical explanations: South African entrepreneurs admit that it is difficult for them to get a foot in the lucrative Angolan economy because of that country's lack of a basic service infrastructure and its unofficial requirement that Angolan partners are included in any joint ventures pursued, as reported by the *Mail & Guardian* on 25 November 2011. The language barrier is another problem. Brazilian, Chinese and Portuguese businesses dominate the Angolan market, with many of them benefitting from state-to-state credit lines (Honorary Consul of Angola, pers. comm., 24 March 2010).

Botswana

Botswana is a sparsely populated country with only 3.4 inhabitants per square kilometre. A railway line, built in the 1890s, passes through the Gaborone– Francistown area. It has, until today, served as an axis of development. Francistown and Gaborone host 65 per cent of all business and investment in processing industries. Together with Lobatse, they account for 85 per cent of the employment in relevant sectors. The Gaborone–Francistown corridor lies in the middle of a regional line of transportation and serves as a means of transit from the Congolese– Zambian Copperbelt to South Africa. The transport infrastructure constitutes a first centripetal force that ties Botswana into southern Africa. An agreement with the Namibian government has allowed Botswana to acquire land in Walvis Bay and to build its own port facility there, as a public–private partnership. Upgrading the Trans-Kalahari Corridor with a railway line has been discussed, as reported by *Mmegi Online* on 12 February 2008. No progress has been made until today though. Another article by the same news site, published on 25 July 2011, suggests that Botswana may also soon cooperate more closely with Mozambique, building a new deepwater port close to Maputo for coal exports, as well as for imports of crude oil, natural gas and fertiliser.

A second centripetal force that ties Botswana, not to the entire region but, instead, specifically to South Africa, is migration. Labour migration from Botswana to South Africa began with diamond mining in Kimberley and increased up until the 1970s. Botswana's rural areas were most affected. Up to 40 per cent of the rural male population aged between 15 and 54 years worked abroad in those years. Amongst the inhabitants of Gaborone, less than 10 per cent of the same age group migrated (Klimm et al. 1994). From the early 1980s onwards, the decline of mining in South Africa and the policy of favouring unemployed South Africans over foreign workers have led to a decline of labour migration. Whilst about 15,000 Batswana were working in South African mines in 1990, this figure had declined to 4,000 by the beginning of this century. Still, 99 per cent of all Batswana who work in mining abroad go to South Africa. The primary destination of those working on farms is South Africa too. Sixty-five per cent of the Batswana who study abroad, meanwhile, attend South African universities (Gwebu 2008).

Diamond mining constitutes a third centripetal force operating between Botswana and South Africa. It generated almost half of Botswana's gross domestic product in the 1980s. Its share therein fell to 30 per cent in the 1990s and has remained at this level until this day. The entire mining sector accounts for 70–80 per cent of export earnings and half of all Botswana's state revenues (Musyoki and Kwesi Darkoh 2002). For many decades, the national diamond mining company Debswana had to export unprocessed diamonds to De Beers's Diamond Trading Company in London. This business monopoly of De Beers ended in 2005. Botswana's current efforts to bring diamond cutters and polishers to Gaborone are promising as regards economic development (Basedau and von Soest 2011). Such steps will not reduce the country's dependence upon diamonds though. Other economic sectors that matter for Botswana's economy – most importantly manufacturing, offshore finance and tourism – depend upon the performance of the South African economy. Trade relations with other neighbours, and especially Zimbabwe, play a secondary but nevertheless still important role (Grobbelaar and Tsotetsi 2005).

The DR Congo

Agriculture accounts for 38 per cent of the gross domestic product of the DR Congo. Two-thirds of Congolese citizens work as full or part-time, mostly semisubsistence, farmers. Mining of cobalt and copper characterises Katanga Province. Gold and tin are found in the Kivus (Smith, Merrill and Meditz 1994). The mining sector accounts for about 70 per cent of the DR Congo's foreign exchange earnings, meaning that it matters much more for the economic and political elite than agriculture does. Taxes are, however, not fully paid by mining companies because of insufficient governance structures (Tull 2010). Mining is also associated with corruption and the DR Congo's war economy. When the Second Congolese War began in August 1998 with an uprising of the Banyamulenge in Goma against the government of Laurent-Désiré Kabila, Burundi, Rwanda and Uganda intervened in order to grab resources in the eastern DR Congo. A few weeks later, Angola, Namibia and Zimbabwe launched a pro-Kabila intervention, which was driven by their political elites being already entangled in resource extraction in the DR Congo (MacLean 2002; Samset 2002).

The Congolese mining sector is totally internationalised though. Most prominently, China and the DR Congo signed a minerals-for-infrastructure agreement in 2007. It guarantees China 10.6 million tonnes of copper and almost 630,000 tonnes of cobalt, which are exported there in order to pay back the loans taken with the Chinese to cover the costs of building roughly 3,800 kilometres of roads and 3,200 kilometres of railway lines (Jonasson 2011). Anglo American and BHP Billiton were amongst the first major mining companies to return to Katanga Province after the civil war. The *Mail & Guardian* reported on 24 October 2007 that traditional mining towns like Kolwezi, which had resembled a ghost town at the end of the 1990s, were experiencing a new boom because of revived international investment and the presence of local informal miners. Western mining companies that operate in the DR Congo often cooperate with South Africans, who are well informed about the DR Congo's mineral potential, its mining legislation and who already know how to do business in the country (Kabemba 2007).

A key challenge to closer Congolese–South African interaction is transport infrastructure, which is virtually swallowed up by the rainforest. The so-called 'voie nationale' connects Katanga Province to Kinshasa to the country's main port in Matadi, 148 kilometres inland from the Congo's mouth and 8 kilometres below the last navigable point – where rapids make the river impassable. The voie nationale consists of rail transport from Lubumbashi to Ilebo, river transport from Ilebo to Kinshasa and rail transport from Kinshasa to Matadi. The construction of the 1,015 kilometre-long railway line from Kinshasa to Ilebo by China Railway is still not guaranteed to happen (Senior official of TradeMark Southern Africa, pers. comm., 2 March 2012). In theory, a railway network interlinks the major towns in southeastern DR Congo. There is not only a railway line from Lubumbashi to Ilebo in Kasaï Occidental Province, but also – since 2004 – one to Kindu in Maniema Province and another one to Kalemie at Lake Tanganyika. Sakania on the Zambian border is connected via Lubumbashi to Kolwezi. The track from Kolwezi to Dilolo on the Angolan border has become overgrown and is therefore currently not in use (Senior official of the DBSA, pers. comm., 1 December 2011).

Transport by rail is further hampered by administrative shortcomings. The roughly 12,000 employees of the National Railway Society of the Congo are rarely paid by the state. Train drivers will only set their locomotives in motion if those who want their goods to be transported pay them both directly and in advance. Locomotives and wagons are in short supply and a poor condition. An executive of Transnet told me that they could not take goods any further than Kolwezi and Lubumbashi (pers. comm., 18 October 2011). In sum, the country's transport infrastructure – reflective of local physiogeographical conditions – fragments the DR Congo. Katanga Province is already tied to Southern Africa. Thinking about the prospects for upgrading the regional connectivity of the Kivus, future links to East Africa appear to be more realistic than ones to the western DR Congo do.

Lesotho

Due to its geomorphology and soils, only 13 per cent of Lesotho's terrain is suitable for agriculture. Unpredictable weather conditions and frost hamper farming. The industrial and service sectors remain weak, also because of the country's small domestic market. Formal employment is available for only 20 per cent of jobseekers. Almost half of the labour force works mainly in agriculture, mostly subsistence farming (Lundahl, McCarthy and Petersson 2003). Seventy per cent of the population derive their livelihoods at least partly from agriculture (Sandrey et al. 2005). These push factors, in combination with the pull factor of better economic prospects in South Africa, explain why Lesotho is dependent upon labour migration to South Africa. The share of Basotho miners in South African gold mines increased from 20 per cent in the 1970s to 50 per cent in the 1990s. By then, one-third of government revenue came from migrant remittances (Lundahl, McCarthy and Petersson 2003). The relevance of labour migration has recently declined though. The share of income from abroad in overall national income dropped from 42 per cent in 1990 to 18 per cent in 2002. Since 2001, remittances from labour migrants no longer constitute the main source of foreign currency (Sandrey et al. 2005). Less strict border controls and a growing demand for unskilled farm workers in the Free State have, however, caused an increase in unregistered migration since 1994.

The clothing and textile industry complements migration as a second pillar of Lesotho's economy. It contributes 19 per cent of the country's gross domestic product and accounts for 74 per cent of its exports, excluding water pumped to South Africa (Bennet 2006). For years, the Basotho government has been encouraging South African entrepreneurs to invest in this sector. In contrast to the South African clothing and textile industry, Lesotho's is export-oriented and benefits from free market access to the EU and the US. Global players such as Levi's and Russell Athletic run factories in Lesotho because of low costs of labour combined with access to said markets. Regardless of the internationalisation of the clothing and textile sector, Lesotho is still tied to South Africa for climatic and geomorphological reasons. One of the few large rivers that flow through

South Africa, the Orange River, receives 41 per cent of its water from Lesotho's mountains. There, dams have been built in order to produce electricity and store water for both countries. The envisaged Lesotho Highlands Power Project – which, according to an optimistic report published in *Engineering News* on 27 October 2011, aims at generating 6,000 MW of wind energy and 4,000 MW of pumped-storage hydropower – will also be dependent upon the demands of South African consumers.

Malawi

Similar to Lesotho, Malawi became a labour pool for South Africa's mines during the colonial era. After independence, the Malawian government promoted export-oriented agriculture instead. Today, the country's economy is still focussed on cash crops. Tobacco accounts for 70 per cent of all export earnings. Ninety per cent of all Malawians work in the primary sector. In 2004, Malawi's former president Bingu wa Mutharika launched an internationally recognised agricultural programme in response to food insecurity concerns: peasants received subsidised fertilisers and seeds. Their output rose significantly. Malawi became an exporter of cash crops and maize. The output of the latter doubled within two years of subsidies first being granted. Yet, agricultural productivity suffers from short-term changes of weather and price fluctuations. The 2011 unrest in Malawi resulted from declining world market prices for tobacco. They deprived Malawi of much of its foreign exchange capital and, thus, of the ability to import and subsidise fertilisers and fuel. Malawi's stagnation in terms of agricultural productivity is reflected in its limited trade relations with South Africa. The most significant categories of products imported from South Africa are: chemicals, which constitute 18 per cent of Malawi's imports from South Africa; vehicles, which account for 12 per cent; and processed metal products, which stand at 8 per cent. Prepared foodstuffs (including tobacco) and textiles are the most important exports to South Africa, constituting 39 and 30 per cent respectively of Malawi's exports to the regional powerhouse (Banda 2005).

However, overland transport to South Africa is expensive and unreliable because of the East African Rift Valley. Steep slopes cause frequent washaways there. The Zambezi River has to be crossed via a poorly maintained suspension bridge in Tete Province. Malawi's government is seeking to build an inland deepwater port in Nsanje, located on the Shire River, which will connect Malawi to the Indian Ocean via the Zambezi. It is not clear whether the Shire is deep enough for larger ships though. Mozambique also has not yet given its permission for container vessels to use the Zambezi. Moreover, the country's low volume of foreign trade makes the project economically unfeasible: Malawi does not export many containerised goods, meaning that containers sent to Nsanje loaded with imports for Malawi would have to return empty. A far better option for Malawi would be to upgrade the ports of Beira or of Nacala, which could be linked to Malawi by rail and road at relatively low costs.

The *Daily Times* reported on 23 December 2011 that Brazilian mining giant Vale, which is driving the upgrade of the port of Nacala, had recently signed an agreement with the government of Malawi on the course of the envisaged railway line from Nacala to Moatize in Tete Province. According to this agreement, the Nacala–Moatize railway line will cross southern Malawi. Aside from transport issues, the Malawian government has, for almost 20 years, also tried to come up with an energy policy that will reduce the country's dependence upon foreign trade or at least reduces import prices (Mhone and Nguira 1993). In addition to exploiting domestic coal reserves, hydropower generation appears to be a sound way of meeting this goal because of the advantageous land configuration of the Shire Valley – it is narrow and decreases in altitude by 434 metres between Lake Malawi and the Mozambican border.

Mozambique

Three railway lines link the ports of Nacala, Beira and Maputo to Malawi, Zimbabwe and South Africa respectively. A pipeline, dating back to the infrastructure projects of the 1980s, connects landlocked Zimbabwe with the port at Beira. High-voltage transmission lines run from the Maputo area to South Africa and from Tete Province to Zimbabwe. The only north-to-south connection is a highway that stretches from Maputo to the Tanzanian border. During the civil war, Mozambique's transport infrastructure significantly deteriorated as a result of its destruction being a core objective of South African raids. Since the early 1990s, the Mozambican government has sought to repair it. The key project in this regard is the road corridor that links Maputo to Gauteng. Just like other spatial development initiatives, this corridor aims to optimise infrastructure so as to promote foreign investment – which is also encouraged by custom duty and tax breaks being offered (de Beer and Arkwright 2003; Nuvunga 2008).

Whilst the Maputo area has seen a significant upgrading of its transport infrastructure, the regeneration of Mozambique's second major port in Beira is dependent upon the unreliable prosperity of Zimbabwe and the recent mining boom in Tete Province. The Sena Line – which connects Beira to Tete – and the Machipanda Line to Zimbabwe cannot currently reach sufficient capacities for the envisaged levels of coal exportation. The Nacala Corridor further north constitutes an alternative gateway for Tete Province. Its reconstruction is being supported by Vale, which is also – together with its Australian rival Rio Tinto – driving the restoration of the Sena Line (Senior official of TradeMark Southern Africa, pers. comm., 2 March 2012). With regard to regional contiguity, these developments in central and northern Mozambique do not suggest that ties to South Africa are about to become closer. On the contrary, a successful upgrading of the Beira and Nacala Corridors will divert trade from the North–South Corridor and thus South Africa's harbours.

Central Mozambique is closely linked to the regional power for another reason besides: 60 per cent of the electricity generated at the Cahora Bassa Hydropower

Station is exported to South Africa. Twenty-nine per cent goes to Zimbabwe (Schröder 2005). Exports of electricity to South Africa amounted to USD 221 million in 2008, being Mozambique's second-largest foreign currency earner – followed by natural gas, being worth USD 152 million. The largest source of exports was (and still is) the aluminium smelter Mozal near Maputo: it accounts for USD 1.45 billion of a total of USD 2.65 billion (Hanlon 2010). Mozal's largest shareholder is BHP Billiton. The works gets its electricity from South Africa. Aside from this, South African commercial farmers have invested all over Mozambique, which makes sense given the proximity of the two countries and the similarity of their climatic conditions. About 800 South African farmers have hitherto acquired 100 million hectares in Mozambique, making the country the primary destination for South African agricultural investment amongst the 22 African countries mentioned in an article in the *Mail & Guardian* on 13 December 2010.

Labour migration is another centripetal force in the Mozambican–South African relationship. The migration of people from the former to the latter began with the commencement of mining in the Witwatersrand. In the 1970s, about 110,000 Mozambican labour migrants went to South Africa every year. They represented 25 per cent of Mozambique's industrial labour force then (Castel-Branco 2002). The number of Mozambicans legally working in South Africa remained at between 42,000 to 52,000 throughout the 1990s and into the early years of this century. Their remittances to relatives in Mozambique rose from ZAR 160 million in 1992 to ZAR 433 million in 2005. The latter figure equals 3.6 per cent of Mozambique's gross domestic product (Raimundo Oucho 2008). Whilst southern Mozambique benefits from labour migration because remittances significantly increase the income of poor rural households, central and northern Mozambique is rather detached from this dynamic (de Vletter 2006).

Namibia

Economic activity in Namibia is concentrated along two corridors heading inland from the harbours of Lüderitz and Walvis Bay and one that stretches through the country, from north to south. Some towns possess a special economic role due to mining and related industrial activities – metal smelting in Tsumeb, for instance. Others, like Windhoek, were founded and developed as administrational, commercial and military centres. Rainfall is essential to the distribution of the Namibian population because it determines the land's potential suitability for agricultural use. In the early 1990s, 60 per cent of the populace lived in the north, where precipitation exceeds 400 millimetres per annum and rain-fed agriculture is possible (Chimhowu et al. 1993). Since independence, many of them have migrated to Windhoek, whose population increased from 120,000 in 1991 to 323,000 in 2011. Officially, 16 per cent of those employed work in the primary sector (excluding mining). They generate 7 per cent of the gross domestic product.

Eighty per cent of Namibia's agricultural sector is livestock farming and 80 per cent of its meat is exported, mainly to South Africa. Slaughtering usually takes place in South Africa. Slaughterhouses in Namibia are often owned by South Africans (Senior official at Namibia Agricultural Union, pers. comm., 25 July 2010). In southern Namibia, the output of certain products is far too large for the local market so that much has to be sold to wholesalers in Cape Town, who supply retailers in Namibia (Official at the Chamber of Commerce of Keetmanshoop, pers. comm., 23 July 2010). Namibia covers half of its corn consumption by imports from South Africa. Its relevance is reinforced by the fact that Namibian farmers consider their South African partners reliable, whereas, in the recent past, maize imports from Zambia have suffered from frequent export bans imposed by the Zambian government (Advisor to the Agricultural Trade Forum in Windhoek, pers. comm., 2 August 2010). Namibia's fishing sector is, contrariwise, internationalised. The most important foreign companies involved in fishing in Namibia are Portuguese and Spanish. Behind mining, the fishing sector is the second largest contributor to exports. Just like Angola's oil sector, Namibia's fishing industry does not depend upon land transport. The proximity to South Africa also does not matter much for the Namibia's fish exports, because transporting fish is not hampered by any physical barriers.

Mining in Namibia is not dominated by South Africans either. Companies from all over the world are involved, in particular those coming from Australia, Canada, China and India. The sector accounts for 53 per cent of Namibia's foreign exchange earnings and triggers investments larger than the government's annual budget. Royalties – especially for diamond mining – amount to NAD 1.9 billion, which is significant considering that the total government budget is NAD 37.7 billion (*The Namibian*, 29 September 2011). Nevertheless, one should not completely dismiss the importance of the role of South African companies: diamond mining is carried out by a 50:50 joint venture of De Beers and the Namibian government. In the construction sector, which is closely linked to mining, government tenders are given to Chinese and North Korean companies rather than to South African ones (Melber 2011).

Yet, Namibia is tied into the region and to the regional power because of transport infrastructure needs. The government seeks to promote foreign investment in the industrial and service sectors, not only by granting export processing status but also by upgrading the transport infrastructure that interlinks the country regionally and globally (Senior advisor to the Namibian President, pers. comm., 29 July 2010). The port of Walvis Bay is essential to meeting this goal. No more than 20 per cent of its capacity is used for Namibian overseas trade. Sixty per cent of the cargo unloaded here goes via the Trans-Cunene Corridor to southern Angola (Senior official at the Offshore Development Company in Windhoek, pers. comm., 30 July 2010). Yet, Namport has also convinced the South African factories of BMW, Mercedes and Volkswagen to ship materials from Europe via Walvis Bay. Namibia's main harbour benefits from the fact that Durban and Luanda are currently the most congested ports in the region.

Swaziland

The Swazi population is concentrated on the Midveld, due to this part of the country being highly suitable for agriculture. Sugar is the main crop cultivated. Around 11 per cent of the country's population are directly dependent upon the sugar industry, which is the largest employer and produces the leading export item. The manufacturing sector is only an appendix of agriculture: 80 per cent of the value generated by manufacturing derives from industries that process agricultural products (Miles-Mafafo 2002). Swaziland benefits from being geographically close to South Africa and having free access to the markets of the region's economic powerhouse. Most prominently, Coca Cola produces the sugar powder for its soft drinks in Swaziland. Whilst no official figures are available, Coca Cola's activities are estimated to account for 40 per cent of Swaziland's gross domestic product. Without free market access to South Africa, Coca Cola would not be active in Swaziland (Honorary Consul of Swaziland, pers. comm., 18 March 2010).

Beyond agriculture, Swaziland's economy is rather weak. Africa's largest manmade forest is located on the Swazi Highveld. It generates some export revenues. Coal and diamonds have been sold abroad in modest quantities since the mid-1980s. Iron ore is no longer mined, because lucrative deposits were already depleted by the end of the 1970s (Miles-Mafafo 2002). The textile industry is much weaker than in Lesotho. It is not difficult to conclude that there are insufficient domestic job opportunities for Swaziland's labour force. Young men migrate to the nearby mining regions of South Africa, where they usually stay up to 10 months a year (Mdluli 1993).

Swaziland's infrastructure – from electricity and water supply to railway lines and roads to telecommunication networks – is integrated into South Africa's. The national railway network links Swaziland to the harbours of Durban and Richards Bay. The four small hydropower stations owned by the Swaziland Electricity Company, which each have a capacity of between 10–20 MW, serve to meet peaking and emergency demand. Eighty to 85 per cent of the electricity used in Swaziland is bought from Eskom (Swaziland Electricity Company 2012).

Tanzania

One may argue that Tanzania complements its fellow SADC members economically because of its physical geography. Onshore resources are already exploited by South African companies. Offshore oil- and gasfields have also attracted the interest of the regional power. Tanzania's potential for agriculture is considerable, because water is not as scarce there as in many parts of Southern Africa (Senior Tanzanian diplomat, pers. comm., 3 February 2011). The Southern Agricultural Growth Corridor of Tanzania supports agriculture and is meant to develop the southern border region. Yet, Tanzanian officials interviewed for an article published in *The Citizen* on 30 January 2012 acknowledge that the current small-scale transport infrastructure – ferries to cross minor rivers for instance

– is insufficient. On a larger scale, the Tanzania–Zambia Railway connects Dar es Salaam to Zambia but is affected by the unfavourable geography of the East African Rift Valley: mudslides frequently block the track. Tanzania Railways Ltd presently operates at 50 per cent of its capacity. The Tanzania–Zambia Railway Company is presently in debt (Hirschler and Hofmeier 2010). Traffic from the Copperbelt to Dar es Salaam has, nevertheless, grown tremendously (Curtis 2009). One negative consequence of this is that the port of Dar es Salaam suffers from heavy congestion, causing long delays (Ranganathan and Foster 2011). In sum, Tanzania hardly offers an alternative and viable gateway to global markets for the landlocked countries of Southern Africa. Presently, the said geographical and nongeographical factors explain why Dar es Salaam can barely compete with Durban and Richards Bay.

With transport infrastructure being upgraded all over the region and the prospect of a Tripartite Free Trade Area – consisting of COMESA, the EAC and SADC – being founded, geographical factors may, however, lose some of their relevance in this particular case. A more likely scenario than Dar es Salaam competing with South Africa's harbours is its emergence as a well-positioned gateway specifically for East Africa. The Central Corridor links Dar es Salaam to Mwanza on Lake Victoria and Kigoma on Lake Tanganyika. These two lake ports are connected to Burundi, the eastern DR Congo and Uganda. Isaka Dry Port, located between Tabora and Mwanza, handles transhipments from Burundi and Rwanda. Tanzania and Uganda are creating a railway line from the port of Tanga to Uganda, which will be operational in 2016 according to articles in *Engineering News* on 8 April 2011 and *The Citizen* on 22 February 2012.

There are, nevertheless, obstacles to Tanzania becoming an East African transport hub. *Engineering News* reported on 4 November 2011 that the EAC needed about USD 900 billion to be invested in it so as to modernise and transform its railway networks. The national railway lines of the EAC member states operate with gauges of different width. In the very south of Tanzania, Mtwara remains poorly connected to its hinterland. A scheduled tarred road to Mbamba Bay on Lake Malawi has not yet been built. However, a 420 MW coal-fired power station is currently being constructed by a Chinese company in Mchuchuma, in the context of the Mtwara Corridor. It will use locally mined coal and provide electricity to the national grid (Economist Intelligence Unit 2012). Although originally envisaged as a project of integration between Malawi, Mozambique, Tanzania and Zambia, the Mtwara Corridor will, most likely, never become anything more than a national project – with the possible exception of it playing a minor role in helping connect landlocked Malawi to the Indian Ocean.

Zambia

The Copperbelt, a 140 kilometre-long and 50 kilometre-wide zone of mining on the Congolese–Zambian border, has been Zambia's ecumene since the beginning of the twentieth century. Its relevance is often exaggerated though. Most Zambians work, in fact, in the agricultural sector. At the end of the 1990s, only around 2 per cent of the country's workforce was employed in copper mining (Drescher 1998). Today, agriculture still accounts for 85 per cent of employment and 22 per cent of gross domestic product. The industrial sector, including mining, provides jobs for 6 per cent of the labour force and contributes 35 per cent to gross domestic product. These figures reveal that mining constitutes a highly productive part of Zambia's dual economy. What matters most about mining is its contribution to Zambia's export volumes and to government revenues. Copper generated almost 90 per cent of the country's foreign exchange earnings until the 1980s. Crises of the sector and efforts by the government to promote farming affected the dominance of copper only slightly (Banda and Nyirongo 1993). With copper prices recently rising again, mining has cemented its place in the Zambian economy. A modernisation of the agricultural sector – something that might generate trickledown effects for the majority of the population – remains to be realised. In order to achieve this goal, the Zambian government continues to encourage investment by South African commercial farmers (Senior Zambian diplomat, pers. comm., 18 August 2010).

Given that Zambia is landlocked and exports copper in large quantities, regional transport is essential. In the colonial era Zambia was controlled by the British, whereas the neighbouring territories to the east and west were Portuguese. Hence, the main railway lines went (and still go) from the Copperbelt to South Africa. Commercial farmland, formerly owned by whites, remains concentrated along this railway line. About 55 per cent of Zambia's population live in a strip of 60 kilometres width on each side of the line (Banda and Nyirongo 1993). Between the independence of Zambia and the beginning of Angola's civil war the Benguela Line experienced a short boom, serving an alternative route to the Atlantic Ocean. In the late 1970s and throughout the 1980s, Zambia's dependence upon South Africa was reinforced. The Tanzania–Zambia Railway, built by the Chinese as a new corridor to the sea for landlocked Zambia and Zimbabwe, only moved 452,000 tonnes of Zambian goods in 1979 despite its nominal maximum freight capacity of 2 million tonnes. Via South Africa, 637,000 tonnes of Zambian goods were shipped (Chitala 1987). Presently, Zambian copper is mainly shipped via the ports of KwaZulu-Natal because of the aforementioned problems with the Tanzania–Zambia Railway, and the fact that the regeneration of the Benguela Line and the corridors in central and northern Mozambique has not yet been completed.

Moreover, airports in the Congolese–Zambian border region are well linked to Johannesburg, which subsequently connects them to the rest of the world as well. According to an article in *Mining Weekly* on 6 October 2011, South African Airways is about to expand its number of flights to destinations in sub-Saharan Africa, especially those in mining areas. As said, Johannesburg appears to serve as a hub for transnational companies and various corporate service providers because of its economic sufficiency (Draper and Scholvin 2012). Thus, although mining in Zambia is internationalised and Chinese companies play a much more important role than their South African rivals do, the country is still closely tied to South Africa because the business sector of Johannesburg serves to interlink it globally.

In spite of this dependence upon South Africa as its gateway to the world, Zambia is more than just the end of the North–South Corridor. It is also linked to Beira, Dar es Salaam and Walvis Bay. Railway lines from the Copperbelt to Lobito and Nacala will, most likely, be available in only a few years. If Kenya and the Great Lakes region were to be linked to Southern Africa by transport corridors, Zambia would be the main transit country – thereby becoming a transport node between East and Southern Africa and between Southern Africa's east and west coasts. A similar nodal role is likely in a regionally integrated electricity grid: transmission lines along the North–South Corridor could make a further 35,000 MW available to the region in the near future, at least according to an optimistic scenario developed in an article in *Engineering News* on 31 March 2009. The grids of the DR Congo, Malawi, Mozambique and Tanzania are, moreover, likely to be interlinked via Zambia.

Zimbabwe

Zimbabwe shared and shares many of the economic characteristics of South Africa. At the time of independence, Zimbabwe was better positioned in terms of economic structures than its big neighbour was 14 years later. When white minority rule ended in 1980, many expected Zimbabwe to become the powerhouse of the Southern African Development Coordination Conference (SADCC). Being rich in mineral resources, it had gone through a process of industrialisation during the Second World War. Zimbabwe's industrialisation was later reinforced by import substitution and also, unintentionally, by international sanctions. The share of agricultural outputs used as inputs for domestic manufacturing rose from 13 per cent in 1965 to 44 per cent in 1981 (Jenkins 2002). Industrialisation did not, however, end dependence upon agriculture and mining. Capital goods were mostly inputs to farming, mining and the transport sector (Katerere, Moyo and Ngobese 1993; Ndlela 1987). In spite of these structural problems, Zimbabwe accounted for 49 per cent of all intra-SADCC exports and 38 per cent of all intra-SADCC imports in 1981 (Wagao 1987).

Today, Zimbabwe is a key site of South African investment, being an important market for South African products and an essential transit country in the SADC region. Connecting Gauteng to the Copperbelt, Zimbabwe's railway lines have been an important means of transport for mineral products ever since the colonial era. Zimbabwe is linked to Beira in Mozambique – but the Machipanda Line urgently needs restoration. Plans to upgrade and more closely integrate the regional transport infrastructure – not only by railway lines and roads but also by pipelines and transmission lines for electricity – almost always include Zimbabwe, as a hinge between South Africa and the rest of the region (Senior officials at Eskom's Trade and Regional Development Department, pers. comm., 11 October 2011).

Zimbabwe has not, however, lived up to the aforementioned expectations of the 1980s. One may reason that the post-2000 farm invasions along with ongoing political instability have ruined the country to such an extent that it has become a 'South African colony', as one researcher of the Ebert Foundation in Johannesburg put it (pers. comm., 12 August 2011). A senior representative of the Adenauer Foundation similarly argued that the recent 'invasion' by South African businesses had cast Zimbabwe into an economically subordinate role vis-à-vis South Africa (pers. comm., 12 July 2010). Being its direct neighbour and suffering from the same problems regarding landownership, South Africa has strongly felt the impact of the Zimbabwean crisis. South African security policy experts estimate that about 4 million Zimbabweans, out of a total population of 17 million, were both legally and illegally living in South Africa in 2010 (Senior researcher at the Institute of Security Studies, pers. comm., 11 August 2010). Zimbabwe-style farm invasions, furthermore, may serve as a model for some in South Africa to emulate: in 2000, peasants in Mpumalanga announced that they had prepared plans for exactly this (Lee 2003).

The Comoros, the Seychelles, Mauritius and Madagascar

The four island countries of the SADC region are marked by economic aspects that clearly distinguish them from the continental mainland. Most importantly, their economies are highly globalised. They export cash crops to former colonial powers and serve as export processing and business hubs. These economic structures speak against close ties existing with South Africa. Those structures aside, the transport infrastructure also does not bind any of the island countries to South Africa for obvious physiogeographical reasons.

Seventy-three per cent of the labour force of the Comoros work in the primary sector and contribute 41 per cent of the gross domestic product. In the coastal areas, cash crops – especially vanilla and ylang-ylang, an essential oil – are grown. Vanilla accounts for almost 80 per cent of the export figures of the Comoros (Ercolano 1995). The largest single contribution to the national budget is the financial support granted by France, a former colonial power. South African tourism is becoming more important. Except for a climate favourable to tourism and relatively short flights to South Africa, the economic geography of the Comoros does not induce ties with South Africa though. The predominance of extraregional actors is best demonstrated by French and Spanish fishing fleets. Exploration rights for offshore oilfields have recently been granted to Bahari Resources from Kenya. Companies from the US have also been involved in the search for oil in the territorial waters of the Comoros (Economist Intelligence Unit 2012).

The Seychelles, meanwhile, are economically more advanced. Medium- and large-scale industries are alien to the islands though. Many Seychellois work in the state-sponsored and tourism-driven service sector. The primary sector accounts for only 3 per cent of gross domestic product. Ninety per cent of all necessary inputs for the primary and secondary sectors are imported from overseas (Tartter 1995). Because of its higher level of development, the Seychelles attract labour migrants from other members of the Indian Ocean Commission – that is, from the Comoros, Madagascar, Mauritius and Réunion. These countries appear to collectively form a region that is far more important to the Seychelles than continental Southern Africa is. The Seychelles, moreover, are seeking to become an international business hub, following the Mauritian example. This strategy aims at global instead of regional integration. Recent and future economic developments may, thus, tie the Seychelles rather to China and India than to their fellow SADC members (Honorary Consul of the Seychelles, pers. comm., 7 January 2010).

Mauritius is different from all other regional states because of its comparatively unique prosperity, which may, at least partly, be explained by one particular geographical factor: being an island, Mauritius was not affected by the decolonisation and proxy wars that marked continental Southern Africa from the 1960s until the 1990s. The economic rise of Mauritius has resulted from the presence there of export processing zones for the clothing and textile sector. In the 1960s, Mauritius was a sugar-based monocrop economy. Then, its government decided to instead support the clothing and textile industry, which benefitted from the low costs of labour on the island. Until the decline that began in 2000, the sector's share of total employment in manufacturing rose to 71 per cent. Clothing and textile products prior to that accounted for 80 per cent of all products coming from Mauritius's export processing zones. Because of lower labour costs, Mauritian companies started to outsource their production to Madagascar in the 1990s and became important investors there (Joomun 2006). Today, the Mauritian export processing zones comprise electrical equipment, financial services and telecommunications – Mauritius has thus upgraded it exports. Preferential treatment by the EU, which is the key customer, and investment from Hong Kong are central features of the export-oriented and globalised Mauritian economy. South Africans play a relevant role as tourists, but only to the same extent as guests from France and Germany do.

Madagascar's foreign trade is mainly about vanilla. Half of the world's vanilla exports come from there alone. The Malagasy export processing zones are dominated by French companies. France accounted for almost 30 per cent of all foreign direct investment that went to Madagascar in the early 2000s. For the reasons noted, Mauritius was the second most important investor – with a share of slightly less than 20 per cent. South Africa did not play a major role as an investor at that time. Before political instability began with the 2009 coup, clothing and textiles was by far the most important branch of Madagascar's export processing zones. Sixty-four per cent of all foreign companies were active in this sector, which accounted for 94 per cent of the employment generated by the export processing zones (Maminirinarivo 2006).

4.4 Overview and QCA

The analysis of the regional transport infrastructure and socioeconomic aspects has revealed various factors that tie the SADC countries to South Africa. Transport infrastructure appears to be a very apt indicator not only for the state of economic relations between the regional countries but also for their geostrategic relevance. The limits of Realist Geopolitics have become apparent, most importantly in the case of Angola – which has proven difficult as a location for South African investment for reasons lying beyond the scope of a materialist, geopolitical approach. The internationalisation of the mining sector – especially in the DR Congo and Namibia – seems to contradict what Realist Geopolitics suggests. One may, however, explain some characteristics of the mining sector geopolitically: South Africa – and in particular Johannesburg and the ports of KwaZulu-Natal – is the regional gateway to global markets. Included in this role is the transportation of regional goods in large quantities by rail and ship, the provision of knowhow by South African experts and flight connections from mining areas via Johannesburg to the cores of the global economy. With regard to the QCA paths, three of four theoretically possible combinations of the two conditions analysed in this chapter appear in reality:

- A first group of cases is marked by its members having good transport connections to South Africa and socioeconomic aspects that also favour links with that country. There are thus transport corridors that bind Botswana, Namibia, Zambia and Zimbabwe to South Africa and its harbours. Lesotho and Swaziland are well integrated into South Africa's transport infrastructure simply because of their location and size. The transport links of the DR Congo and Mozambique to South Africa are, however, of a different nature: only Katanga Province and the Maputo area are well connected with South Africa. Moreover, all these cases possess socioeconomic aspects that suggest close interaction with South Africa. Their agricultural sectors depend upon inputs from South Africa. Mining offers opportunities for South African investment and creates a huge need for transportation via South Africa's harbours. The energy sector also calls for tight cooperation. Only Lesotho's clothing and textile industry, which is bound to the market of the US, constitutes a clear exception to the observable pattern of regionally interlinked economies. Labourers and refugees who migrate to South Africa from elsewhere in the region are another centripetal force, although this phenomenon has significantly declined since the 1980s.

- A second group of cases consists of the island states in the Indian Ocean and the DR Congo (except for Katanga Province). Regarding the latter country, the rainforest of the Congo Basin virtually swallows up the transport infrastructure. Existing and envisaged spatial development initiatives rather fragment the country. Katanga Province is, for example, unique in its being already tied to Southern Africa. The Kivus will probably in time develop close links to East Africa. Maritime transport from the Comoros, the Seychelles, Mauritius and Madagascar to South Africa is possible and certainly no more expensive than transportation by rail and road in continental Southern Africa. However, in contrast to the latter, maritime transport does not create any need for interaction with South Africa. It links the island countries directly to their trading partners all over the world. South Africa is thus not a gateway for them. What is more, the analysis above did not identify any significant socioeconomic aspects of the island countries that imply their close linkages to South Africa. The latter's nationals come as tourists to Mauritius and to the Seychelles. Other than that, there are some links between the islands countries in terms of labour migration and investment – however, what really characterises their economies is globalisation not regional integration. Given, meanwhile, that the Congolese mining sector is concentrated in Katanga Province, there appear to be no socioeconomic aspects of the DR Congo beyond that province that imply close links existing with South Africa either.
- The three remaining cases are Angola, Malawi and Tanzania. Mozambique, with the exception of the Maputo area, is comparable to these three. The economic geography of Angola, Mozambique and Tanzania suggests that huge potential exists for their greater economic cooperation with South Africa, but the locations of their resources – which are mostly found offshore – speak against such ties emerging. The case of Malawi is different. Malawi relies on energy imports from South Africa. Economic not physical geography – meaning the development gap between Malawi and South Africa – explains this dependence. However if the development strategies of Malawi are successfully implemented, these incentives for close relations with South Africa will cease to exist. Regarding transport infrastructure, none of these countries are well connected to the regional power. The absence of a good transport infrastructure between Malawi, Mozambique, Tanzania and South Africa reflects physical geography: the East African Rift Valley and the Zambezi River. In the case of Angola, there are no significant physical barriers to transport to South Africa; history and not geography accounts for this situation.

Table 4.1 provides an overview of the analysis undertaken in this chapter. It also lists the main centripetal forces that I have addressed. The principles behind the ratings are identical to those applied in Chapter 3.

Table 4.1   Data for the QCA, also including transport and socioeconomic links

Case	Location	Physical geography			Transport	Economy (main centripetal forces)
		Climate	Minerals	Movement		
Angola	0	1	1	1	0	1 (oil, lucrative market)
Botswana	1	0	1	1	1	1 (labour migration and mining)
Comoros	0	–	0	0	0	0
DR Congo (except for Katanga Province)	0	1	0	0	0	0
DR Congo (Katanga Province alone)	0	1	1	1	1	1 (mining)
Lesotho	1	1	0	1	1	1 (labour migration, LHWP)
Madagascar	0	–	0	0	0	0
Malawi	0	1	0	0	0	1 (energy imports)
Mauritius	0	–	0	0	0	0
Mozambique (except for Maputo area)	0	1	1	0	0	1 (agriculture, labour migration, Cahora Bassa)
Mozambique (Maputo area alone)	1	0	0	1	1	1 (labour migration, Maputo Development Corridor)
Namibia	1	0	1	1	1	1 (agriculture)
Seychelles	0	–	0	0	0	0
Swaziland	1	1	1	1	1	1 (electricity, Coca Cola)
Tanzania	0	0	1	0	0	1 (agriculture, gas)
Zambia	0	1	1	1	1	1 (mining)
Zimbabwe	1	1	1	1	1	1 (investment, especially in mining)

Source: Author's own compilation.

Chapter 5
Key Projects of Regional Integration

In this chapter, I analyse regional cooperation on water, electricity and transport in order to divulge the importance of geographical conditions. The objective of the following sections is not to derive economic and political features of the continental SADC region deterministically from geography. By applying Process Tracing, I seek to show that geographical conditions in combination with social factors shape the economics and politics of South Africa's regional relations. Following the concept of INUS causality, the geographical conditions that I address are necessary but insufficient components of larger causal factors. In other words, geography matters.

5.1 Regional Cooperation on Water

South Africa is a water-scarce country. In the semiarid parts of the country, droughts are frequent. There, lakes and rivers that permanently hold water are rare. The variability of rainfall is high. Groundwater has to be used for agriculture and drinking, although it is often of dubious quality. On the regional scale, the four economically most diversified member states of SADC – that is, Botswana, Namibia, South Africa and Zimbabwe – all receive less precipitation than the global average amount of 860 millimetres per year. Climate change will further reduce rainfall in these countries. The stream flow of the major rivers will decrease. Already 13 years ago, 12.9 billion cubic metres of water were consumed in South Africa – which is only slightly less than the 13.2 billion cubic metres available (Department of Water Affairs and Forestry 2004). South African water suppliers expect to run into serious problems by 2030. They argue that water pipelines running from the DR Congo must be ready by then because there is not much capacity left for dealing with the water shortage domestically (Ashton and Turton 2005). Socioeconomic developments further increase water scarcity: since 1994, 12 million South Africans have been provided with access to water; another 3 million will be connected in the coming years.

Some regional countries possess an abundance of water, however. The DR Congo lies entirely in the humid tropics; Angola, Mozambique, Tanzania and Zambia partly so. Regional cooperation on water appears to be rational. Provided that intensive agricultural continues in the semiarid parts of the region, it will have to be transferred from surplus areas to where it is most needed (Pazvakavambwa 2005). Following Hartshorne, one may argue that the continental SADC region is functional as a political unit because the complementarity of the regional states

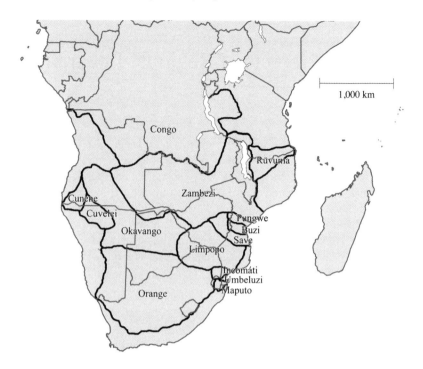

Map 5.1   International river basins in the continental SADC region
Source: Adapted from Ashton and Turton (2005: 8).

in terms of water supply and demand enables it to fulfil key economic functions on its own. This naturally- and economically-induced rationality of cooperation is reinforced by the fact that many watercourses in East and Southern Africa are shared by different states. The SADC region comprises 14 international river basins – meaning that in 14 cases a river or a river system crosses the territory of at least two states. Map 5.1 shows the international river basins found in the SADC region.

Amongst South Africa's international river basins, the most important one is that of the Orange River. It is not only the biggest in terms of physical size and water volume, it is also essential because Gauteng relies on water transferred from there to the Vaal River system. As analysed later, the LHWP is the key component of this transfer scheme. Further downstream, dams have been erected in order to generate electricity and provide water. Southern Namibia depends upon the Orange River too. Plans to transfer water to Namibia's Fish River Basin date back to the late 1940s. Botswana – and the Gaborone area in particular – may also benefit from transfer schemes in the near future. The second largest basin in South Africa is that of the Limpopo River. It is highly relevant for Botswana because the national North–South Carrier provides much needed water to the dry Gaborone area. Transfers from South Africa complement what is pumped through the North–South Carrier. Further east, this basin coincides geographically with South Africa's mining areas and has been essential for providing water to them for more than a century. The basins of the Incomáti and Maputo Rivers, meanwhile, are much smaller. They are shared by Mozambique and South Africa. The Incomáti River Basin supplies water to many of Eskom's coal-fired power stations, which generate about 90 per cent of the electricity used in South Africa (Turton et al. 2004).

The most extraordinary project of regional cooperation on water is the LHWP. In the late 1940s, the British colonial administration considered building dams in Lesotho in order to supply the neighbouring provinces of South Africa with water and so as to generate electricity. A consultation study published in 1951 stated what was hard to miss: South Africa was (and still is) the ideal buyer for water and electricity from Lesotho. The Free State – which directly borders with Lesotho – was already then South Africa's agricultural heartland, as industrial production boomed in the nearby Johannesburg–Pretoria agglomeration. The South African government at the time, however, showed little interest in the project for fear of becoming dependent upon foreign suppliers. The victory of the National Party (NP) in the elections of 1948 meant the end of close cooperation with Britain and Lesotho. Without South Africa's support, large-scale water projects could not be realised in the latter. Even today, the mountain kingdom possesses neither enough capital nor the necessary knowhow for such ventures. The construction and maintenance of hydropower stations exclusively for Lesotho is, moreover, not rational because of its small domestic market (Senior Basotho diplomat, pers. comm., 17 February 2010).

In the late 1970s, the attitude of the South African government changed, also because projects with Lesotho constituted a way to circumvent the antiapartheid sanctions that had been imposed on the regime. Such projects provided South Africa with much-needed access to international credits and foreign direct investment. Yet, a Basotho–South African treaty on the water project was only signed after a coup in 1986, which brought to power an anti-Communist junta that favoured cooperation with South Africa. The end of the apartheid regime, which is correctly seen as the turning point for regional relations, did not mean much to the LHWP. It had begun at a time when no one expected the NP to give up power.

By 2020 the LHWP will include six dammed lakes, 225 kilometres of tunnels for the transfer of water, 650 kilometres of tarred roads and two hydropower stations (Waites 2000). The first and already completed phase was about damming the Bokong and Malibamatso Rivers. Construction works on the Katse Dam, the central reservoir of the project, were completed in 1998. The Muela Dam became operational four years later. Water is diverted from Katse to a third dam, Mohale, through a 32-kilometre-long tunnel. From there, it supplies Muela via an 82-kilometre-long tunnel. Muela is linked to South Africa; 20 cubic metres of water per second are pumped from Lesotho to its neighbour in this way. A newly built hydropower station at the Muela Dam has a maximum capacity of 72

MW (Nel and Illgner 2001). In the phases of the project that are still to come, the amount of water transferred will increase to 70 cubic metres per second – half of Lesotho's average annual runoff. For these purposes, three more dams (Mashai, Ntoahae and Tsoelike) still have to be constructed and interlinked, which will be done by underground pipelines.

It is obvious that the LHWP has become a reality because of South Africa. The region's economic powerhouse not only has a crucial influence by being the buyer of Lesotho's water and electricity, its government also acts as guarantor for all external project-related loans. The DBSA works as the channel for the transfer of money from international agencies and donors to the Basotho government (Matlosa 1998; Nevin 1998). South African interest in the LHWP is induced by geographical conditions, because the regional power runs short of water under natural conditions. Manmade climate change is now increasing the extent of this shortfall. Lesotho's proximity to South Africa's main agricultural and industrial areas, its comparatively high rainfall and its geomorphological structures – which make building dams relatively easy – constitute further necessary geographical conditions for the LHWP. Such factors do not completely explain it though. As South Africa's disinterest in the project in the 1950s and 1960s demonstrates, geography provides opportunities that politicians may choose to forego.

Beyond the analysis of geography as a condition for social processes, the LHWP is revealing with regard to both the benefits and problems that the countries of Southern Africa experience in their relationship with the regional power. The most obvious benefit to Lesotho of the project is the income generated by selling its water, which increased from ZAR 80 million in 1997 to ZAR 440 million in 2010 (LHWP 2011b). Moreover, the first phase of the project created around 7,000 jobs, half of them for people from the disadvantaged highlands. The upgraded infrastructure is also beneficial to Lesotho's economy, its people and the tourism sector (Matlosa 1998). Hundreds of kilometres of tarred roads have been built to and from the construction sites along with countless gravel roads around the dams, which serve to connect remote villages to the rest of the country. Newly established telecommunication networks, especially for mobile phones, are reliable. Pipelines for water have been constructed or upgraded (Nel and Illgner 2001). As mentioned, the LHWP also generates electricity for Lesotho itself. This means that the country – which used to import 95 per cent of its electricity from South Africa in the early 1990s (Tabirih 1993) – is now able to meet a significant share of its demand. The Muela Hydropower Station generates up to 72 MW. Lesotho's peak demand stands at 121 MW (Senior official of the Southern African Power Pool, pers. comm., 19 September 2011).[1] Because some electricity is sold to South Africa at times of low domestic consumption, another ZAR 175,000 to

---

1   'Peak demand' or 'peak load' are terms used in energy demand management. They describe a period in which electrical power has to be provided at a significantly higher than average supply level. This means that the justmentioned 121 MW have to be put on the grid in Lesotho at the time of peak demand in order to avoid blackouts occurring.

ZAR 2 million per year went into the national budget of Lesotho between 2001 and 2010 (LHWP 2011a).

However, extreme side effects on the natural environment – such as declining biodiversity, increased evaporation, loss of grazing land and soil erosion – have also occurred as a consequence of the project (Matlosa 1998). Furthermore, building artificial lakes in Lesotho's mountains is likely to in future deprive the Orange River of water that is needed by those living along its course, as *Business Day* reported on 4 October 2011. Only the areas close to the dams have so far significantly benefited from the upgraded infrastructure, especially in terms of water supply. Distant parts of Lesotho, meanwhile, have not yet experienced any positive benefits from it at all (Bogetić 2006). Other negative socioeconomic consequences of the project range from corruption and nepotism to discrimination against Basotho workers to alcoholism, prostitution and sexual violence. In a broader context, the development strategy behind the LHWP is based on the expectation that there will be trickledown effects that help modernise the Basotho economy. Such an approach has come along with economic liberalisation. Hence, import restrictions have been lifted. Prices are no longer controlled by government institutions. Taxes on big business have been reduced in order to attract export-oriented companies (Seiffert 1997). The economic rationale behind the LHWP is, furthermore, aligned with South Africa's goal of gaining market access in the region, something that I will come back to in Chapter 6.1.

Crossborder water transfer schemes of a smaller size than the LHWP are already common in Southern Africa. Without these, water resources would be insufficient in many areas of Botswana, Namibia and South Africa. The latter can transfer about 4.2 billion cubic metres of water per year between its catchment areas. It exports 9 million cubic metres to Botswana. The transfer capacity from Angola to Namibia is about 90 million cubic metres. Namibia and Zimbabwe can transfer 60 million and 1.2 billion cubic metres from one catchment to another within their own borders. Several larger projects are also being envisaged (Heyns 2002): water may be transferred from Angola's Calueque Dam to northern Namibia. Central Namibia will most likely receive water from the Okavango Basin. Botswana's North–South Carrier is to be expanded from the Limpopo Basin to the Zambezi Basin. Gauteng may be linked to it as well. A 1,200-kilometre-long pipeline from the confluence point of the Chobe and the Zambezi Rivers, near Victoria Falls, via Botswana to South Africa's Vaal River system was discussed 20 years ago. Yet, in addition to the probable difficulty of negotiations between the three states involved, physical geography also hampers the transfer of water from the Zambezi to Gauteng because the river flows at an elevation of 600 metres – whereas Gauteng itself is located 1,400 metres above sea level.

In South Africa, linking rivers in KwaZulu-Natal and the Eastern Cape with the Orange River is being considered. Zimbabwe's government would like to supply Bulawayo with water from the Zambezi. By far the most impressive idea is the transfer of water from the Congo River system – specifically from the Cassai and Lualaba Rivers – to the headwaters of the Okavango and Zambezi. One may of course wonder whether such projects are sensible, given their enormous costs and certain negative environmental impact. Moreover, the water scarcity of South Africa and its neighbouring countries is not only due to insufficient precipitation. Theft of water accounts for an annual loss of 230 million kilolitres in the Vaal catchment area alone. The *Mail & Guardian* reported on 22 March 2012 that 180 million kilolitres of water would be saved every year if leaking pipelines were fixed. In some areas, up to 30 per cent of water is lost because of aging infrastructure (Centre for Development and Enterprise 2010). A working paper by the DBSA accordingly concludes that South Africa would not face a water crisis if water management were 'sound' (Muller et al. 2009: 36). Considering, however, that authorities in South Africa have not been able to fix water pipelines for decades, and that those who use water for their swimming pools and lawns can still afford water despite this impressive level of waste, it is unlikely that South Africa will cope with water scarcity by using domestic resources in a more sensible way. Regional cooperation projects on water can, as such, be expected to gain much relevance in the near future.

Such cooperation is framed by the SADC Protocol on Shared Watercourses, signed in 1995 and revised in 2000. The fact that it was the first sector-specific protocol adopted by the community stresses the key relevance of water to regional relations. The protocol goes back in origin to efforts to jointly manage the Zambezi Basin. The common management of the Zambezi had been initiated two years before the protocol was ratified. The core of the protocol is the stated desire of member states of SADC for 'close cooperation for judicious, sustainable and coordinated utilisation of the resources of the shared watercourses' in the region. They are convinced 'of the need for [the] coordinated and environmentally sound development of the resources of shared watercourses' (2000). Until today, numerous institutions have been set up bi- and multilaterally in order to bring together technocrats from the states concerned. They deal with jointly conserving, developing and utilising water (Heyns 2005; Pazvakavambwa 2005).

In the mid-1990s, armed conflicts over water appeared more likely to occur than regional cooperation did. Namibia's government announced plans to divert water from the Okavango River regardless of the impact on neighbouring Botswana. Zimbabwe considered supplying dry Matabeleland with water from the Zambezi, which would have caused a conflict with downstream Mozambique (Swatuk 2000). Botswana and Namibia have still not settled the Okavango issue yet. Their dispute over five small islands in the Chobe and Zambezi Rivers also remains unresolved. Namibia and South Africa are at odds regarding water access rights at the lower Orange River (Ashton 2000). Although these conflicts are unlikely to escalate, water will certainly remain a core element of national power. Angola holds a pivotal position concerning regional cooperation on water, and in particular on hydropower. The former Portuguese colony not only links its southern neighbours to the Congo River but also controls access to the Zambezi. If climate change continues to reduce the availability of water south of the Cunene River, Botswana, Namibia and South Africa will come to depend upon Angola for access to this resource. Regional food security will also not be maintained unless Angola promotes domestic agriculture and effectively integrates into the regional economy (South African expert on water resources, pers. comm., 28 November 2011).

What these remarks on water as a basis of national power and on conflicts over water show is that geographical conditions alone do not explain social outcomes. There is regional cooperation on water in Southern Africa because of a combination of both geographical and nongeographical factors. Had there been a war over water between Botswana and Namibia in the mid-1990s, geographical factors would have been necessary but insufficient causes for that conflict. In order to explain regional cooperation on water, geographical conditions thus have to be taken in combination with political factors – namely, the generally cooperative relations that exist between the different states of the region today.

5.2 Regional Cooperation on Electricity

South Africa faces serious difficulties to meet its current level of domestic electricity demand. In January 2008, Eskom – which generates 95 per cent of the electricity used in South Africa – had to ask its largest customers, mostly gold and platinum miners, to shut down their operations and reduce their use of electricity to minimum levels, using only a sufficient amount to get all remaining staff out of their mines. Platinum and palladium hit record prices because South Africa normally supplies 85 and 30 per cent respectively of these two metals to the world market. In the following months, energy-intense businesses – steelworks for example – had to scale down their production because of power rationing, as *Business Day* reported on 14 and 22 February 2008. The reason for the 2008 crisis is that Eskom had both neglected the transmission system and failed to significantly increase its generation capacity. According to another article in *Business Day* on 3 March 2008, Eskom's reserve capacities fell from 30 per cent in 1994 to 10 per cent in 2005 on account of an investment moratorium. From 1992 to 2004, electricity demand for the production of nonferrous metals tripled. It doubled for nonmetal minerals. In the iron and steel sector, more than twice as much electricity was used (Department of Minerals and Energy 2006).

Large-scale industrial projects, for example in aluminium production, indicate that this trend will continue or even accelerate in future. In 2006, Eskom (2006) estimated that South Africa's annual 2–3 per cent growth in electricity use would threaten the company's ability to meet excess peaking capacity in 2007 and excess baseload in 2010. Data collected by the Southern African Power Pool confirms that the entire region has run into a supply deficit because of low levels of investment in power stations, large-scale electrification programmes, ongoing economic growth and high metal prices – the latter of which boost the energy-intense mining sector (pers. comm., 19 September 2011). Such developments in its neighbourhood directly affect South Africa, because Eskom sells electricity to the continental member countries of SADC and has so far kept its agreements even in times of domestic shortage. Even more troublesome is the fear that the 2008 crisis may only have been a foretaste of future energy shortages. Meeting the ANC's goal of an annual growth rate of 6 per cent in terms of gross domestic product will require about 47,000 MW of additional capacity being produced within the next 20 years (McDonald 2009), which is an impressive ambition considering that current peak demand is only about 36,000 MW. Given that South Africa hardly ever meets the government's growth targets, the Department of Energy (2011) expects peak demand to rise to 68,000 MW by 2030.

Beyond South Africa's borders, economic growth and modernisation also come along with a higher demand for electricity. In the late 1990s, experts predicted the share of noncommercial energy – meaning predominantly biomass and charcoal – to decrease from the 43 per cent of the time to around 15 per cent by 2020. The share of electricity and liquid fuels was expected to increase accordingly (Horvei 1998). Seeing these developments and projections, Eskom (2010) plans to reach an output of 80,000 MW by 2026 – a goal that appears to be far beyond what is actually feasible given current capacities and the time that it takes to build new power stations.

In addition to measures taken on the national level – that is, the expansion of coal-fired power generation and investment in renewable and nuclear energy, developments that I have assessed elsewhere (Scholvin 2014c) – the region also plays an important role for South Africa's chosen energy strategy. There are coal reserves lying beyond South Africa's borders that Eskom may exploit jointly with junior partners from neighbouring countries. Mozambique and Namibia possess gasfields close to South African consumers in Gauteng and the Western Cape respectively. Liquefied natural gas may be shipped from Tanzania to already existing processing facilities in Port Elizabeth. Most importantly, the DR Congo holds tremendous potential for hydropower generation. Angola, Mozambique and Zambia offer smaller but still relevant opportunities in this regard as well.

By cooperating with its neighbouring countries, South Africa could acquire much more energy than it will actually need in the coming decades. Its neighbours may benefit from national electrification, incentives for development and revenues from selling electricity. Regional cooperation also provides a way to reduce the impact of droughts, which undermine the generation capacity of hydropower stations. If the regional electricity grid is sufficiently interconnected, Eskom will be able to cover shortages elsewhere in the region with its coal-fired power stations (Stephan and Fane Hervey 2008). Moreover, though, hydropower is based on a forever reusable resource – whereas coal, as a finite one, does not offer any such long-term solutions. The global peak for coal will probably occur in 2026 regarding energy output and in 2034 concerning the quantity extracted (Mohr and Evans 2009). South Africa's coal peak will be reached in 2020 (Hartnady 2010). Any coal-centred strategy is worsened by the fact that global prices for coal are likely to increase dramatically with peak oil coming ever nearer.

Such thinking is already part of South Africa's energy strategy (Scholvin 2015). The South African government declared in its White Paper on Energy Policy that such policy ought to be made regionally compatible. It rejects a strategy aimed at autarky, as was pursued by the apartheid regime. Regional cooperation is expected to lead to a diversification of energy sources – or, in other words, to give South Africa access to the energy resources of the region. The aforementioned gasfields in Mozambique and Namibia are described in this document as an opportunity for South African companies, for example. The South African government states that it will facilitate the expansion of South African firms by setting up regional bodies that regulate the natural gas sector. The Southern African Power Pool is mentioned as a tool to widen market access. Moreover, an oil refining hub for the SADC region is to be promoted – it will be located somewhere on South Africa's coast (Department of Minerals and Energy 1998). A 400,000-barrels-per-day crude oil refinery in the Coega Industrial Development Zone near Port Elizabeth has been discussed, as reported in *Engineering News* on 17 July 2009. Such a project is likely to strengthen the ties between South Africa and its neighbours in the energy sector. Together with water, energy constitutes the core driver of interstate cooperation in the SADC region. Energy and water are, as such, two essential centripetal forces that bind the continental SADC states together.

There are three geographical factors that suggest greater future regional cooperation on energy is likely. First, climate and geology provide opportunities for Eskom in the region. Reinforcing the need to realise these opportunities, climate change and diminishing coal reserves can be subsumed as a geographically induced need to decarbonise the South African energy sector. Second, the economic structures of South Africa and its neighbouring states are compatible in the sense that the former possesses the capital and know-how to make use of the energy potential of its neighbours, two key assets that they themselves lack. The high demand for energy in South Africa is a reflection of the country's economic geography, meaning its energy-intense industries (Scholvin 2014c). Third, an agenda of regional cooperation – which has marked South Africa's approach to the SADC region since 1994 – constitutes the necessary political condition for regional cooperation on energy. The will to cooperate regionally on energy was expressed, for example, in a recent policy paper by South Africa's Economic Development Department (2010).

Today, regional cooperation on energy looks different to the ideas just presented – although it is also shaped by geographical conditions. Geology is the key to understanding South Africa's energy sector in general and Eskom's regional trade in particular. First of all, South Africa possesses a large amount of coal – about 4 per cent of global reserves (Energy Information Administration 2011a). Coal can be mined at a relatively low cost and provides a cheap and reliable way to meet baseload demand. Moreover, South Africa is economically more advanced than its neighbours.[2] The combination of geology – that is, the aforementioned abundance of easily-minable coal – and of South Africa's strong industrial sector, have led to a path-dependent development of the large-scale, carbon-based generation of electricity in the country (Scholvin 2014c). Sasol's coal-to-liquids processing fits into this context as well. The resulting vested interests and actor network – namely the aforementioned minerals–energy complex – currently privilege coal-fired power stations over other sources of electricity. With regard to regional relations, this means that South Africa possesses the necessary physiogeographical foundations and manmade geographical structures that allow Eskom to export electricity to the region. Table 5.1 shows Eskom's recent regional trade in electricity.

Table 5.1   Eskom's trade in electricity from 1 April 2005 until 31 March 2011

Trading partner	Imports (in gigawatt-hours)	Exports (in gigawatt-hours)
Botswana	0	15,334
DR Congo	1,815	0
Lesotho	109	420
Mozambique	64,927	58,454
Namibia	105	11,551
Swaziland	0	4,866
Zambia	677	683
Zimbabwe	282	1,259

Source: Information provided by Eskom in 2013.

For the process of present-day regional cooperation on energy, geographical conditions can, once again, be identified as necessary: if South Africa did not possess so much coal and if its economy were not so highly industrialised, the regional power would not be able to export electricity. In this specific case, geographical factors are probably sufficient for that outcome to occur because there appear to be no political factors that need to be considered in explaining the region's dependence upon South African electricity. What matters to South Africa's role as a regional power in this regard is that the trade patterns, shown by Table 5.1, indicate that some regional countries are highly dependent upon Eskom. Table 5.2 further brings together the available capacities and the peak demand in the continental SADC countries, which indicates to what extent every regional country relies on South Africa's surplus generation of electricity – because each

2   Following Fairgrieve's (1917) thinking, one may argue that South Africa is highly industrialised and can generate so much electricity because of its coal reserves. It was natural that energy-intense industrialisation occurred in South Africa, Fairgrieve would say.

gap between peak demand and available capacity must be met by transmissions from South Africa.

Mozambique's considerable surplus, generated by the Cahora Bassa Power Station, is mostly sold to Eskom. Zimbabwe also buys electricity generated there. Angola and the DR Congo transmit smaller amounts of electricity to some of their direct neighbours, whenever their power stations are fully operational. Even though this dependence is certainly risky for Botswana, Namibia, Swaziland and Zimbabwe, electricity bought from Eskom is cheaper than electricity produced domestically is. Connecting up with South Africa is, therefore, economically beneficial (Honorary Consul of Namibia, pers. comm., 9 December 2009). Lesotho has become less dependent upon South Africa because of the LHWP. In Mozambique, the Maputo area will no longer have to rely on South African electricity once adequate transmission lines from there to Cahora Bassa have been built. Tanzania, which suffers from frequent blackouts, is not sufficiently connected into the regional grid. Domestic projects there, in Angola and in the DR Congo suggest that the degree of dependence upon Eskom will decrease in future (Senior official of the Southern African Power Pool, pers. comm., 19 September 2011).

Table 5.2   Capacities and peak demand for electricity in the continental SADC region

Country	Available capacity (in MW)	Peak demand (in MW)
Angola	870	668
Botswana	90	503
DR Congo	1,170	1,028
Lesotho	70	108
Malawi	246	260
Mozambique	2,249	416
Namibia	360	444
South Africa	38,384	35,959
Swaziland	50	200
Tanzania	680	694
Zambia	1,200	1,495
Zimbabwe	1,080	1,397

Note: Data for 2008 and 2009.
Source: Information provided by the Southern African Power Pool in 2011.

The efforts taken to boost domestic electricity generation within the regional states do not hint at their future decoupling from South Africa though. They are rather an indicator for the change occurring in regional cooperation on electricity

that I just explained. The expansion of the regional electricity grid confirms this
assessment. Whilst coal and natural gas can be transported to power stations in
South Africa, trade in electricity depends upon high-voltage transmission lines.
As the first major project of postapartheid regional cooperation, a 400 kilovolt
line from South Africa via Botswana to Zimbabwe became operational in 1995.
Zimbabwe already possessed transmissions lines to the DR Congo via Zambia.
The project linked the coal-centred southern states with the hydro-centred northern
states of the region.

Mozambique and Namibia are individually connected to South Africa.
Envisaged transmission lines will bind Angola (via Namibia), Malawi and
Tanzania (via Mozambique and Zambia) and even Kenya and Uganda (via the DR
Congo or Tanzania) to the regional grid (McDonald 2009). As shown by Map 5.2,
this network of transmission lines can be divided into three major south-to-north
corridors: a western one from the DR Congo via Angola, Namibia and Botswana
to South Africa, a central one from the Congolese–Zambian Copperbelt via
Zimbabwe to South Africa and an eastern one from Kenya via Tanzania, Malawi
and Mozambique to South Africa. Under the auspices of the Southern African
Power Pool, priority is being given to better linking Malawi to neighbouring Tete
Province in Mozambique, Katanga Province in the DR Congo to Zambia, and
Botswana to Namibia and Zimbabwe (pers. comm., 19 September 2011). Tanzania
and Mozambique as well as Tanzania and Zambia, meanwhile, are to become
sufficiently connected at a later point in time.

The western corridor used to be seen as the most lucrative one because of the
DR Congo's Inga Dam, where up to 44,000 MW can be generated. The entire DR
Congo has a theoretical hydropower potential of 100,000 MW. Regardless of the
still rather vague upgrade plans for Inga, 3,000–4,500 MW could be transferred
from the power stations that already exist there to Southern Africa if sufficient
transmission lines existed. En route, another 6,500 MW would be added at the
Kwanza River in Angola (McDonald 2009). Eskom has already been involved
in the rehabilitation of the existing hydropower station at the Inga Dam. The
Congolese government would like the South African giant to work on its other
hydropower stations and on its domestic electricity grid as well (Kabemba 2007).
According to a senior official of the Southern African Power Pool, the western
corridor project is no longer being pursued because of technical obstacles (pers.
comm., 19 September 2011). A relaunch, agreed upon by Jacob Zuma and his
Congolese counterpart Joseph Kabila in October 2013, remains an uncertain
prospect (Maupin 2015; Scholvin 2015).

Officials from Eskom, meanwhile, told me that the failure of the western
corridor was due to differing national legislations and political quarrels over the
distribution of expected revenues (pers. comm., 11 October 2011). They agreed
with a senior official of the Power Institute for Eastern and Southern Africa that
connecting South Africa to the Inga Dam was not a problem technically (pers.
comm., 11 October 2011). Remarks by the aforementioned official of the Southern
African Power Pool appear to confirm that it is political factors that currently

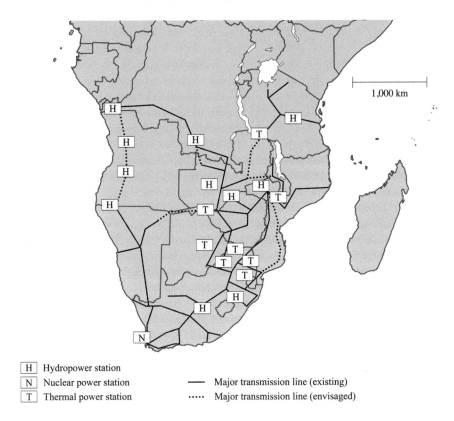

H   Hydropower station
N   Nuclear power station   ——— Major transmission line (existing)
T   Thermal power station   ····· Major transmission line (envisaged)

**Map 5.2   The electricity grid and major power stations in
the continental SADC region**

Source: Scholvin (2014c: 197).

hamper regional cooperation on electricity: he said that governments 'often pursue political goals' and their own national interests, which are not always compatible with what is best for the region as a whole. As a replacement for Westcor – the joint venture company that was created in 2004 by the utility companies of Angola, Botswana, the DR Congo, Namibia and South Africa – individual projects are now being carried out. Angola and Namibia will be better linked by 2017. Angola and the western DR Congo are to be connected by a 400 kilovolt line by 2015. Without these transmission lines, Angola remains the only country that is barely connected to the rest of the region. Thus, connecting the DR Congo to South Africa will depend upon the utilisation of the central corridor. This is problematic because the Inga Dam is located in the western DR Congo, and transmission lines within the country are few in number and of poor quality. The senior official of the Southern African Power Pool with whom I discussed these matters argued that the DR Congo should first solve the maintenance problems vis-à-vis its own power stations before thinking about building additional transmission lines though, claiming such problems currently reduce its export potential by 50 per cent.

In sum, a regional electricity grid that is based on sufficient transmission lines will not be established overnight. The aforementioned officials of Eskom told me that the most prominent project of regional cooperation on energy – expanding the DR Congo's Inga Dam and linking it to South Africa – would become a reality 'someday in our lifetime'. One must, therefore, be cautious regarding any optimistic plans voiced. Nevertheless, the vision of high-voltage transmission lines running from Zambia via Tanzania to Kenya and to Ethiopia, as recently articulated by TradeMark Southern Africa (2012b), may motivate the South African government to now speed up negotiations on the Tripartite Free Trade Area.

We are thus currently witnessing the construction of manmade structures in geographical space that constitute centripetal forces, ones tying together continental Southern Africa – and possibly also East Africa and the Horn of Africa. They reinforce South Africa's position as the regional economic powerhouse and reveal how closely this position is associated with naturally given and manmade geography. At the same time, nongeographical obstacles – such as the issues that led to the failure of Westcor and the poor maintenance of power stations in the DR Congo – indicate that geographical explanations alone do not reveal all that matters with regard to the current state of regional economic and political relations.

5.3 South Africa as the Region's Transport Hub

Reasons for South Africa's Centrality in Transport Corridors

As noted, the former British colonies in Southern Africa depend upon South African harbours for their overseas trade. This dependence is reinforced by the fact that the regional countries rely on the export of extracted or produced primary sector products. They furthermore need to transport goods in large quantities. Today, exports from the Congolese–Zambian Copperbelt – which are mostly shipped through the two major ports of KwaZulu-Natal, Durban and Richards Bay – best demonstrate that South Africa connects the region to the rest of the world. It is the only African country that possesses shorelines on both the Atlantic and Indian Oceans. It can easily be reached by cargo ships coming from Europe, the Far East and North America. Regional geomorphology moreover suggests that every place south of the Congolese rainforest and southwest of the East African Rift Valley can easily be tied to South Africa by a transport infrastructure.

Yet, lacking centrality on both the global and regional scale, South Africa is not well positioned as either a hub for transport or as Africa's gateway to the cores of the global economy. South Africa shares borders with only a few other countries. Crossing borders hampers the movement of goods. For instance, Botswana and Namibia possess one-stop border posts that it takes lorries 20 minutes to cross, but transport from Namibia's capital Windhoek to Lubango in southern Angola

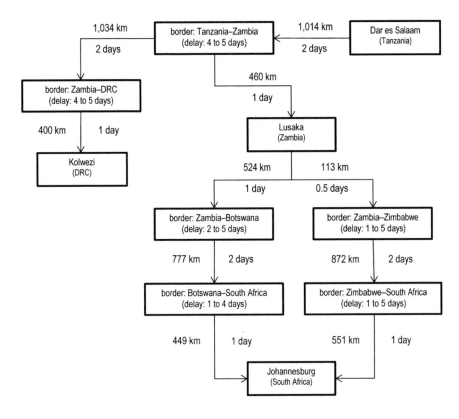

**Figure 5.1   Distances and transportation times along
the North–South Corridor**

Source: Adapted from TradeMark Southern Africa (2012a: 17).

can take up to 15 days because of border controls (involving corrupt practices) and poor roads in Angola (Advisor of the Agricultural Trade Forum in Windhoek, pers. comm., 2 August 2010). Reports of the World Bank indicate that delays at Beitbridge on the border between South Africa and Zimbabwe are 34 hours for traffic heading north and 11 hours for traffic going south. At Chirundu, on Zimbabwe's border with Zambia, freight vehicles wait another 39 and 11 hours respectively (Curtis 2009). Taken together, delays at Beitbridge and Chirundu are equal to the imposition of a 25 per cent surcharge on transport costs (Teravaninthorn and Raballand 2008). Goods transported along the North–South Corridor spend about one-third of their total transport time waiting at borders (Curtis 2009). Lorries that take the western branch of the corridor from Zambia to Botswana have to cross the Zambezi River by ferry near Kazangulu. The governments of Botswana and Zambia agreed in 2006 to build a bridge there, but have not actually followed through on this yet. Figure 5.1 gives an impression of how extensively distances and border issues slow down transport in both East and Southern Africa.

Due to the legacies of colonialism and in accordance with the aforementioned locational disadvantages of South Africa, there are some considerable centrifugal – meaning disuniting – effects that arise from the transport infrastructure present in Central, East and Southern Africa today. Railway lines link harbours in Angola (Lobito, Luanda and Namibe), the two Congos (Matadi and Pointe Noire), Kenya (Mombasa), Mozambique (Beira, Maputo and Nacala), Namibia (Lüderitz and Walvis Bay) and Tanzania (Dar es Salaam) to their respective national hinterlands. These corridors, stretching from east to west, are poorly interconnected at the national level. They fragment most regional countries, and especially the two former Portuguese colonies. Only the Coast2Coast Corridor from Maputo to Johannesburg to Walvis Bay and the North–South Corridor from Durban via Johannesburg, Francistown, Harare and Lusaka to Lubumbashi and Dar es Salaam bind the regional countries somewhat together.

In contrast to the corridors that bypass the regional power, the Coast2Coast Corridor and the North–South Corridor are in good shape. The World Bank rates 59 per cent of the road between Lubumbashi in the DR Congo and Durban as 'good', with problems occurring rather in the DR Congo and Zimbabwe. Only 27 per cent of the road between Lilongwe in Malawi and Nacala in Mozambique is in a good condition. Seventy-two per cent of the road from Zimbabwe's capital Harare to Beira is in a 'fair' condition, meaning that maintenance work on it will be necessary in the next couple of years (Ranganathan and Foster 2011). Railway lines that bypass South Africa are in an inadequate condition, except for the newly rehabilitated Benguela Line and, with some restrictions, the Sena Line (Pearson and Giersing 2012). Comparing transport from Dar es Salaam and Durban to Zambia's capital Lusaka, delays at the port of Dar es Salaam make the latter the faster option, even though the former is closer to Lusaka. In comparison to Beira, the advantages of Durban in terms of time and costs are even clearer. Dar es Salaam can compete with Durban because of lower costs of rail transport though (Ranganathan and Foster 2011). Still, experts from TradeMark Southern Africa reason that corridors that bypass South Africa are economically barely feasible, because of the low quantities of goods that can be transported – and especially by rail (pers. comm., 2 March 2012). These features of the regional transport network bestow centrality on South Africa despite its peripheral location.

Conducting interviews with senior officials from South Africa's major transport company Transnet, I gained the following additional information: southbound rail and road transport dominates in the SADC region (pers. comm., 16 August 2010 and 18 October 2011). Firstly, this is because the ports of Durban and Richards Bay possess greater capacities to handle cargo than non-South African harbours do and offer, therefore, better prices. Maputo has become an alternative. Lobito in Angola is about to be linked again to the Copperbelt. The upgrades that are being made to the port of Dar es Salaam, the Tanzania–Zambia Railway and the nearby Tanzania–Zambia Highway are impressive. Nonetheless, a study published by TradeMark Southern Africa (2012c) indicates that most parts of the Tanzania–Zambia Highway remain in a poor condition. Regardless of the upgrading of railway lines and roads, Dar es Salaam, Lobito and Maputo will, according to my interviewees from Transnet, never reach the size of the two giant ports in KwaZulu-Natal.

The second reason for South Africa's dominant position in the regional transport network is that the country provides good maritime connections to Europe, the Far East and North America. The harbours in its neighbouring countries meanwhile only offer access to one of these three possible options, for the locational reasons apparent. Thirdly, South Africa's harbours benefit from their being integrated into a reliable railway network. Botswana, for instance, cannot export mining products via Walvis Bay because it is not connected by rail to Namibia's main port. Where railway lines do exist, most of South Africa's neighbouring countries nevertheless run short of actual locomotives and wagons. Upgrading existing infrastructure or building new railway lines is beyond their current financial reach. The volume of trade passing through regional ports, summarised in Table 5.3, demonstrates the dominance of South African harbours. Even Kenya – the leading economy of the EAC – does not come close to South African dimensions of maritime transport. Economies of scale go hand-in-hand with technological advantages: South Africa's ports need less time to handle the same amount of cargo. Containerisation was introduced there already in the 1970s, whereas in neighbouring countries first attempts to use this key shipping method were only made in the 1990s (Ahwireng-Obeng and McGowan 1998a).

South Africa's dominance as the regional transport hub is reinforced by the fact that the country provides an advanced business environment. The World Bank's Logistics Performance Index reveals that South Africa is way ahead of its neighbouring countries in terms of logistics sophistication. In a global comparison on the Logistics Performance Index – which operates on a scale from 1 to 5, and brings transport infrastructure together with aspects of the operational management of transport – South Africa belongs to the first tier of states and is on the same level as New Zealand and Thailand. As shown by Table 5.4, its neighbouring countries belong only to the third and fourth tiers – which are almost exclusive to Least Developed Countries. South Africa's exceptional role in maritime transport is further proven by the Liner Shipping Connectivity Index. Published by the UN Conference on Trade and Development, this measures on a scale from 0 to 100 how well connected internationally the ports of a country are.

South Africa's high rating, shown in Table 5.4, reflects the good regional and global connectivity of its harbours. They serve as intersections between regional ports and the rest of the world. Overseas goods unloaded in Walvis Bay, for example, have often been first shipped on a large vessel to Cape Town, where some of the cargo has then been reloaded onto a smaller ship heading for Namibia (Senior representative of the Hanns Seidel Foundation, pers. comm., 12 July 2010). Angola's main port, Luanda, has recently entered into a pairing agreement with South Africa's port of Ngqura, 20 kilometres northeast of Port Elizabeth,

Table 5.3   Annual port traffic volumes of major harbours in East and Southern Africa

Port	Container port traffic in 20-foot equivalent units	Total port traffic in tonnes
Beira	100,000	3,000,000
Cape Town	740,000	13,700,000
Dar es Salaam	250,000	7,400,000
Durban	2,000,000	45,000,000
Lobito	30,000	300,000
Luanda	90,000	2,100,000
Lüderitz	1,000	200,000
Maputo	100,000	10,000,000
Matadi	40,000	1,600,000
Mombasa	500,000	16,000,000
Nacala	45,000	700,000
Namibe	0	700,000
Port Elizabeth	370,000	8,100,000
Richards Bay	0	80,000,000
Walvis Bay	100,000	3,000,000

Note: Data is for 2009.
Source: Information provided by TradeMark Southern Africa in 2012.

Table 5.4   Logistics performance in East and Southern Africa

Country	Liner Shipping Connectivity Index	Logistics Performance Index
Angola	11.27	2.25
DR Congo	3.73	2.68
Kenya	12.00	2.59
Mozambique	10.12	2.29
Namibia	12.02	2.02
South Africa	35.67	3.46
Tanzania	11.49	2.60

Note: Data on the Liner Shipping Connectivity Index is for 2011; data for the Logistics Performance Index is for 2010.
Source: UN Conference on Trade and Development (2011), World Bank (2010).

in order to coordinate vessel schedules and custom processes (Senior official of TradeMark Southern Africa, pers. comm., 2 March 2012). Ngqura complements Richards Bay and Saldanha Bay as the third deepwater harbour of the country. Its location is geographically favoured by Nelson Mandela Bay, which protects it from the prevailing southwesterly winds. Its present capacity for transhipment is 1,300 20-foot equivalent units per day. The capacity of Cape Town in this regard is going to be expanded up to the same volume. The largest non-South African transhipment harbours in the region are Maputo and Walvis Bay, with capacities of 100 and 250 20-foot equivalent units respectively (Senior official of Transnet, pers. comm., 18 October 2011).

Understanding South Africa's role as the region's transport hub is not possible without taking historical developments into consideration. Until the independence of Angola and Mozambique, South Africa cooperated with the colonial regimes in both. Maputo handled 40 per cent of the cargo for Gauteng. It was a major port for landlocked Nyasaland, Rhodesia and even the southern tip of Belgian Congo (Jourdan 1998; Waller 1988). After 1974, this changed dramatically. South Africa sought to maintain its economic and political dominance by keeping its neighbours dependent upon its transport network. South African imports and exports through Maputo declined from 4.2 million tonnes in 1977 to 2.2 million in 1982 (Gibb 1991). Zimbabwe – inheritor of the trade relations of Rhodesia – only transported 15 per cent of its foreign trade through the ports of Beira and Maputo in the mid-1980s (Waller 1988). One reason for this it that South Africa and its proxies – the Mozambican National Resistance, or RENAMO, and the National Union for the Total Independence of Angola, also known as UNITA – started sabotaging railway lines in the former Portuguese colonies in the early postindependence years. The South African army intervened in Angola. The Benguela Line stopped linking the landlocked countries of the region to the seas, as did the Limpopo Corridor running from Harare to Maputo.

Only the Beira Corridor, protected by 12,000 Zimbabwean soldiers, and the Tanzania–Zambia Railway served as gateways to overseas markets for Zimbabwe, which was then the leading power of the antiapartheid bloc (Gleave 1992; Price 1984; Smith 1988). South Africa also used nonviolent means to disrupt the transport corridors that bypassed its harbours. It prevented its independent neighbouring countries from acquiring sufficient rolling stock and personnel for their national railway companies. In 1981, South Africa withdrew 25 locomotives leased to National Railways of Zimbabwe. To a certain degree, the apartheid regime did not even have to actively encourage the decline of transport infrastructure in the region. The postindependence crisis of the Angolan and Mozambican railway systems resulted at least partly from the fact that those trained to control and repair the trains and tracks were whites, who left after the watershed of 1974. The apartheid regime's decision to keep prices of transportation via South Africa artificially low further hampered the development of non-South African ports (Gibb 1991).

Until Robert Mugabe's Zimbabwe African National Union won his country's first democratic elections in 1980, the apartheid regime tried to cement South

African local dominance institutionally – specifically via a regional organisation called the Constellation of Southern African States (CONSAS). CONSAS was initially proposed by Prime Minister Pieter Willem Botha. It refined John Vorster's 'outward policy', which appeared to have failed with the antiapartheid resolutions adopted by the Organisation of African Unity (OAU) in the early 1970s and South Africa's military intervention in Angola. The outward policy, firstly formulated in 1967 as a continent-wide strategy, aimed at establishing friendly relations with black-ruled states by providing them with economic and technical assistance. It was anticipated that this support would reinforce their dependence upon South Africa for technical knowhow. Botha took up the basic idea of Vorster's strategy. He wanted to make the countries of Southern Africa a new *cordon sanitaire* for the apartheid regime.

CONSAS was supposed to consist of Botswana, Lesotho, Malawi, Namibia, Rhodesia, South Africa and Swaziland. The DR Congo and Zambia were scheduled to be considered for later admission. Angola, Mozambique and Tanzania would have become members if South Africa had enforced a change of government in them. CONSAS was based on the conviction that South Africa and so-called 'moderate African states' faced a common threat: Communism. They were thus meant to form an alliance, remaining formally sovereign but economically dominated by – and, thus, politically dependent upon – South Africa (Centre for African Studies 1980; Geldenhuys 1991). Yet, Mugabe won Zimbabwe's first post-independence elections, CONSAS was subsequently rejected and South Africa's neighbours founded SADCC instead. Botha reacted with the so-called 'total strategy' – a maximum response to what the South African regime considered an onslaught by Communist-inspired black governments and resistance movements. The *cordon sanitaire* was replaced by a cordon of instability (Hanlon 1986).

SADCC – founded by Angola, Botswana, Lesotho, Malawi, Mozambique, Swaziland, Tanzania, Zambia and Zimbabwe in 1980 – was meant to help strengthen its members' hand vis-à-vis the South African apartheid regime. Reinforcing the international isolation of the apartheid regime was SADCC's major achievement. The most prominent project aimed at easing South Africa's economic grip on the region was the Tanzania–Zambia Railway, which had already been launched in the late 1960s. The 1,860 kilometre-long railway line runs almost parallel to an oil pipeline stretching from Dar es Salaam to Kapiri Mposhi, where it connects up with the Zambian system. In the late 1970s, the Tanzania–Zambia Railway suffered from an inefficiency of service. Given the poor quality of the Chinese materials imported and difficulties to get supplies for making repairs, half of its wagons were always out of service. Locomotive availability decreased from 40 per cent in 1980 to 25 per cent in 1983. Many locomotives could barely manage the steep route across the East African Rift Valley. The difficult terrain between Dar es Salaam and Kapiri Mposhi necessitates 22 tunnels, 300 bridges and almost 2,200 culverts (Gleave 1992). Until today, landslides along the East African Rift Valley frequently lead to track closures. The Tanzanian government invests heavily to repair the damages that these landslides cause. Its Zambian counterpart however has not done the same, which is, in addition to upgrading locomotives and wagons, something that will need to be done if the Tanzania–Zambia Railway is to run smoothly – as pointed out by that company's managing director in *The Post* on 29 January 2011.

Not only did the Tanzania–Zambia Railway perform poorly in the era of SADCC. The few railway lines that existed in the SADCC region in the late-1980s were single-track ones and dated back to the pre-First World War era. National railway companies ran short of locomotives and wagons. Only 10 per cent of the roads in the SADCC region were tarred. Few vehicles for road transport could be obtained. Having reached a port like Beira or Dar es Salaam, one had to then deal with their insufficient cargo handling capacities (Mongula and Ng'andwe 1987). In consequence, half of Zimbabwe's overseas trade transited through South Africa in the early 1990s. For Zambia, the according figures were 65 per cent for imports and 40 per cent for exports. Botswana's, Malawi's and Swaziland's figure for this reached 90 per cent. During the drought in 1992 and 1993, the vast majority of relief maize passed through South Africa for lack of alternative transport corridors (Ahwireng-Obeng and McGowan 1998a). Former Prime Minister Botha was right when he declared in 1989 that the strategy of destabilisation had been effective; regional integration against South Africa had proven impossible.

Transport Corridors as Spatial Development Initiatives

Given the failure of SADCC to upgrade the local transport infrastructure sufficiently, intraregional railway lines and roads constituted one of the most pressing regional needs when South Africa became a democracy in 1994. Even today, 56 per cent of the final average price of Malawi's exports results from transport costs. The equivalent average for all developing countries is only 8 per cent (Mills 2008). Although the regional states have not yet found a way to finance infrastructure projects jointly, they are at least managing to coordinate them together. The DBSA promotes spatial development initiatives that have the potential to ease transport restrictions, facilitate investment and bring about economic development. The rationale behind spatial development initiatives is that sustainable jobs depend upon global competitiveness, which triggers overseas investment. Policy planners trace the lack of overseas investment back to an undeveloped business environment.

In order to overcome this fundamental barrier to economic growth, the state has, in cooperation with the private sector, to now get that environment right (Jourdan 1998). The DBSA hence provides state agencies with a package of measures to attract investors for various economically sustainable projects. This means that spatial development initiatives are a method by which to facilitate economic development along transport corridors. They focus on private investment in sectors that could potentially be competitive on the global scale. Infrastructure that matters for these sectors has to be developed in public–private partnerships. Nontariff barriers to investment – bureaucratic obstacles for example – will have to be reduced (Senior official at the DBSA, pers. comm., 1 December 2011). South Africa's regional economic policy, accordingly, does not reflect an ethos of pure neoliberalism, as it is often criticised for, but rather brings the state back in. The state assumes the role of a partner to the private sector. It facilitates investment and rectifies what the invisible hand of the market does not automatically remedy on its own (Thompson 2000).

The promotion of a spatial development initiative starts by establishing an institutional framework that ties the relevant national authorities to the DBSA. Afterwards, opportunities for the spatial development initiative are assessed. An according strategy, based on anchor projects, is then drafted. Feasibility studies are conducted; trickledown strategies to unlock economic potentials along the corridor follow. Regarding the role of South Africa, it is most interesting that the programme of the DBSA that deals with spatial development initiatives receives its funding from the South African Department of Trade and Industry (Senior official at the DBSA, pers. comm., 1 December 2011). South Africa's leadership role is further exemplified by Jacob Zuma having been crowned the 'Presidential Champion of African Infrastructure', a formal title that was bestowed on him by the African Union (AU) in 2010.

Presently, the DBSA is actively involved in eight spatial development initiatives: it supports Mozambique's Ministry of Transport and Communication on the Maputo and Limpopo ones. Tanzania's National Development Corporation is advised on the Central and Mtwara ones. In the DR Congo, several state agencies cooperate with it on the Bas-Congo Spatial Development Initiative. The Namibian Walvis Bay Corridor Group receives advice on the Trans-Caprivi Initiative. There is also cooperation with the governments of Angola, Namibia and South Africa on a corridor stretching from south to north through Angola, known as the ANSA Spatial Development Initiative. The most prominent and – regarding the quantity of traffic – most important spatial development initiative supported is the one relating to the North–South Corridor. Map 5.3 shows these different spatial development initiatives, as well as another 13 corridors identified by the DBSA as potential future projects.

The progress made for the eight aforementioned spatial development initiatives varies considerably. The staff affiliated to the Bas-Congo Initiative are currently reviewing feasibility studies and drafting strategies on anchor projects. The Walvis Bay Corridor Group has confirmed its support for ANSA but a recent strategy paper – in which anchor projects are identified – still needs to be adapted by the Angolan authorities. For the Tanzanian spatial development initiatives, there are national strategies in place. Work on anchor projects and transport infrastructure has already begun. The DBSA is trying to link them to transport corridors in the Great Lakes region. The Maputo Spatial Development Initiative dates back to the mid-1990s and serves as a role model for such endeavours. The Limpopo one is less advanced. It will be incorporated into a new strategy addressing the entire south of Mozambique. Information on the current status of the Trans-Caprivi Spatial Development Initiative and the North–South Corridor could not be obtained.

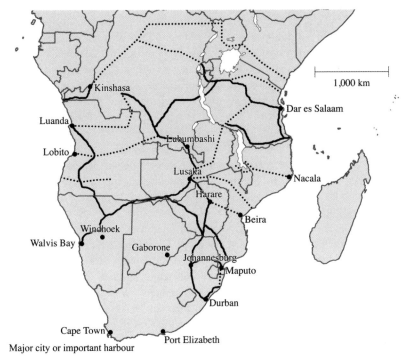

Map 5.3   Spatial development initiatives in Central, East and Southern Africa

Source: Author's own draft, based on information provided by the DBSA in 2011.

A comparison of all corridors shows that those in which South Africa is directly involved are more successful, both in terms of easing transport and of generating economic growth. The reason for this is that the success of spatial development initiatives depends upon a large market, which regionally only South Africa can provide. Corridors that bypass South Africa rely on investment from large overseas companies that seek to exploit resources in the hinterland, for example in central and northern Mozambique. Only two corridors exist that could ease the region's dependence upon South Africa: the Benguela Line from Angola's port of Lobito to Katanga Province in the DR Congo and the aforementioned Tanzania–Zambia Railway. The Benguela Line has recently been reopened on the Angolan side. Chinese investment was essential for its restoration. It does not yet connect the port of Lobito to the Copperbelt because the tracks between the border station Dilolo and Kolwezi in Katanga Province has, as noted, become overgrown. Given the economic boom of Angola, which is no longer limited to the oil sector as development has been triggered in other areas as well, the country possesses the greatest potential out of all states in the region to form an economic counterweight to South Africa (Honorary Consul of Angola, pers. comm., 24 March 2010).

For the further development of the Tanzania–Zambia Railway, China is the essential partner. With Chinese loans, Tanzania may be able not only to revive the Tanzania–Zambia Railway but also to connect the Great Lakes region to Dar es Salaam. Tanzania thus has the potential to become a regional transport hub. This role will probably, as noted, ultimately be limited to only East Africa though. For the landlocked Great Lakes region, Kenya and Tanzania provide – for locational and physiogeographical reasons – the easiest means of access to the world's oceans. As a gateway for Zambia and Zimbabwe, Tanzania will, most likely, play a secondary or tertiary role due to the cemented dominance of South Africa, the priority that SADC and South Africa give to the North–South Corridor and the current rapid development of corridors in central and northern Mozambique (Senior official at the DBSA, pers. comm., 1 December 2011).

Beyond issues of connectivity, spatial development initiatives are revealing with regard to patterns of dominance and subordination. The Maputo Spatial Development Initiative or 'Maputo Development Corridor' – which connects Gauteng to the port of Maputo – is the oldest and most advanced such initiative transregionally. It exemplifies how South Africa takes a superior position in the regional transport network and its associated economic activities. Transport from the Johannesburg area to Maputo has a long-standing history given that the latter – and not Durban or Richards Bay – is the natural gateway to South Africa's economic heartland. Maputo is closer, and passing the Great Escarpment in South Africa's east is easier than crossing the Drakensberg and the Great Escarpment in KwaZulu-Natal. Thus, a transport corridor to Maputo (as noted, then called Lourenço Marques) emerged when industrialisation began in the area around Johannesburg in the late nineteenth century. It lasted up until the independence of Mozambique. Forty per cent of the exports of the Johannesburg area were shipped via Lourenço Marques in the first half of the 1970s (Jourdan 1998). The corridor also provided cheap labour to South Africa's mining industry. From the beginning of the twentieth century until the independence of Mozambique, around 100,000 Mozambicans came to the mines of the Witwatersrand every year (Söderbaum 2002). As explained above, transport via Mozambique declined tremendously during the country's civil war years. As soon as Mozambique became more stable, however, the informal trade of clothes, fruits, small home appliances and vegetables began to flourish once more between Mozambique, Swaziland and South Africa (Söderbaum 2002; Söderbaum and Taylor 2001).

Anchor projects of the Maputo Development Corridor – such as the aluminium smelter Mozal and the Maputo Iron and Steel Project (MISP) – indicate that a core purpose of this initiative is industrialisation in and around Maputo. In order to achieve this goal, the Maputo Development Corridor facilitates the inflow of private capital from South Africa. Seven of the 10 largest investment projects in Mozambique in the mid-2000s were directly linked to South Africa's minerals–energy complex. The remaining three served it indirectly (Nuvunga 2008). The biggest shareholder of Mozal is the South African-founded company BHP Billiton. The smelter depends upon cheap electricity generated by two coal-fired power stations in South Africa. Most materials used for building Mozal came from South Africa (Lee 2003). The Matola Coal Terminal at the port of Maputo is owned and operated by the South African company Grindrod. The Pande and Temane Gasfields are exploited by the South African chemicals giant Sasol, with the energy-intense MISP being closely linked to its operations in Mozambique.

With regard to the business sector, the Maputo Development Corridor exemplifies that South Africa has positioned itself as an intermediary between international capital – including donors of foreign aid – and its neighbouring countries. In general, spatial development initiatives are a means by which the South African government can make its business sector benefit from playing the role of a middleman. The uneven relationship between South Africa and Mozambique is also demonstrated by the fact that all spatial development initiatives in Mozambique rely on South African technical support. The daily management of the Zambezi Valley Spatial Development Initiative, which is mostly about energy generation and mining, lies in the hands of the DBSA meanwhile, with the project manager being accountable to that institution. Only the overall plan and its broad realisation are jointly carried out by officials from Mozambique and South Africa (Nuvunga 2008).

In sum, even though the Maputo Development Corridor is certainly beneficial for the people of southern Mozambique, the fact that it is tailored to the needs of South African big business can hardly be denied. Rogerson (2001) argues that spatial development initiatives reflect the objective of the 'Growth, Employment and Redistribution Plan', or GEAR, which is to place South Africa in a favourable position within the international division of labour – doing this requires the country to take a superior role in the regional parts of globalised production chains. Reflecting this structural imbalance between South Africa and its neighbouring countries, an unnamed government official from Mozambique is quoted by Milissão Nuvunga as saying that spatial development initiatives are a tool for 'the realisation of all apartheid goals in the region [in one word, hegemony] under a black regime' (2008: 83). Spatial development initiatives are thus an example of how a regional power shapes the manmade geography of its region in order to achieve – partly with the backing of its neighbouring states – its national goals, as well as to reinforce its own local dominance.

5.4 Overview

By applying Process Tracing to three domains of regional cooperation – water, electricity and transport – I have shown that geographical conditions are a necessary aspect of understanding some of the phenomena essential to South African regional powerhood:

- Several states in Southern Africa cooperate on water because natural conditions limit the availability of this resource for the economically most diversified countries of the region, including South Africa itself. Whilst demand has been increasing and will continue to do so, climate change is simultaneously reducing the availability of water. Various watercourses in the SADC region are shared by several states anyway, which is a locational factor that requires interstate cooperation regardless of water stress. The LHWP exemplifies how geography provides essential conditions for regional cooperation on water: Lesotho is close to South African consumers in the Free State and Gauteng. There is a compatibility of supply and demand because Lesotho receives significant rainfall, whereas the Free State and Gauteng are relatively dry and consume lots of water. Moreover, Lesotho's geomorphology is suitable to building dams and artificial lakes.
- Similarly, there would not be cooperation on electricity in the SADC region if geography did not provide opportunities for that. Eskom can presently supply much-needed electricity to the region because of South Africa's abundant coal reserves and its high level of economic development – the latter factor constitutes a manmade structure in geographical space. Sasol's regional trade in liquid fuels, which I have not addressed in detail, is possible for the same reasons. Future regional cooperation on electricity will also be shaped by geographical conditions. Eskom is likely to import electricity from South Africa's neighbouring countries because of their considerable potential for hydropower generation. Coal and natural gas will also be either imported for processing in South Africa or burnt close to mining sites so as to generate electricity for South African consumers.
- The boundaries of a region integrated by South Africa as a transport hub can be derived from the physiogeographical barriers: the Congo Basin and the East African Rift Valley. On the interior plateaux south of these boundaries, geomorphology provides almost ideal conditions for railway lines and roads. The Great Escarpment and coastal geomorphology significantly limit the number of locations suited to being used as harbours. South Africa's ports are the largest and most efficient ones in the region. Transport corridors interlink South Africa relatively well with most regional countries. Corridors that bypass the regional power are of poor quality and will, most likely, never become as important as the Coast2Coast and the North–South Corridors. Due to its advanced stage of economic development, South Africa moreover provides the best business environment regionally and a lucrative domestic market. The manmade geography that is being built via spatial development initiatives will further boost the nodal role of the regional power vis-à-vis global markets.

These processes cannot be explained by geographical factors alone. In general, the observed outcomes are not comprehensible unless one also takes into consideration the cooperative regional relations that have marked Southern Africa since 1994, with the will thereafter of the ANC to engage in intense economic interaction with the regional states. Moreover, geographical conditions can hardly explain the precise form that local policies take. The same geographical setting accounts for both present-day regional cooperation on spatial development initiatives and the previous efforts of the apartheid regime to damage transport infrastructure in the Frontline States. These two phenomena are thus so different in nature rather because of nongeographical factors. The LHWP demonstrates that opportunities provided by geography will be foregone if they are not compatible with the strategic objectives pursued by businesspersons and politicians. What is more, taking every opportunity provided by geography is not necessarily the most rational course of action. Using water more efficiently, for example, would safeguard South Africa's water supply, probably at much lower costs than those incurred by diverting water from more humid parts of the SADC region to the country.

Chapter 6
The Economics and Politics of
South African Regional Powerhood

The last empirical chapter deals with the dependent variable or outcome – that is, the economic and political interaction between South Africa and other African countries. I first present economic aspects of South Africa's regional relations, in particular its economic expansion into Africa since 1994, and then elaborate on political aspects. The latter range from as SACU and SADC – two essential organisations that advance regional integration – to South Africa's regional security policy. In the third part of this chapter, I explain the regional political strategies of South Africa's neighbouring states, concentrating on South Africa's role therein. The chapter concludes with the final QCA and its interpretation.

6.1 Economic Aspects

South Africa's Regional Economic Expansion

After the end of the apartheid regime, South African capital – which had been extensively accumulated within the country during the decades of sanctions – virtually burst out into Africa. From the first democratic elections in April 1994 until the beginning of the year 1995, 22 new trade missions were established in other African countries. The African Business Development Group, a branch of the private South African Foreign Trade Organisation, grew from 12 to 80 members within two years (Ahwireng-Obeng and McGowan 1998a). At the height of Thabo Mbeki's African agenda, the continent benefitted from about USD 1.3 billion of South African foreign aid. In 2002, South Africa became the biggest foreign investor in Africa. This role has, since then, been based on six key sectors: construction and manufacturing; financial services; mining; retail; telecommunications; and, tourism (Le Pere 2009). In 2008, South African companies were active in 27 African countries and employed more than 70,000 people there (Stephan and Fane Hervey 2008). Since the mid-2000s, there is practically no sector of the South African economy that does not do business with Africa (Games 2004).

In addition to the end of antiapartheid sanctions, the regional expansion of South African firms is due to a fundamental change in South Africa's trade policy. Seeking autarky, the apartheid regime discouraged exports and tried to substitute imports. As soon as the ANC took over, it liberalised the foreign trade regime – especially for financial markets (Blumenfeld 2006). From a social–social scientific perspective, there are five more causes of the success of South African business in Africa.[1] First, South Africans are experienced in Africa and/or have employees who are enthusiastic about doing business there. South African products are, partly for this reason, highly competitive in terms of both price and quality. Second, foreign investment in sub-Saharan Africa declined in the 1980s and 1990s, leaving a vacuum for South African businesses to fill. Third, the adoption of neoliberal policies has opened up formerly state-controlled markets to South African companies. Many African states went through a wave of privatisation just when South African capital was ready to expand out into the continent. Fourth, major Western states, international organisations and nongovernmental organisations see South Africa as the driver of economic development in Africa. They consider South Africa's regional economic dominance beneficial to the continent, and thus are supportive of it. Fifth, for many African governments South Africa appears to be the main beacon of hope for economic development and political stability (Ahwireng-Obeng and McGowan 1998a). Even though there is criticism of so-called 'South African neoimperialism', my interviews with diplomats from the member states of SADC – summarised in Chapter 6.3 – suggest that most of their governments actually long for South African investments.

Yet, geographical factors matter too. As shown above, physical geography – specifically, South Africa's lack of water supplies and its need for electricity – generates an ongoing necessity for regional cooperation. Already in the mid-1990s South African agribusiness made use of its sophisticated financial and marketing resources to move into regional markets (Atkins and Terry 1998). Energy companies from all over the world started to invest in the SADC region then. Cooperating with firms from South Africa, they intended (and still intend) to use the vast naturally given potential for energy generation in Angola, the DR Congo and Mozambique to produce electricity for the South African market (Horvei 1998). These examples not only highlight that physical geography matters, manmade material structures in geographical space that cannot be altered in the short run also have a comparable impact on regional economic and political processes. The expansion of South African companies into the region would not have occurred if South Africa's economy was not larger and more advanced than those of its neighbouring countries – this greater level of sophistication endows South African entrepreneurs with a regionally incomparable business knowhow and significant financial resources.

Geographical conditions – those both provided by nature and built by man – only set a frame of opportunities and constraints. South African businesspersons and politicians either take these opportunities or forego them. In fact, South Africa's government has played a proactive role in promoting the expansion

---

1   As noted in Chapter 2.2, approaches that refer to nature as a set of independent variables in order to explain social phenomena can be labelled 'natural–social scientific'. Concepts and theories that are based on social factors as independent variables, for example on business strategies or political ideologies, are termed 'social–social scientific'.

of South African companies across the continent. The DBSA and the Industrial Development Corporation run and support development projects in Africa. The South African state covers a maximum of 25 per cent of the costs of these projects north of the equator and up to 50 per cent south of it (Games 2004). South African embassies and the Department of Trade and Industry advise any South African companies that are seeking to expand regionally. Business delegations almost always accompany high-ranking politicians on their trips abroad (Researcher of the Ebert Foundation, pers. comm., 12 August 2011). The ANC explicitly referred to these measures as part of its foreign policy strategy in the resolutions agreed upon at its Polokwane Summit in 2007. The private sector facilitates the regional expansion of South African firms too: public relations campaigns depict South African businesses as being African. Giants like Shoprite and Woolworths promote the idea that their activities concur with the vision of mutually beneficial cooperation and are an expression of the New Partnership for Africa's Development (NEPAD) (Söderbaum 2002).

Still, one should not misunderstand the role played by the South African government itself, which is not about giving step-by-step advice. South African businesses tend only to ask for support from the government when they run into problems abroad (Senior researcher at DNA Economics, pers. comm., 10 October 2011). What matters is the regional business environment that their government has created. As I show below, the ANC has quite successfully pursued a partisan agenda of economic liberalisation continent wide. Regional markets have been opened for South African products, whilst foreign competitors are still kept out of the South African market (Alden and Soko 2005). With regard to an assessment of the relevance of short-term political changes – such as the end of the NP's rule in 1994 – it is, nevertheless, revealing that the present grand strategy of the ANC does not differ from what Prime Minister Jan Smuts declared in 1940: 'If we wish to take our rightful place as the leader in pan-African development [...] all Africa [must] be our proper market' (quoted in Vale and Maseko 1998: 274).

Smuts's quote not only indicates that South Africa's economic relations with Africa are driven by forces that are more enduring than party politics, it also hints at the fact that South Africa needs Africa to realise its export-oriented development strategy. The *White Paper on Reconstruction and Development* (1994), passed into a law in the same year, sets a clear priority for the country: high and sustainable economic growth in order to overcome poverty and social inequality. South Africa's integration into the global economy is to be grounded on a strong export-oriented manufacturing sector, which is expected to create many jobs. A greater outward orientation is stated to be a central objective. Vis-à-vis imports and inward foreign direct investment, postapartheid South Africa has pursued rather protectionist policies though.

With regard to the regional level, the authors of the Reconstruction and Development Programme argue that South Africa cannot build its economy in isolation from its neighbours. Striving for regional economic dominance is rejected. Neither South Africa nor its neighbours would benefit from the pursuit of either of these strategies because they would restrict growth in the neighbouring countries, diminish their potential as markets for South African products and, as a consequence, increase poverty-driven migration to South Africa. Hence, the Reconstruction and Development Programme calls for 'an effective growth and development strategy for all Southern African countries' (Parliament of the Republic of South Africa 1994: 10). Benefits from cooperation on energy, transport and security are explicitly mentioned, so is the potential for a unified and, hence, larger regional market. The 'Growth, Employment and Redistribution Plan' of 1996 confirms that the expansion of trade and investment flows in Southern Africa as well as the integration of the regional economies are important goals in South Africa's economic policy (Department of Finance 1996). As a side note, this reveals that the ANC's approach to regional economic cooperation was rather realist than idealist already in the mid-1990s. Regional prosperity was seen as the path towards prosperity for South Africa.[2]

Hentz's (2005a, 2005b) analysis of South African–African relations captures the ambiguity of mutually beneficial development and the pursuit of South Africa's national interests. He argues that the ANC seeks to promote South Africa's development within a framework that also helps the neighbouring countries but it has to adjust, at least partly, to the interests of the South African business sector. The outcome is some sort of middle course between mutually beneficial cooperation and the pursuit of national interests. At the end of the apartheid regime years, South Africa's gross domestic product was almost four times that of Southern Africa. It produced 30 per cent of the goods imported by the regional countries. They depended upon South African transport infrastructure and the electricity provided by Eskom. Given that the ANC was morally indebted to the regional states that had supported it during the struggle against the apartheid regime, many expected that postapartheid South Africa would give something back to the region. However, in the years of democratic transition, a fundamental disagreement between the ANC and the white business sector became apparent: the ANC favoured institutionalised forms of developmental cooperation, whilst business associations preferred ad hoc cooperation on a bilateral level – fearing that institutionalised integration would tie South Africa too closely to its poor neighbours. In addition to pressure from the business sector, the ANC soon realised that it could only meet its domestic economic goals by addressing the economic needs of South Africa through strengthening South African companies themselves.

Meeting South Africa's economic needs required ad hoc cooperation, in particular on energy, transport and water. What is more, the ANC has, since 1994,

---

2   The region appears to have lost some of its relevance in South African policy planning though. The 'Accelerated and Shared Growth Initiative', or ASGISA, is limited to the national level. No references to Southern Africa or regional cooperation can be found in the overview document provided by the government (The Presidency 2005). The annual reports also neglect to mention the regional level (The Presidency 2007, 2008, 2009).

chosen to concentrate on the manufacturing sector as the driver of domestic economic development. Because manufactured goods are traded internationally and boosting the sector therefore requires export-oriented strategies, foreign trade has become essential to South Africa. First efforts to launch an export-oriented strategy based on manufacturing can be traced back to the 1980s. The potential of Southern Africa as a market for manufactured goods from South Africa was and is considered tremendous, argues Hentz. As a consequence, various government bodies and policy mechanisms have been set up since the late 1980s – and especially since 1994 – to ease the export of such goods, usually favouring therein large, capital-intense industries. The resulting agenda for regional economic relations is one aimed at market-oriented integration – the strategy preferred by the Afrikaner-dominated state bureaucracy.

Yet, the ANC has aligned itself with the working class and thus supports labour-intense industries. Some of South Africa's can, however, hardly survive in open competition with those of neighbouring countries because the wage levels of the latter are lower. Thus, South Africa under the ANC has only partly pursued market-oriented integration. It compensates its neighbouring countries with some developmental policies for the negative effects of market-oriented integration. Benefits for South Africa in one sector – the protection of car manufacturing for instance – are offset by concessions being made to neighbouring countries in other sectors, such as the reliable provision of cheap electricity by Eskom.

The Impact of South Africa's Regional Economic Expansion

Because of the massive expansion of its business sector across Africa, South Africa has frequently been accused of acting like a neoimperial power. A senior diplomat from Zambia told me that if it were not for the 'white economy', South Africa would be on the same economic level as any other regional country (pers. comm., 18 August 2010). Regional trade patterns highlight the special – and, from a certain viewpoint, problematic – role of South Africa. Intra-SADC trade is marked by a growing trade surplus for South Africa. South Africa mainly exports to the SADC countries, whereas they on the other hand predominantly import from one another. The most important South African goods exported to the region are machinery and mineral fuels. Vehicles, electrical goods and electronic products as well as processed iron and steel are of secondary relevance. The neighbouring countries export unprocessed primary sector goods to South Africa, especially copper, cotton, oil and natural gas (Draper and Scholvin 2012).

Given these characteristics of regional trade, Lesufi (2004, 2006) argues that the Mbeki government advanced the NEPAD as a neoliberal grand design only in order to gain greater market access on the continent. He maintains that the regional economic expansion of South Africa is carried out by white capitalists who obtain legitimacy by operating under the umbrella of a democratically elected black government. This black government promotes an economic agenda tailored to the interests of the white capitalists. Whilst Lesufi sees South Africa as an imperialist power acting independently, Bond (2005, 2006) argues instead that South Africa is a subimperialist one. South Africa collaborates with the US and uses its leading role in Africa to push forward a neoliberal agenda, which reflects the objectives of European and US imperialists. Still, Bond stresses that South Africa's regional policy does also serve the interests of South African capital. The NEPAD enables South Africans as well as Europeans and North Americans to appropriate valuable assets in Africa, ranging from mining concessions to formerly state-owned service providers. At the same time, South Africa's business associations, trade unions and government have prevented any changes from being made in the regional structural imbalances. They protected South Africa's status as regional hub for car manufacturing when Hyundai and Volvo built fairly efficient assembly plants in Botswana in the mid-1990s. Because of South African pressure, Volvo relocated to Pretoria and Hyundai's plant was sold at an auction to South African bidders (Good and Hughes 2002). In less prominent cases, South Africa has derailed plans for a fertiliser factory in Swaziland, breweries in Lesotho and Swaziland, a television assembly plant in Lesotho and car assembly plants for Citroën and Peugeot in Namibia (Lee 2003).

Contradicting Lesufi and Bond, various scholars have emphasised the positive role that South Africa has played for Africa – and Southern Africa in particular – since 1994. Hudson (2007), for example, argues that South African enterprises do not so much push small business out of the market but rather buy inefficient, often state-owned, firms and modernise them. South African retailers operating in Southern Africa not only import many products from South Africa but also trigger local dynamics, as dairy farming in Zambia demonstrates (Kenny and Mather 2008). In her study on Mozambican–South African economic relations, Grobbelaar (2004) shows that South African investment in Mozambique has generally had positive effects. The lowest wage paid at the metal smelter Mozal, which is the flagship project of Mozambican–South African cooperation, is 10 times higher than the statutory minimum wage for Mozambique's industrial sector. Productivity per worker is 18 times higher than for the average Mozambican firm. Mozal and Sasol's projects in Mozambique will, most likely, generate spinoffs and transfer technology to Mozambican companies in the long run. Moreover, South African enterprises apply relatively good labour standards, sometimes including medical aid schemes and pension funds. Grobbelaar quotes in her report the chairperson of the Mozambican–South African Business Chamber, who expects higher labour standards to trickle down to the entire Mozambican formal sector.

However, South African investment is capital intense and knowledge based. This means that linkages to domestic businesses remain poor. South African companies operating in Mozambique obtain less than 10 per cent of their materials from local suppliers. The level of job creation is marginal compared to the volume of investments that are made. Even in the case of megaprojects such as Mozal and Sasol's pipeline from Johannesburg to the Mozambican gasfields, most jobs are only created for the duration of the construction phase. South African investment has also worsened disparities between Mozambique's affluent south and the rest of the country, and between rural and urban areas. Nevertheless, South African investment does drive economic growth in Mozambique. When Mozal came online in 2002, it increased Mozambique's gross domestic product by 2.1 per cent and accounted for 53 per cent of the country's exports and 28 per cent of its imports. This and the various other projects based on South African investment apparently also generate increased tax revenues.

In sum, the title of Grobbelaar's report – *Every Continent Needs an America* – captures the way in which she and many other South African researchers see the role of their country: being economically more advanced, South Africa serves as the regional growth engine. Close economic relations cause mutual benefits. For South African firms, there are various incentives for doing business in the region. By investing in Mozambique, they seek access to a lucrative market – something that applies to MTN and Shoprite for example. They try to get hold of important resources, as exemplified by Sasol's investment in gasfields. Low-cost labour – which increases global competitiveness, as in the case of Mozal – is another motive. South African parastatals have been active in Mozambique because of strong political support, in particular from Mbeki's African agenda.

In contrast to Grobbelaar's interpretation, such a mutually beneficial relationship does not, however, mean that the economic gap between South Africa and its neighbourhood will necessarily shrink. The structural imbalances involved in South African–African economic interactions will, most likely, persist. Grobbelaar herself points out that Mozambique may be considered 'a South African province' because of the dominant role of South African business there – it accounted for 49 per cent of all foreign direct investment in the country at the beginning of this century. As a general pattern, South African companies in Mozambique assume high up positions in commodity chains. When Grobbelaar wrote her report, South African investors controlled three out of four sugar estates, three out of four breweries, all soft drinks bottling plants and large cereal mills, and most tourism facilities. Mozambicans, meanwhile, provided only basic raw materials and cheap labour.

Delineating South Africa's Regional Economic Impact

Taking a closer look at the business sectors that matter most for South Africa's regional economic expansion reveals a pattern that explains how South Africa shapes the geography of its region. As noted, construction, financial services and telecommunications are major domains of South African investment in Africa. This means that South African companies are constructing railway lines, roads and harbours. They export and repair vehicles, provide loans and carry out international transmissions and provide mobile phone networks and internet connectivity. In other words, the investment of South African pioneers enables the expansion of other South African firms into Africa.

The provision of electricity is facilitated by South Africa too. Since 1994, Eskom has expanded into Africa. In many African countries, Eskom builds what private capital needs in order to operate successfully. For instance, Eskom was assigned to rehabilitate the electricity grid of Sierra Leone's capital Freetown in 2006. This project, worth ZAR 30 million, was funded by the South African government. Feasibility studies for electrification have been carried out in Angola and in the DR Congo. Algeria has received technical assistance from Eskom. In 2008, Eskom staff met with colleagues from 14 different African countries. A four-party power system has been discussed for Botswana, South Africa, Zambia and Zimbabwe (Koen and Bahadur 2010). South African banks and telecommunication providers have invested massively in Africa. They have upgraded the service infrastructure in numerous countries, paving the ground for investment by other (South African) firms.

Telecommunication providers, and in particular MTN and Vodacom, are important players in all SADC countries and in the most rapidly growing markets elsewhere in sub-Saharan Africa, especially Nigeria – but also Cameroon, Rwanda and Uganda. Between its entrance into the Nigerian market in August 2001 and June 2002, MTN gained 400,000 subscribers. The company then expected its revenues to rise by 35 per cent, mostly because of its Nigerian business (Games 2004). Today, MTN is the biggest mobile operator in Africa with 126 million subscribers, of whom 45.6 million are in Nigeria. Vodacom counts 50 million subscribers, of whom 20 million are in South Africa (Mthembu-Salter 2012).

South African-based banks have been equally successful. In the early 2000s, Absa Bank held more than 80 per cent of the shares of the Mozambican Banco Austral and 55 per cent of those of the National Bank of Commerce, Tanzania's largest retail bank. It possessed a stake of 26 per cent in the Commercial Bank of Zimbabwe. In 2010, Absa Bank failed to acquire the majority of the shares of Bank Windhoek. Two years later, it succeeded in purchasing 49.9 per cent, whilst 50.1 per cent of the last non-South African-owned bank in Namibia remain in Namibian hands, as the *Allgemeine Zeitung* reported on 8 June 2012. In the early 2000s, South African Nedbank Group possessed 40 per cent of the Commercial Bank of Namibia, 20 per cent of the State Bank of Mauritius and 29 per cent of the Merchant Bank of Central Africa, based in Zimbabwe. First National Bank was (and still is) a key player in Botswana, Namibia and Swaziland (Games 2004).

The expansion of its banks and telecommunication providers to the continent reflects South Africa's competitive advantages in these sectors. This expansion fosters South Africa's role as an economic hinge between Africa and the rest of the world by first creating African networks and then interlinking them globally. The acquisition of South African banks and telecommunication providers by overseas rivals – Absa Bank by Barclays PLC and Vodacom by Vodafone for example – has to be seen in this context. Overseas companies making such purchases not only acquire South African enterprises with major shares in rapidly growing markets but also their extensive business networks (Draper and Scholvin 2012).

Beyond Southern Africa, only certain individual countries hold a particular relevance to South African business. AngloGold Ashanti goes, according to one of its senior officials, 'where the minerals are' (pers. comm., 19 August 2010). MTN realises, as noted, a large share of its profits in Nigeria. PetroSA exploits oil in Algeria, Nigeria and Sudan. Sasol is active in Gabon. The primary destination for South African foreign direct investment is, however, the member states of SACU. The remaining Anglophone members of SADC, Kenya and Uganda, are partners of secondary relevance, followed by new growth poles: Angola, Mauritius, Mozambique and the Seychelles. Further north, South Africa's influence declines considerably. It remains above average in the DR Congo, Gabon, Ghana and Nigeria (Thomas 2006). Alden and Soko (2005) conclude that South Africa's economic hegemony is strongest within SACU, also because of the deeply entrenched structural inequalities that exist between its different member states. In the rest of SADC, there is less South African investment and trade and as a result the country's influence becomes weaker.

Up north, South African companies invest but do not dominate. Several North African and West African countries realise trade surpluses with South Africa – a sharp contrast to the situation with the member states of SACU and SADC. In contrast to the aforementioned authors, who ascribe a primary relevance to SACU, Games (2004) argues that Mozambique and Zimbabwe matter most as economic partners of South Africa. Basic data on imports and exports underlines that South Africa's exceptional role is currently limited to the SADC region. As shown by Table 6.1, Botswana, the DR Congo, Malawi, Namibia, Swaziland, Zambia and Zimbabwe are highly dependent upon South Africa. South Africa reaches enormously high shares of the imports and/or exports of these countries. They should be considered the core of South Africa's economic impact region.

Using South Africa's share of imports and exports as an indicator, one cannot conclude that SACU is the inner circle of South Africa's sphere of influence and SADC its outer one. Botswana and Lesotho, both members of SACU, appear to have globalised economies. This is not surprising: Lesotho's clothing and textile industry is tied to the US market. Botswana's diamonds are also sold overseas. Angola, Kenya, Tanzania, Uganda and the island states are on the edge of a region demarcated by South African economic influence because that country is a significant – but not, by a large margin, the most important – trading partner of these countries. For all African countries not listed in Table 6.1 South Africa play an unimportant – sometimes not even a significant – role as a trading partner.

Taking a critical overview of this data, one may argue that whilst South Africa apparently matters a lot to many of its neighbouring countries they themselves only play a small role in South Africa's foreign trade. China is the most important destination for South African exports with a share of 13.7 per cent, followed by the US (10.1 per cent) and Japan (8.7 per cent). South Africa's imports, meanwhile, come predominantly from China (13.4 per cent), Germany (11.2 per cent) and the US (7.0 per cent) (*World Fact Book* 2012). Yet, such a critique only demonstrates that South Africa's economy cannot rely exclusively on the SADC region for its prosperity. The regional market is small and cannot be compared to those of the cores of the global economy.

Table 6.1   Trading partners of countries in East and Southern Africa

	Imports	Exports
Angola	1. Portugal 17.4% 5. South Africa 6.0%	1. China 42.8% –
Botswana	1. South Africa 80.1% 2. United Kingdom 6.9%	1. United Kingdom 58.2% 2. South Africa 17.1%
Comoros	1. Pakistan 16.2% 7. South Africa 4.2%	1. Singapore 36.0% –
DR Congo	1. South Africa 19.2% 2. China 12.5%	1. China 46.9% –
Kenya	1. China 14.8% 4. South Africa 7.8%	1. Uganda 10.0% –
Lesotho	1. South Korea 26.9% –	1. United States 58.4% –
Madagascar	1. China 14.6% 3. South Africa 6.4%	1. France 26.3% –
Malawi	1. South Africa 41.4% 2. Zambia 7.8%	1. India 10.4% 3. South Africa 7.5%
Mauritius	1. India 20.3% 4. South Africa 9.7%	1. United Kingdom 19.0% 6. South Africa 6.0%
Mozambique	1. South Africa 28.6% 2. China 10.3%	1. Netherlands 47.6% 2. South Africa 11.6%
Namibia	1. South Africa 69.4% 2. United Kingdom 9.3%	1. South Africa 33.4% 2. United Kingdom 17.2%
Seychelles	1. Saudi Arabia 21.1% 2. South Africa 8.4%	1. United Kingdom 19.0% –
Swaziland	1. South Africa 95.6% 2. Japan 0.9%	1. South Africa 59.7% 2. United States 8.8%
Tanzania	1. China 17.3% 3. South Africa 7.9%	1. China 15.6% –
Uganda	1. Kenya 15.3% 5. South Africa 5.6%	1. Sudan 15.0% –
Zambia	1. South Africa 35.0% 2. DR Congo 23.5%	1. Switzerland 51.3% 3. South Africa 9.2%
Zimbabwe	1. South Africa 58.0% 2. China 8.7%	1. DR Congo 14.8% 2. South Africa 13.4%

Note: Data is for 2010 and 2011.
Source: World Fact Book (2012).

From the perspective of regional powers analysis, these objections are not relevant anyway. When studying the impact of the dominant power on its region, one should first ask how much the regional power matters to the region and only then inquire how much the region matters to the regional power. Moreover, regional markets do play an important role for South Africa. Many South African companies are too small and inefficient to compete in global markets. However, they produce too much for the South African market alone. By gaining access to regional markets, they can sell there what cannot be sold domestically (Hudson 2007). The resulting regional trade surplus partly compensates for South Africa's trade deficit with Europe, the Far East and North America – a phenomenon going back to the 1960s and 1970s, when South Africa first started to sell its uncompetitive products in the region in order to finance its growing number of high-tech imports (Hentz 2005b). Present policy planning by the Economic Development Department (2010) is based on the idea that the region may widen South Africa's domestic market and, thus, facilitate greater consumption, economic growth and job creation for South Africa. The country's role as a financial, logistics and services hub is emphasised in this regard, so is the region's need for investment in infrastructure, ranging from electricity to transport to water.

6.2 Political Aspects

South Africa's Regional Foreign Policy under the ANC

At the end of the apartheid era, Rob Davies (1992) – who is today South Africa's Minister of Trade and Industry – laid out three possible future scenarios for Southern Africa policy: South Africa could unilaterally pursue its national interests, therein neglecting political cooperation and ignoring the negative consequences of that for the region. Alternatively, it might opt for establishing regional institutions and egoistically push through its own interests therein. It would favour some of its neighbours over others. Benevolent cooperation and integration was, following Davies, a third but unlikely option. It would require South African entrepreneurs – and, one may add, the government – to forego some short-term gains in order to realise the mutual benefits of regional cooperation in the long run.

The third scenario reflects the vision that the ANC had for Southern Africa in the 1990s. Under the ANC, South Africa joined numerous international organisations. Within a month of the country's first democratic elections being held, South Africa was admitted to the OAU, became a member of SADC and agreed to renegotiate decision-making processes within SACU. South Africa's rapprochement with Africa was framed by a new rationale in its foreign policy, the nature of which Nelson Mandela explained in an article published in *Foreign Affairs* (1993). According to Mandela, South Africa had to overcome its isolation and transform itself into a 'responsible global citizen' (1993: 86–7). Given the experience of the struggle against apartheid, human rights would serve as 'the light that guides our foreign policy' (1993: 88–9). Democracy was the second pillar of South Africa's new foreign policy. Bringing in a spatial perspective, Mandela wrote that Africa mattered more to South Africa than the rest of the world because of its potential for economic cooperation, which he depicted as the way to overcome poverty. Southern Africa had an even more important role to play because it offered various opportunities for interstate cooperation, in particular on hydropower and water supply. Such projects, Mandela reasoned, depended upon a consensus being reached between all regional states. Summing up these thoughts, Mandela wrote that South Africa's fate was 'linked to that of a region that is much more than a mere geographical concept' (1993: 93).

A more recent online discussion paper by the Department of Foreign Affairs accordingly states that South African policymakers should bear in mind how 'to promote the interests of the SADC region or the African continent' (2008). This discussion paper takes up declarations by former foreign minister Alfred Nzo on the priority of Africa and the 'paramount importance [... of] the promotion of economic development of the Southern African region'. The authors of the document point out that the promotion of economic growth through private sector investment and intraregional trade is the key objective for South African–SADC relations. For equatorial Africa and the Indian Ocean islands, similar goals – albeit on a more basic level – are stated. South Africa's diplomatic network needs to support the expansion of the South African private sector there, creating employment and investment opportunities for South Africans – especially in infrastructure projects.

Seeing the paradigms for South African foreign policy laid out by Davies and Mandela, political scientists mostly agreed at the end of the 1990s that South Africa should likely become a benign hegemon and promote economic development in the SADC region. By offering its neighbours some collective goods, South Africa would acquire followership – leading to mutually beneficial arrangements in regional economics and politics (van Wyk 1997). Since the end of the Mandela presidency, however, South Africa has shifted towards the more pragmatic pursuit of national interest. According to the Strategic Plan 2003–2005 published by the Department of Foreign Affairs (2003), foreign policy has to serve specifically South African interests, economic growth and security. The Strategic Plan 2005–2008, meanwhile, states that 'we are committed to promoting South Africa's national interests and values' (2005: 18). As the Strategic Plan 2006–2009 further demonstrates, domestic economic interests have become a key driver of foreign policy: 'South Africa's foreign policy incorporates economic diplomacy [...] in order to grow the economy faster and create more jobs to address the challenge of poverty eradication' (2006: 7).

An odd fact about South Africa's recent history is that this shift towards the pursuit of national goals has come along with a decline of regional contestation of South African leadership. Mandela's idealist approach revolved around spreading democracy and human rights. It was revisionist because Mandela aimed at fundamentally changing the regional order. He thus sought to place democracy and human rights above national sovereignty and the principle of noninterference. This threatened the rule of authoritarian elites, who would have to face criminal prosecution if human rights laws were successfully pushed through by the South Africans (Scholvin 2013). Hence, Mandela met with resistance from some African governments, as the Saro-Wiwa incident in 1995 best exemplifies (more details on this later). In the late 1990s, the atmosphere became often chilly – if not outright hostile – towards South Africa whenever issues related to bad governance were raised (Cilliers 1999), meaning whenever the regional states feared that South Africa would interfere in their domestic affairs. Under Thabo Mbeki and even more obviously under Jacob Zuma, South Africa has not challenged the national sovereignty of other African states. Especially the Zuma government has pursued South African interests – instead of idealist African ones – and is status quo-oriented regarding the regional order. This way, it avoids contestation and even gains regional followership (Scholvin 2012, 2013).

Regardless of the shift from idealism to realism, Africa has remained the essential arena for South Africa's foreign policy. Diplomats from the Southern Africa Division at the Department of International Relations and Cooperation told me that there were 'no questions about a prominent role of South Africa' in the SADC region (pers. comm., 18 August 2010). Their state possessed a 'leading role' because of its dominance, as demonstrated by its share in the overall gross domestic product of the region. My interviewees explained that South Africa had to find the right balance between pushing for its own interests and what it considers to be those of the region, and to show some self-restraint in order not to overwhelm others with its assumption of this regional role. A senior diplomat from South Africa's High Commission in Windhoek reasoned that South Africa 'is walking on thin ice' because the postapartheid euphoria about democracy and human rights still influenced its foreign policy, implying that the other states of the region are not always comfortable with these values (pers. comm., 30 July 2010).

Other diplomats from the SADC division at the Department of International Relations and Cooperation referred to Southern Africa as South Africa's 'prime entry point into global affairs' and 'the basis of our foreign policy' (pers. comm., 17 October 2011). They argued that South Africa needed regional stability because 'this is where we live'. The senior diplomat from the High Commission in Windhoek added that South Africa supported economic development in its neighbourhood, also in order to reduce migration flows to South Africa. He described the xenophobic riots in South Africa in 2008 as a result of insufficient levels of development in the countries of origin of the migrants.

His colleagues from the Department of International Relations and Cooperation argued in this context that a key goal of South Africa's regional policy was regional industrialisation. They also hinted at regional cooperation on transport infrastructure and on energy. A senior official at the Department of Trade and Industry told me that he and his colleagues saw Africa as a market where South Africa has comparative advantages in manufacturing (pers. comm., 17 October 2011). The Department of Trade and Industry hence supports the expansion of South African manufacturers into Africa. My interviewee referred to Africa as South Africa's 'natural market', but voiced dissatisfaction with the performance of South African businesses in postconflict countries – namely Angola, the DR Congo, Mozambique and South Sudan, with overseas competitors instead benefitting from the stability that South Africa had created there.

These convictions have found their clearest expression during the Mbeki presidency, when he tried to establish himself as the leading politician of the African continent. Following his political vision, South Africa was to play a continental leadership role. The 'African Renaissance' and the NEPAD were, according to the Department of Foreign Affairs (2003), the key means of realising South Africa's objectives on both a continent-wide level and in the SADC region. Hence, an entire 'toolbox' for economic cooperation under South African control was developed (Erdmann 2010; Schoeman 2003).

Those who argue that South Africa is a (sub)imperialist power point out that the institutions created in the context of the NEPAD promote a neoliberal agenda for the benefit of South African enterprises. One of the core objectives of the permanent, completely South African-financed, secretariat that coordinates the NEPAD is to advance the privatisation of infrastructure. This not only includes spatial development initiatives but also information and telecommunication technologies. The inclusion of the latter reflects the interests of South Africa's sophisticated service sector, which as explained above has been one of the drivers of South Africa's regional economic expansion. Yet, similar to the regional expansion of South African businesses, the institutional framework created by Mbeki offers other African states better prospects. The African Renaissance can be interpreted as a promise made by South Africa to Africa that the continent will prosper if it opens its gates to South African companies. Opening up Africa in economic terms, and interlinking regional and global economic processes, South Africa serves as the agent of Africa's globalisation. This intermediary role includes a preferential option for South Africa vis-à-vis African resources and markets some may reason (Vale and Maseko 1998). In realising this vision of politically driven regional economic cooperation, intergovernmental organisations with a focus on economics are essential.

South Africa's Role in SACU and SADC

SACU is the world's oldest still-existing customs union. It was founded in 1910, and first consisted of South Africa and the three British administrated territories that later became Botswana, Lesotho and Swaziland. Namibia joined after the First World War, when it became a South African mandated territory. Originally, the purpose of SACU was only to oversee the distribution of custom revenues. The organisation did not seek to facilitate the economic development of its smaller member states. Their subordinate integration into a regional economic system dominated by South Africa was a fait accompli. Before Afrikaner nationalism became the dominant political force in South Africa, SACU appeared to be the first step towards the incorporation of Botswana, Lesotho and Swaziland into South Africa as provinces. The needs of the smaller members were given special consideration from 1976 onwards, when a new basic agreement introduced a stabilisation factor to fix their share of the common revenue pool. This fixed share is more than what the small members would obtain as customs income if they were not part of SACU (Gibb 2002, 2006; Sidaway and Gibb 1998). Granting customs-free market access to all other member states, Botswana, Lesotho and Swaziland lost however USD 20 to 30 million per year during the 1970s and 1980s. They also suffered as a result of importing overpriced South African goods, paying for them with hard currency, and from an economic polarisation that helped make South Africa's economy more and more regionally dominant (Hentz 2005a).

After the end of the apartheid regime, decision-making processes in SACU were democratised. Regarding revenue sharing, national interests eventually outweighed benevolent considerations though. Botswana, Lesotho, Namibia and Swaziland sought to maintain the de facto compensation paid to them by South Africa, whilst it wanted to decrease the level of compensation (or at least limit it). An agreement reached only seven years after the democratisation of South Africa guarantees compensation for the four smaller members – through the so-called 'development component', which constitutes the revenue sharing formula together with a customs component and also an excise one (Gibb 2006; SACU 2002). In consequence, compensation for the smaller members cannot fall below a certain level, nor can South Africa's share exceed a certain level either. South Africa still contributes disproportionately to SACU: the smaller SACU members receive 40 per cent more money than they should get according to their trade activity. Given that South Africa surpasses the fixed minimum tariffs, the amount of compensation given is even higher (Adelmann 2003). Additionally, SACU grants Botswana, Lesotho, Namibia and Swaziland the right to protect nascent industries. Intra-SACU protectionism is limited to a period of eight years (McCarthy 1999). Its prolongation depends upon the consent of all member states, which has often been reached in relevant cases (Senior advisor to the Namibian President, pers. comm., 29 July 2010).

It is important to note that Botswana, Lesotho, Namibia and Swaziland do not have much of a choice when it comes to membership of SACU. Income from the common revenue pool presently covers about 30 per cent of the national budgets of Botswana and Namibia, and about 80 per cent of those of Lesotho and Swaziland (Official at the SACU Secretariat, pers. comm., 5 August 2010). One of my interviewees from Namibia's High Commission in Pretoria said that delinking from South Africa would be 'self-destructive' (pers. comm., 20 August 2010). Given this dependence of the smaller members upon South Africa and the considerable advantages that the regional power grants them, it is not surprising that present budget constraints in South Africa have heightened calls for an end to South Africa's disproportionate contributions to the common revenue pool (Official at the SACU Secretariat, pers. comm., 5 August 2010).

However, decision taking in SACU lies practically in South African hands. The other members apply customs and exercise laws similar to those of South Africa (McCarthy 1999). Lesotho and Swaziland have pegged their currencies to the South African rand at a fixed exchange rate of 1:1 since 1974, thereby creating the Common Monetary Area (CMA), previously, the Rand Monetary Area, or RMA. In 1992, Namibia joined the CMA. The South African rand is legal tender in Lesotho, Namibia and Swaziland. The currencies of these countries are not, however, accepted in South Africa. Given that monetary policy in the CMA follows the steps taken in South Africa, that country not only directs the tariff policy of SACU members but also the monetary policy of the members of the CMA. The South African Reserve Bank acts as a de facto central bank for the CMA (Professor at the University of Stellenbosch, pers. comm., 1 November 2011).

When it comes to advancing the economic goals of the smaller members of SACU, South Africa hardly acts as the benevolent-minded spokesperson of the community. In negotiations with the EU, South Africa has pushed through its own national interests without considering what matters to its fellow SACU members (Ahwireng-Obeng and McGowan 1998b; Erdmann 2010). Intra-SACU relations were shattered by the failure of the member states to negotiate jointly on the Economic Partnership Agreements (Official at the SACU Secretariat, pers. comm., 5 August 2010). In personal discussions with me, a senior official at the Namibian Agricultural Union (25 July 2010) and an advisor to the Agricultural Trade Forum in Windhoek (2 August 2010) criticised the fact that South African companies frequently 'dump' agricultural overproduction on the markets of other SACU members in order to keep prices stable in South Africa. In other words, the CMA and SACU create a nearby market with preferential access for South African businesses (McCarthy 1994).

The other intergovernmental organisation that is essential for cooperation on economic and political issues in Southern Africa is SADC, founded in 1992. Its precursor, SADCC, had united the regional states in their struggle against the apartheid regime during the 1980s but failed to overcome the economic dependence of its members upon South Africa, as noted above. South Africa's incorporation into SADC from 1994 marked the point when regional relations turned from confrontation to cooperation. Despite much rhetoric being aired about peace, security and common values, SADC in reality concentrates on economic issues. Its Protocol on Trade, signed in 1996, aims at a tariff reduction adapted to each country's level of development, the elimination of nontariff barriers, liberalisation and harmonisation in service industries and the harmonisation of various associated policies. The purpose of regional economic integration is 'marketing [... the] region as an attractive option for international trade and investment'. This requires 'the easing of regional trade barriers, enlarging regional markets and promoting investment' (1996: 20–21).

In the mid-1990s, the organisation also emphasised neoliberal principles such as the right to repatriate capital, profits and dividends. Private management capacities, an investment-friendly environment and tax exemptions were stressed as means of promoting economic growth. Government interference in the economy should, it posited, be minimised (1996). Söderbaum (2002) concludes that regionalism in Southern Africa is about boosting the role of the private sector and synchronising regional market integration with globalisation. From a neoliberal perspective, regional integration and globalisation are necessary because Southern Africa is too small in economic terms and does, thus, not see much growth. External impulses are thus necessary. This is why South Africa's incorporation into SADC in the mid-1990s came along with much optimism. South Africa was – and still is – expected to serve as the region's growth engine. With South Africa's inclusion, the regional market attains a collective size that makes it of interest to overseas investors. South Africa's business and industrial sectors provide much needed capital and knowhow. However, South Africa's membership has also polarised SADC in economic and political terms. The regional power dominates decision making on economic issues, whilst its elites also control key sectors of the economies of the other SADC countries (Adelmann 2003; Peters-Berries 2001).

Until now, SADC has advanced less quickly than it was originally envisaged it would. A de facto free trade area has been in existence since 2008, in which Angola and the DR Congo are currently not included. According to senior diplomats at the Department of International Relations and Cooperation, SADC's common market – which was initially scheduled to become operational in 2015 – will probably not become a reality in the near future (pers. comm., 17 October 2011). Efforts to establish a SADC customs union are 'not going well'. A monetary union is 'somewhere on the horizon'. Even free trade within SADC remains a conflict-laden issue because South African firms out-compete their non-South African rivals. For mutually beneficial trade liberalisation, South Africa must open its market more swiftly at least for some products and allow market protection measures to be enacted in its neighbouring countries. In practice, access to the South African market is still hampered by South African protectionism (Senior researcher at Trade and Industrial Policy Strategies, pers. comm., 16 October 2011).

Moreover, customs provide a major share of the national budgets of many SADC states given that they collect few taxes from citizens and domestic businesses. These states have lost much of their import duty revenue as a result of regional integration. This is particularly problematic because, in contrast to SACU, SADC does not possess a mechanism for revenue sharing or compensation – and South Africa is neither willing nor able to compensate its fellow SADC members for integration (Peters-Berries 2001). At the same time, it is uncertain how much the regional countries have to gain from integration because their economies are hardly complementary: they depend upon South Africa and overseas trading partners. Nevertheless, many diplomats from the region told me that they expected economic progress to occur in their countries because of regional integration and South African investment, as summarised in Chapter 6.3.

It appears though that such investment will not be accompanied by a deepening of regional integration, for example by the forming of a monetary union or the concluding of a common economic policy. A recent policy paper by the Economic Development Department states that 'South Africa should be the driving force behind the development of regional energy, transport and telecommunications infrastructure' – meaning ad hoc cooperation (2010: 25). These efforts are to be directed towards SADC and its links with COMESA and the EAC. A strategy paper by the Department of Trade and Industry (2010) stresses the relevance of regional markets, referring therein to the entire continent and in particular to the envisaged convergence between COMESA, the EAC and SADC. With regard to the SADC region, spatial development initiatives are presented in this strategy paper as a key policy tool; regional industrial policy is posited as a way to overcome the growing trade imbalance between South Africa and its fellow SADC members. In other words, South Africa will in future concentrate on getting the infrastructural conditions right for investment in its wider neighbourhood. The regional power's interests appear to require only rather superficial regional integration though.

Paradigms of South African Security Policy

By standard indicators such as military spending and the number of available troops, South Africa is one of the most powerful states in the whole of Africa. It should, accordingly, theoretically be able to intervene in armed conflicts beyond its borders. In East and Southern Africa, only Angola comes close to having South Africa's military might. Further north, Ethiopia, Kenya and Nigeria each possess significant military capacities. If African solutions for African problems are to be found in security affairs, South Africa will have to take an active role therein – not only because of its military strength, but also because South Africa is accepted as a mediator and has the diplomatic capacities to act accordingly. South Africa's capabilities vis-à-vis security provision are limited though, and policy advisors warn of a potential overstretch (Spence 2007) – something that would probably occur if one considered the entire sub-Saharan region to be an appropriate domain for South African mediation and security operations.

Given this risk, Cilliers (2007) and Gamba (2007) suggest that close cooperation between African states should be enacted within the frameworks provided by the AU, the UN and various regional organisations like SADC. The South African military has to be transformed into a prevention and intervention force: it needs to be able to protect civilians and politicians, guarantee smooth elections, disarm combatants, beat armed opponents in low-intensity conflicts, participate in reconstruction projects and train the security forces of postconflict states. These suggestions concur with the 1996 White Paper on National Defence, wherein civil wars in the region and resulting crossborder insecurities are described as the most important challenges faced. Consultation and common doctrines, joint exercises and training, assistance in disaster relief and clearing of minefields are mentioned as issues requiring cooperation. Southern Africa is defined as the area for regional cooperation; it appears to be considered the focal point of South African security policy (Ministry of Defence 1996).

Yet, the regional power has been reluctant to commit itself to transnational security affairs. Some I interviewed referred to the legacy of the apartheid regime in order to explain why the ANC has been trying 'not to flex its muscle' (Senior diplomats at the Department of International Relations and Cooperation, pers. comm., 18 August 2010). The problems associated with this course of action were, as noted above, first highlighted when Mandela's agenda of democracy and human rights met with fierce resistance in 1995. After having failed to prevent the execution of Ken Saro-Wiwa and eight prodemocracy activists, the South African government sought Nigeria's expulsion from the Commonwealth of Nations, called on Britain and the US to impose an oil embargo on the country and urged sanctions the UN to impose sanctions. Whilst the West maintained a pragmatic stance vis-à-vis Nigeria, thus practically ignoring the South African position, governments all over the African continent chastised Mandela for behaving in an 'un-African' way. Even a discussion of the Nigerian issue at a SADC meeting broke down. Some ANC politicians went as far as to remind Mandela of Nigeria's supportive role during the fight against the apartheid regime (Barber 2005; Kagwanja 2006).

Against this background, it may, at first glance, be surprising that South Africa has in fact participated in a number of security operations in Africa, particularly during the Mbeki presidency years. South Africa has stabilised postconflict situations by sending its troops in and by acting as a mediator – from Burundi (1999–2005) and the DR Congo (2002–) to Sudan (2005–). Currently, the regional power plays a key role in the mediation between government and opposition forces in the Comoros, Madagascar and Zimbabwe. What is more, South Africa has signed numerous agreements on military cooperation with all members of SADC. At second glance, these forms of commitment to regional security do not contradict South Africa's general reluctance to participate in it. When successful, South African regional security policy has been marked by the compatibility between the policy-specific interests of the regional states and a common vision for the general order of international relations in the region (Scholvin 2012, 2013). As noted, the latter has, during the Mbeki and Zuma presidencies, shifted in focus from democracy and human rights to national sovereignty.

In other words, South Africa does not use its military power unilaterally. Its army is an implementation tool for policies agreed upon on a (sub)continental level. One may conclude that both South Africa and its neighbouring countries adopt a cooperative and inclusive approach to regional security issues. This cooperative attitude reflects the fact that South Africa under the ANC has 'always opted for negotiated solutions' (Senior diplomats at the Department of International Relations and Cooperation, pers. comm., 18 August 2010). Additionally, it appears that many issues considered by the West to be security problems are seen by the South African government rather as political problems, which thus require diplomatic and not military solutions to be applied to them.

In the following sections, I shed light on three key South African security interventions that exemplify the aforementioned characteristics of the regional power's contemporary security policy. In line with the broader argumentation, I also reveal the role played by geographical factors in each of these interventions.

The 1998 Intervention in Lesotho

Following elections in Lesotho in August and September 1998 violent protests and a mutiny by members of the army occurred – with soldiers refusing to intervene against the ongoing protests of demonstrators. Four years earlier, unrest in the army had led to the arrest and assassination of cabinet members. Having been unable to stabilise the country for several weeks during the crisis in 1998, the government of Lesotho finally called on SADC for help in crushing what it labelled a coup. One day later, 600 South African soldiers crossed the border. They not only captured the Royal Palace and the headquarters of the Lesotho Defence Force in Maseru, forcibly ending sit-in protests there, but also occupied the Katse Dam. Details that have emerged about Operation Boleas suggest that securing this dam was the prime objective of the intervention: shortly after Basotho opposition groups had threatened to blow it up, South African elite forces were flown by helicopter from Bloemfontein to the dam, where they killed 16 Basotho soldiers.

The South Africans then guarded the dam, whilst the first troops deployed to bring order to Maseru were from Botswana. They arrived late and did little to stop looting and violence. South African soldiers in Maseru did not prevent such incidences of disorder either (Bond 2002). Some sources have even suggested that the looting was started by individual soldiers from the intervention forces (Makoa 1999). South African security experts interviewed a few years later mostly described the intervention as a failure of South African diplomacy and an indicator of the operational shortcomings of the South African army (Schleicher 2006).

Other regional states shared the interpretation of Operation Boleas as driven purely by South Africa's own economic interests. They did not buy into the rhetoric of a benevolent intervention, and must have started wondering whether South Africa under the ANC would stick to multilateralism and peaceful means. The OAU and the UN criticised South Africa for acting unilaterally. Operation Boleas was even compared to the military adventurism of the apartheid regime (Kagwanja 2006). Apart from that, the de jure legitimacy of the intervention is doubtful. SADC's Organ for Politics, Defence and Security (OPDS) constitutes the essential institution of regional security policy. The initial idea behind the OPDS was to create a special forum for conflict management (Neethling 2003). However, according to the *Protocol on Politics, Defence and Security Cooperation* (2001), a wide variety of ways to keep the peace – ranging from an early warning system to fighting crossborder crime – was bestowed on it.

The OPDS may also enforce peace. Since any conflict that 'threatens peace and security in the region or in the territory of a state [... that] is not a party to the conflict' should be addressed by the OPDS, its competences are very broad and hard to delimit in practice (SADC 2001). One can argue that Lesotho's political authorities asked for an intervention and that it was covered by Article 11 of the aforementioned protocol, which calls on the OPDS to resolve any conflict that results from a military coup or from other threats posed to the legitimate authority of a state. Because of an ongoing dispute between South Africa and Zimbabwe over regional leadership, however, the OPDS was not operational when the South Africans intervened in Lesotho. The Mandela government even said that it considered the OPDS to be suspended at that time.

The lack of formal legitimacy matters a lot, because ever since 1994 South Africa has faced enormous constraints to how it engages in regional politics. Given both its ongoing dominance and the legacy of the apartheid era, any unilateral action by South Africa is almost always associated with the malevolent policies previously pursued by the NP. Whilst the West and emerging powers such as Brazil, China and India see South Africa as a representative – or even as the leader – of the African continent, most African states contrariwise call South Africa's benevolence into question (Flemes 2007). When intervening in Lesotho, the ANC government therefore referred to the framework of SADC in order to avoid being perceived in the same mould as the NP, which had launched raids against antiapartheid guerrillas in Lesotho in the 1980s. The symbolic participation of one other regional state, Botswana, was meant to serve as another legitimising factor, although as outlined this strategy clearly failed to succeed.

Regardless of these considerations on the legitimacy of the intervention and the reaction of other African states, Operation Boleas exemplifies how geographical factors sometimes play a key role in international relations. The driver of the intervention was the protection of the Katse Dam. The existence of this site and its relevance to South Africa results from location and physical geography: Lesotho is close to South Africa's economic heartland. Climatic conditions and geomorphological features enable Lesotho to provide water to South Africa, which is in short supply there. Yet, Operation Boleas was not triggered by the Katse Dam per se but rather by the political instability in Lesotho that threatened to harm it. In this sense, the said geographical factors are an insufficient explanation for the observed outcome. Still, they are a necessary condition. If there had been no Katse Dam, South Africa would, most likely, not have intervened in Lesotho – despite the postelection turmoil unfolding in the mountain kingdom. In addition to this interplay of geographical and nongeographical factors, it is important to stress that the latter explain the exact form that the observed outcome took. It is thus geographical conditions that tell us why there was a strong South African reaction to the crisis in Lesotho. Geographical conditions do not inform us, though, why South Africa sought to legitimise the intervention via SADC. This uncertainty does not, however, change the fact that certain geographical conditions were necessary for this outcome to occur.

Peacekeeping in the Great Lakes Region

At the beginning of this century, South Africa was the lead mediator and peacekeeper in Burundi, a country that had gone through decades of ethnic violence. South Africa deployed 1,500 troops on the ground in order to protect returning politicians and linked the peace process there to its mediation efforts in the DR Congo. Stability in Burundi was seen as a precondition for stability in the entire Great Lakes region (Southall 2006). Already in 1999 South Africa had introduced a peace plan for the DR Congo, which proposed a ceasefire agreement, demanded the standing down of all troops, called for a conference on reconciliation and reconstruction, and suggested a transitional government composed of all conflict parties. A new constitution and general elections were envisaged in the South African plan. South

Africa also financed a joint military commission that was sent to the DR Congo. In 2002, Mbeki and UN Secretary General Kofi Annan brokered a deal between the DR Congo's President Joseph Kabila and his Rwandan counterpart Paul Kagame. This deal led to the 2003 Sun City Agreement, which foresaw the coming of a transitional government and democratic elections (Schoeman 2003).

In the DR Congo itself, European powers were the key external actors involved in mediation and peacekeeping. South Africa did not deploy a large number of troops there. Burundi, however, was the first case that saw a relatively well-organised effort by African states to bring peace and stability to a war-torn country. It was the first test for the idea of African solutions for African problems, and symbolised the commitment of the Mbeki government to Africa. Mbeki continuously emphasised that South Africa should give something back to the continent that had supported it during the struggle against the apartheid regime (Rautenbach and Vrey 2010a).

The operational limits of the South African military became apparent during the intervention in Burundi, hinting at the fact that geographical distance is a severe constraint to South Africa's projection of military power. After having been flown to Burundi, South African soldiers had to wait standing in the sun for hours before buses brought them to their bases. The distribution of their equipment, especially their weapons, became a nightmare for their commanders because even light weapons had been flown to Burundi by other airplanes. South African soldiers thus found themselves unarmed in a postconflict situation (Rautenbach and Vrey 2010b). Until today, South Africa's military capacities have continued to somewhat decline. A senior researcher from the Institute of Security Studies argued that South Africa could currently only participate in peacekeeping missions (pers. comm., 11 August 2010); its ability to realise interventions that involve fighting was and is very limited.

Nonetheless, the intervention in Burundi was a success for South African security policy because of its political framing. In comparison to the intervention in Lesotho, South Africa was perceived in this case as a neutral broker both by the conflict parties and its fellow SADC members (Southall 2006). On an operational and strategic level, the South Africans cooperated with the AU and the UN, which subsequently took over the mission in 2003 and 2004 respectively. More importantly, Mandela started acting as a mediator only after a regional summit of the EAC had requested him to do so. Despite this official mandate, he had to struggle to counter fears that South Africa wanted to steal the credit for a successful peace process, which had up to that point been driven by Tanzania's former president Julius Nyerere (Rautenbach and Vrey 2010a). In addition to being widely accepted in the first place, South Africa's success in Burundi resulted from a moderate and – on the level of key personalities – inclusive approach, which was essential given the high relevance that certain individuals and their personal ties hold in African politics (Landsberg 2006). When Mbeki took over from Mandela, he prudently started negotiating with Kabila, Kagame and Mugabe. Even Angola's President José Eduardo dos Santos was integrated into a process that became a complex web of foreign trips for high-ranking South African politicians and meetings with their counterparts from the region. Moreover, Mbeki was less ambitious than Mandela, insisting that South Africa could keep the peace in Burundi but was unable to make peace there – meaning that the conflict parties had to voluntarily agree to a South African-brokered arrangement.

Geographical factors hold a certain relevance for South Africa's commitment to the Great Lakes region. Stabilising it serves South African economic interests, because peace facilitates investment. Political stability as a necessary precondition to economic development induced by South African investment was the basic tenet of Mbeki's approach to Africa. Hence, there would not have been such a strong commitment made to the Great Lakes region if this part of Africa did not provided economic assets that complement South Africa's economy. Katanga Province and the Kivus possess mineral resources that are attractive for South African mining companies. Several years after the end of the Second Congo War, the South African government and its Congolese counterpart signed agreements on economic, financial and infrastructural cooperation. In a separate protocol, the South African government declared its commitment to rebuilding the Congolese mining sector. South Africa has, since then, shared mining technology with the DR Congo (Kabemba 2007). What is more, South Africa's efforts to stabilise the Great Lakes region have contributed to stabilising the entire DR Congo – the threat of rebels, supported by Burundi, Rwanda and Uganda, pushing through the country and overthrowing the government in Kinshasa has become fairly low. This way a basic precondition is met for a regionally integrated electricity grid, with the DR Congo acting as the main provider. As the First Congo War showed, a politically unstable DR Congo cannot be a reliable provider of electricity: one of the main objectives of Rwanda and its Congolese allies was to capture the Inga Dam, when they tried to topple the Congolese government in 1997 (Kabemba 2007).

Hence, Mbeki's policy principle of facilitating economic growth by guaranteeing political stability will only explain South Africa's strong diplomatic and military commitment to the Great Lakes region if it is seen together with the geographical opportunities that make the DR Congo and the Great Lakes region attractive for South Africa from an economic viewpoint. These geographical opportunities are a necessary condition. Their relevance is further indicated by the rising criticism from within South Africa's foreign policy community about unfulfilled expectations with regard to the economic benefits that were supposed to result from the country's commitment to the Great Lakes region (Senior researcher at the South African Institute of International Affairs, pers. comm., 11 August 2010). Daniel and Luchtman (2006) argue that economic opportunities provided by geography sufficiently explain South Africa's political and military role in the DR Congo. What I show here is, however, that geographical factors must be combined with political ones in order to fully understand South African security policy. South Africa would thus have acted differently if President Mbeki had not been pursuing an African agenda.

De-escalating the Crisis in Zimbabwe

The key characteristic of the approach of the Mbeki and Zuma governments to the crisis in Zimbabwe, which began in the early 2000s, is that they have not criticised Mugabe directly – a lesson learnt from the reactions to Mandela's harsh criticism of Nigeria in 1995. Using the words of Mavivi Myokayaka-Manzini, a foreign policy expert of the ANC, South Africa had to avoid repeating Mandela's 'terrible mistake' of behaving like a 'bully', which was why 'everyone stood aside and we were isolated' during the Saro-Wiwa crisis (quoted in Barber 2005: 1095). The way South Africa has addressed the crisis in Zimbabwe is, therefore, labelled 'quiet diplomacy'; behind closed doors, South Africa tries to influence the Zimbabwean government and military. There is speculation about concealed efforts having been made by Botswana, Mozambique and South Africa to isolate Zimbabwe and convince Mugabe to step down shortly after the elections in 2002 (Schoeman and Alden 2003). It was only when the Zimbabwean government refused to allow election monitors into the country that Mbeki publicly called on SADC to take action in order to prevent Zimbabwe from descending into chaos (Lee 2003).

As noted, Mbeki revised the priorities of South African foreign policy. Under him and then later Zuma, respecting the national sovereignty of other states has outweighed criticism of their authoritarian tendencies and violations of human rights. This shift in South African foreign policy is also a reflection of a personal shift by Mbeki, whose African agenda initially reflected Mandela's idealism. With regard to the Zimbabwean crisis, Mbeki declared that South Africa claimed no right to impose its will on anyone. This conviction constitutes a core paradigm of South African foreign policy until today. The regional power has frequently cooperated with pseudo-democratic rulers and firmly shut its doors on those who lobby for democracy and human rights (Olivier 2003). It is hardly surprising that representatives of opposition movements and parties in South Africa's neighbouring countries speak very favourably of the Mandela era and would like South Africa to return to the principles of it (Namibian human rights activist and scholar from Zimbabwe, pers. comm., 27 and 28 July 2010).

What is more, South Africa and the West understand the crisis in Zimbabwe in totally different ways. Mbeki wrote in an open letter to his party that certain actors were using the notion of human rights against the Mugabe government. In that letter, Mbeki referred to Mugabe as a true hero of the common struggle against apartheid and called Mugabe's party – the Zimbabwe African National Union Patriotic Front (ZANU PF) – an allied liberation movement (Matyszak 2009). Given that the willing buyer–willing seller principle had not led to satisfactory results in Zimbabwe's land reform initiative, a forcible process of land redistribution perhaps became inevitable he argued (Barber 2005). Kgalema Motlanthe, then the ANC's secretary general, added that the ZANU PF was in trouble not because it did not care about ordinary people, but because it had cared too much. Mbeki similarly declared that the Zimbabwean crisis had arisen from a genuine concern to meet the needs of the black poor (Phimister and Raftopoulos 2004).

If one dismisses these statements as rhetoric and believes that Mbeki and his colleagues opposed what was happening in Zimbabwe, there is another convincing explanation for quiet diplomacy. When the oppression in Zimbabwe reached its height, the Mbeki government was struggling to make African states accept South Africa as truly African and as a leader – or at least a representative – of the continent (Schoeman and Alden 2003). Mbeki and his cabinet found themselves caught in a dilemma. They knew that Mugabe would depict them as proxies of the West and call their Africanness into question if they strongly criticised him. For many (South) Africans, Mugabe is an anticolonial hero and liberator (Lipton 2009). Various diplomats from the region told me that South Africa could never act against a government that strongly supported the ANC during the struggle against the apartheid regime (pers. comm., 2010 and 2011).

Against this background, one may suggest that South Africa did not possess any better options to move forward with; it had to acknowledge the limits of its regional influence. Senior diplomats at the Department of International Relations and Cooperation accordingly argued that one must accept that some countries in the region were 'not so far yet', meaning that some principles on democracy and human rights still have yet to become common practice in them (pers. comm., 17 October 2011). In order to position his government as a friendly mediator and exert a gentle influence on Zimbabwe in this way, Mbeki emphasised the ANC's historic ties with Mugabe and the ZANU PF, which is odd because the latter's predecessor did not support the Soviet-related ANC but rather the pro-Chinese Pan Africanist Congress of Azania. Mugabe, meanwhile, had during the apartheid years allowed the ANC to open an office in Harare, but the party was not officially permitted to use Zimbabwe for any guerrilla activities.

As these arguments demonstrate, politics has played an important role in South Africa's reaction to the crisis in Zimbabwe. Geographical conditions are, however, necessary to fully understand quiet diplomacy. None of Zimbabwe's neighbours wants to see an intensification of the Zimbabwean crisis. Western states, being far away, can easily criticise Mugabe – whereas the neighbouring states will immediately feel the consequences of imprudent action because of their geographic location. Taking a confrontational approach to Zimbabwe, as preferred by the West, is likely to increase instability – at least in the short run. A total breakdown of Zimbabwe would significantly increase migration to South Africa. Furthermore, regional transport by rail and road is dependent upon Zimbabwe, which is the major transit country between the Congolese–Zambian Copperbelt and South Africa. Plans to better interlink the electricity grids in the SADC region also rely on Zimbabwe, as all existing major transregional transmission lines pass through its territory.

All this would be at risk if South Africa pursued an approach other than quiet diplomacy (Schoeman and Alden 2003). In one sentence, Zimbabwe's central location in Southern Africa is a core geopolitical factor. In addition, economic relations with Zimbabwe are in their present state profitable for both private and state-owned companies from South Africa. They exploit Zimbabwe's vast mineral resources. The relative stability, which is guaranteed by the power-sharing agreement between the ZANU PF and the Movement for Democratic Change, has allowed South African firms to invest massively in Zimbabwe – in the process taking over various companies and entire industries (Lipton 2009). Botswana, Mozambique and Namibia are cooperating with Zimbabwe on electricity, by helping upgrade the coal-fired Hwange Power Station. The USD 30 million that was invested by Namibia in Hwange was repaid by the electricity transmissions made from there to its territory between 2007 and 2012.

Whilst Mugabe's post-2000 policies have practically removed Zimbabwean companies as rivals from the regional market, quiet diplomacy ensures that Zimbabwe still remains a lucrative market for companies from its neighbouring countries (Adelmann 2004). It even makes the weakened Zimbabwean elite dependent upon their regional – mostly South African – partners. From this viewpoint, it becomes clear that the aid South Africa has given to its neighbour has not been donated on the grounds of idealism. When the Mbeki government granted Zimbabwe a rescue package of ZAR 1 billion shortly before the elections in 2000, South African enterprises – and in particular Eskom and Sasol – were the ones to benefit because Zimbabwean parastatals were highly indebted to them. These debts could only be paid off after South Africa had granted Zimbabwe financial support. That aside, the 2000 rescue package financed more than 20 investment projects in Zimbabwe – with South African businesses being the ones to carry out them out (McKinley 2004).

6.3 Country-specific Analysis: Regional Political Strategies

Angola

Oil and natural gas exports are driving the growth of Angola's economy. Because of oil exports, Angola's foreign exchange reserves have risen to USD 33 billion. The country's current account surplus is 13.9 per cent of its gross domestic product. Experts from the Economist Intelligence Unit (2012) predict that Angola will expand credit lines with Brazil and China in order to further upgrade domestic infrastructure. These observations concur with what an honorary consul also told me (pers. comm., 24 March 2010). He said that South Africa's relevance for Angola was limited, first because of the considerable distance between the two countries and second because Angola is, according to him, not interested in playing a subordinated role.

Third, Angola has very lucrative alternative partners: Brazil, China and Portugal. Brazil and Portugal benefit from sharing a common language with Angola. China offers interest-free loans, which amounted to USD 5 billion in 2009. Angola has in exchange granted market access to Chinese consumer goods (Schubert 2010). A representative of the Adenauer Foundation told me that Angola was a special case in Southern Africa because Brazil, China, Portugal and the US matter much more for its economy than South Africa does (pers. comm., 12 July 2010). Data from the website *Who Owns Whom* (2012) confirms that South African investment does not play a major role in Angola. There is some South African investment in oil, natural gas and chemicals. Business services are provided by Imperial Holdings and Standard Bank. Shoprite has recently established an Angolan branch. De Beers is involved in diamond mining. Brazilian and Chinese investment directed at the oil and transport sectors plays the lead role in Angola's economic development strategy though (Schubert 2011).

Angola can be seen as a regional power in the western part of Central Africa or as a regional counterweight to South Africa. In a speech in 2012, Angolan Foreign Minister Georges Rebelo Chikoti said that his state was not only committed to SADC but also to Central Africa, including the Gulf of Guinea. He highlighted Angola's commitment to the stabilisation of the DR Congo and emphasised that Angola wanted regional integration in Central Africa to proceed (Chatham House 2012). Experts from Stratfor (2012) argue that the Angolan government is trying to prevent the rise of nearby regional powers – that is, Nigeria, Rwanda and South Africa. The competition with South Africa occurs in the domain of regional transport, because Angola's best way to successfully take South Africa on is to upgrade – as it is currently doing – its port of Lobito and link it to the landlocked countries, thereby replacing Durban and Richards Bay as the gateway to the world for the Copperbelt. Angolan–South African relations are competitive for historical reasons. First of all, the apartheid regime intervened militarily in Angola, devastating vast parts of the country. In the mid-1990s, the ANC government did little to stop weapons shipments to Angolan anti-government rebels. When the South Africans called for a political and inclusive solution to the civil war, the People's Movement for the Liberation of Angola, or MPLA, criticised them for trying to apply the South African model to everyone else.

Angolan–South African relations have become less conflictive during the Zuma presidency because of his strict adherence to the principle of noninterference and focus on mutually beneficial economic relations (Conchiglia 2007). Schubert (2011) even calls these relations 'amicable'. Given Angola's increasing political relevance and the attractiveness of the Angolan market, which is not limited only to oil extraction, it is not surprising that Zuma went to Luanda on his first trip abroad as South African president – for which he was accompanied by 11 cabinet ministers and 180 businesspersons. South African Foreign Minister Maite Nkoana-Mashabane has pointed to the relevance of Angola for South Africa's 'oil security', as the *Mail & Guardian* reported on 19 August 2009. Yet, the former Portuguese colony does not depend upon regional integration. The honorary consul I interviewed gave the example for this of Angola's infrastructure policy, which aims, according to him, at linking the national hinterland to domestic ports instead of at interlinking the country regionally. The Benguela Corridor – which will soon connect the port of Lobito to the Copperbelt – and bridge and road construction near the Namibian border aside, this assessment appears to be accurate (Schubert 2010).

Botswana

Botswana will, according to experts from the Economist Intelligence Unit (2012), continue to push its privatisation programme. Investment opportunities occur mainly in diamond mining and electricity generation, but sectors as diverse as construction, pharmaceuticals, public transportation, software and computer services, and retail and wholesale also attract foreign investors as well. So far, South African companies are predominant in these sectors (*Who Owns Whom* 2012). With its mining sector growing, Botswana's dependence upon South Africa is likely to increase for another reason besides: Botswana is a landlocked country and its overseas trade passes mostly through its neighbour's territory. A diplomat at Botswana's High Commission in Pretoria agreed with this assessment, arguing that Botswana is, to a certain extent, economically depended upon South Africa – especially because it is landlocked (pers. comm., 13 August 2010). Since Botswana's capital and major agglomeration Gaborone is close to the South African border, there is, according to my interviewee, a preference for transportation via South Africa. The secondary centre Francistown tends instead towards Mozambique and Zimbabwe; the tertiary centre Ghanzi towards Namibia.

With regard to the expansion of South African businesses into the region, my interviewee reasoned that this was beneficial because South Africa's neighbouring countries lacked economic impulses coming from abroad and thus would not develop without South African investment. He mentioned outcompeting locals as a problem, but pointed out that his government tries to make South African firms that operate in Botswana interlink with local companies. This strategy, he argued, reflected the simple fact that 'nobody can remove himself from his region'. Constraints and opportunities provided by the region hence have to be incorporated into economic and political strategies. The diplomat further explained that his state left the Rand Monetary Area in 1977 in order to maintain its political independence, meaning retaining the ability to devaluate its currency. He recognised that South Africa is not only economically but also politically dominant in the SADC region. The influence that South Africa exerts on Botswana's politics is indicated by recent revelations of De Beers having financially supported the ruling Botswana Democratic Party during the 1980s and 1990s (Basedau and von Soest 2011). My interviewee suggested that other regional states 'do not like South Africa's dominance'. They are, however, unable to do anything about it. At the same time, my interviewee was convinced that South Africa 'does not want to appear as big brother' and, therefore, offers incentives to its neighbours so that they accept South African regional dominance.

The DR Congo

The Congolese economy remains problem laden, first of all because of the government's mismanagement of natural resources. The minerals-for-infrastructure deal signed with China in 2007 and a similar, much smaller agreement with South Korea from 2010 demonstrate that the DR Congo is, nonetheless, attractive to investors. Data from *Who Owns Whom* (2012) indicates that the activities of South African enterprises in the DR Congo generate centripetal forces: apart from mining, South Africans are predominantly active in the construction and telecommunication domains. Still, a diplomat at the Congolese embassy in Pretoria pointed out in an interview with me that his country is a part of more than one region: the Kivus drift towards the EAC, whereas Katanga Province is integrated into SADC (pers. comm., 27 August 2010). He argued that South Africa, being a regional power in economic terms, sought to advance development for the entire region and closer integration within the framework provided by SADC. Given that the members of SADC are marked by a considerable development gap between them, reservations regarding free trade and South Africa's economic expansion into the region were understandable he said. SADC should, therefore, try to ease the intra-SADC development disparities. From his perspective, SADC and South Africa hence play a key role for the DR Congo because they are expected to provide opportunities for economic development.

Regarding security affairs, the DR Congo is likely to suffer from further problems in the coming years. President Kabila's de facto control of the eastern DR Congo remains minimal. Acts of violence, mostly against civilians, are committed by the national army and various rebel groups. The latter are said to receive support from Rwanda and Uganda (Tull 2011). Being for certain aware of these threats to stability in his country, the diplomat I talked to reasoned that the quickest way to solve problems is at the EAC or SADC level. Crisis response capacities should be developed there. He argued that the genocide in Rwanda in 1994 would not have happened if the EAC or SADC had possessed the crisis response capacities that they do today. He referred to the intervention of Angola, Namibia and Zimbabwe in the DR Congo in 1998 as an example of how regional cooperation can solve security problems, which is not a very convincing argument because these three countries all intervened only in order to safeguard the stakes of their ruling elites in the Congolese resource economy. Regardless of this issue, it appears that for my interviewee South Africa does not represent a major player in regional security affairs. He suggested that other states – and in particular Angola – were militarily stronger than South Africa is. From his viewpoint, South African regional powerhood is limited to the realm of economic affairs.

Lesotho

Politically, Lesotho is much more stable today than it was in the 1990s. The transition from the Mosisili government to a multiparty coalition headed by Tom

Thabane, the chairperson of the All Basotho Coalition, went smoothly. Thabane and his deputy, Mothetjoa Metsing, served in cabinets of Mosisili – the change of government has thus not meant a change of the ruling elite. Political stability has increased Lesotho's attractiveness to foreign investors, but the global financial crisis hit the country hard because it significantly reduced SACU customs revenue. Job losses in the clothing and textile industry were not prevented, also due to uncertainties about the prolongation of the Africa Growth and Opportunity Act by the US Congress. Orders declined by 30 per cent between 2008 and 2011 (Economist Intelligence Unit 2012). Given the uncertainty about the Africa Growth and Opportunity Act, it is not surprising that a Basotho diplomat told me that Lesotho's economic future lay in Southern Africa (pers. comm., 17 February 2010). The LHWP could provide electricity and water not only to South Africa but to other regional countries as well she argued.

Within SADC, South Africa acts – according to my interviewee – as an enabler and a uniting force. It promotes good governance and regional integration. South Africa should be even more active, sharing its economic potential with neighbouring countries. My interviewee argued that the bilateral relations of Lesotho and South Africa were marked by 'mutual understanding' for cultural and historical reasons, and also by a 'compatibility of needs'. As a consequence, the two countries have established various cross-border projects of which the LHWP is the most prominent example. The Basotho diplomat added that Lesotho – just like all members of the CMA – wanted South Africa's economy to prosper because their currencies and economies depended upon it. Furthermore, she hinted at the simple but crucial fact that Lesotho needs to cross through South African territory to access foreign markets. She recognised that Lesotho maintains key economic relations with the EU and the US because of its clothing and textile industry. The most important sector of the Basotho economy is internationalised and not linked to South Africa, as she pointed out. This is confirmed by data from *Who Owns Whom* (2012). South African investment in Lesotho is primarily directed at retail, with Mr Price and Shoprite being well known examples; Standard Bank and Vodacom are other key South African investors in the mountain kingdom.

Malawi

Since Joyce Banda assumed the presidency in April 2012, relations with foreign donors have been re-established and the foreign exchange rate liberalised. Malawi's fiscal deficit is expected to decrease to 1.6 per cent of gross domestic product. The risk of domestic protests has, however, increased. After an overnight depreciation of the Malawian kwacha by 50 per cent in May 2012, workers at the Kayelekera Uranium Mine went on strike, demanding a 66 per cent increase in their wages. Inflation is high, standing at 18.4 per cent in 2012 (Economist Intelligence Unit 2012). Banda's decision to increase subsidies for the agricultural sector is positive in this context, but these do not help to diversify Malawi's economy. Nor do they solve the problem of the currently inadequate transport infrastructure.

Against this background, regional economic cooperation becomes essential for Malawi – not only for economic development but also for political stability. According to two senior Malawian diplomats, Southern Africa is bound together by SADC – which they described as 'the most successful regional grouping in Africa' (pers. comm., 17 February 2010). They pointed out that South Africa plays an outstanding role in SADC, both economically and militarily, and argued that the SADC region was marked by 'a nature of cooperation', which resulted from the way in which South Africa deals with the regional states. In order to exemplify South Africa's cooperative and inclusive approach, the diplomats referred to the fact that South African universities charge the same tuition fees for all SADC students, regardless of their nationality. However, conflicts may arise because of protectionism, which is, according to them, necessary for Malawi because of the regional gap vis-à-vis development. South African enterprises are active in transport-related activities, tourism and retail in Malawi but there are clearly fewer cases of investment here than in South Africa's direct neighbours (*Who Owns Whom* 2012).

Apart from that, some of the projects that my interviewees highlighted regarding Malawi's economic planning – in particular the development of transport corridors through Mozambique and Tanzania, as well as Malawi's harbour in Nsanje – indicate that Malawi will probably eventually drift away from South Africa. This is supported by the fact that external partners have come to hold considerable relevance to Malawi's transport infrastructure projects: in 2009, Saudi Arabia pledged USD 12 million for road construction in Malawi, which represents, after all, one-third of the money spent by the African Development Bank for this purpose. The fact that China has allowed Malawi to export 95 per cent of its products to the People's Republic without paying any import taxes constitutes another centrifugal force in the Malawian–South African relationship. India supports Malawi as well, by granting development credits and promoting bilateral trade in agriculture and mining (Dzimbiri and Chipaka-Jamali 2010).

Mozambique

Politically speaking, Mozambique has become one of the closest regional partners of South Africa. A senior researcher at the South African Institute of International Affairs argued that Mozambique was the only African state that could be considered an ally of South Africa (pers. comm., 11 August 2010). Economically, Mozambique and South Africa are close too. In 2002, the former Portuguese colony replaced Zimbabwe as South Africa's largest continental trading partner. The rapid expansion of Mozambique's mining sector is driven by investment that originates in or is channelled through Johannesburg. Cooperation on the governmental level – for instance over the Maputo Development Corridor and the Zambezi Valley Spatial Development Initiative – facilitates close economic links and suggests that Mozambique sees South Africa as its growth engine. At the same time, trickledown effects from megaprojects – especially the smelter

Mozal – have remained at a level below expectations. The Maputo Development Corridor, meanwhile, has reinforced disparities between the Maputo area and the rest of the country (Conchiglia 2007).

Mozambique depends so much upon South Africa in economic affairs that it can hardly risk political confrontation. The unequal relationship between the two countries is best demonstrated by the fact that Mozambique's national electricity provider buys electricity from Eskom in order to supply the Maputo area at a higher price than Eskom pays for the electricity that it gets from Cahora Bassa (Conchiglia 2007). South African investment in Mozambique follows the aforementioned typical pattern: construction, business support in banking and telecommunications, and transport are the most important sectors. Related activities such as the provision of car parts and of packaging play a secondary role. Well-known retailers such as Massmart, Shoprite and Spar have recently invested in Mozambique. Mozambique's natural resources – that is, coal, oil and natural gas – are apparently of interest to South African enterprises (*Who Owns Whom* 2012).

Overseas companies play a much more important role than South African ones in the mining sector though. Mozambique's economy will change a lot in the coming decades because of natural resource exploitation. Foreign direct investment is expected to amount to USD 6.4 billion between 2012 and 2016 – a figure that will increase significantly if an envisaged project on liquefied natural gas goes ahead in Pemba, northern Mozambique. Investment in mining will trigger investment in the transport infrastructure because communication services, electricity grids and pipelines as well as harbours, railway lines and roads are presently insufficient to support this project. Although Mozambique's resources are highly attractive to overseas investors, in particular those from Brazil and the Far East, some developments hint at closer regional relations; Sasol has invested in the Pande and Temane Gasfields in southern Mozambique. They are linked by a pipeline to Gauteng. Aluminium smelting and petrochemical industries, especially for the production of fertilisers, may pop up in Pemba. Pipelines will eventually connect Pemba to Maputo – which lies about 2,000 kilometres away – and to consumers in some of the neighbouring countries (Economist Intelligence Unit 2012).

Namibia

According to a Namibian diplomat I interviewed in Pretoria, Namibia and South Africa have a 'reasonably strong' economic partnership – which she derived from the vast presence of South African businesses in Namibia and the fact that South Africa is Namibia's most important trading partner (pers. comm., 20 August 2010). It is quite revealing that she overestimated the share of South African imports, saying that 80 to 90 per cent of Namibia's imports came from that country. The true figure is 69.4 per cent, as shown in Table 6.1. Most of Namibia's economic growth is due to overseas investment in the mining sector, in uranium in particular

(Economist Intelligence Unit 2012). Nevertheless, South African investment affects practically every sector of the Namibian economy, ranging from farming, fishing and mining to electricity and transport to financial services, retail and tourism (*Who Owns Whom* 2012).

My interviewee admitted that Namibia's close economic relations with South Africa involve certain risks. Her country suffers from a vast trade deficit with South Africa and is not independent in its monetary policy because of the CMA. At the same time, Namibia benefits from its proximity to South Africa. Especially in agriculture and property construction, it appears likely that firms relocate from South Africa to Namibia because of lower labour costs. My interviewee also suggested that Namibia was diversifying its economic relations regionally but South Africa would still remain the most important trading partner – partly because other trading partners were unreliable. In this context, an advisor to the Agricultural Trade Forum in Windhoek pointed to Zambia's failure to deliver grain for cattle farming in Namibia (pers. comm., 2 August 2010). Because of domestic shortages, Zambia suddenly stopped its grain exports to Namibia a few years ago.

A policy analyst at the Ministry of Trade and Industry advanced the same ideas on economic diversification and added that Angola mattered most in this regard: the bulk of transhipments at Walvis Bay are destined for Angola (pers. comm., 3 August 2010). For a recently opened cement plant near Otavi, the Angolan market is more important than the Namibian one is. An honorary consul argued in this context that the Namibian government preferred cooperation with Angola, Botswana and Zambia because it saw itself as being on a similar level to these states (pers. comm., 9 December 2009). Yet, he acknowledged that Angola, Botswana and Zambia do not constitute full alternatives to South Africa. My interviewee from the Ministry of Trade and Industry accordingly said that the South African market and the revenues generated by SACU were vital to Namibia, and added that much overseas investment in Namibia occurred only because SACU constituted a sufficiently large regional market.

Swaziland

Because of the extravagant lifestyle of the royal family, the mismanagement of public funds and its extreme budgetary dependence upon SACU's common revenue pool, Swaziland is one of the most unstable states in the region. In reaction to the government's failure to bring public finances onto a sound footing, the International Monetary Fund and the African Development Bank have suspended their cooperation with Swaziland. In this desperate situation, Swaziland relies on South Africa but negotiations over a loan of USD 285 million are currently not making much progress. In order to meet its budgetary crisis, Swaziland's rulers will eventually have to cut wages in the public sector, which account for 45 per cent of public spending. Such a step could provoke protests organised by trade unions (Economist Intelligence Unit 2012).

An honorary consul argued in a discussion with me in March 2010 that the economic development of Swaziland reflected that of South Africa (pers. comm., 18 March 2010). He was very sceptical regarding Swaziland's economic prospects because he expected South Africa's economy and especially its currency to enter a deep crisis after the FIFA World Cup of that year. These negative developments would then cause severe problems in Swaziland. There was no recession in South Africa after the World Cup, but his arguments indicate how closely the economic fate of Swaziland is linked to that of South Africa. Data from *Who Owns Whom* (2012) confirms that the most important sectors of the Swazi economy are strongly affected by South African investment: farming and retail in particular but also construction and transportation. Apart from that, the honorary consul underlined the fact that transnational companies that operate or want to operate in Swaziland usually manage their business from headquarters in Johannesburg, being established where the market is. Major investment projects in Swaziland – for example Coca Cola's involvement in the sugar industry – are only realised because of nearby South African consumers. Economic ties with Swaziland's other neighbouring country, Mozambique, are limited to tourism and transport. In the course of reviving the Maputo Development Corridor, railway lines and roads from Swaziland to the port of Maputo are also being repaired.

Tanzania

Tanzania possesses some untapped natural resources. It may benefit from its location between its landlocked western neighbours and the Indian Ocean. Yet, a poor energy and transport infrastructure has limited Tanzania's economic success until now. The fiscal deficit of 6.2 per cent indicates that the government lacks the necessary means to sufficiently upgrade the national infrastructure. Even though exports of hydrocarbons and uranium are about to begin, they will probably only cause a slight decline in the current account deficit down to 11.0 per cent of gross domestic product (Economist Intelligence Unit 2012). These problems make it unlikely that Tanzania will in future integrate closer with Southern Africa, which would require massive investment in its transport infrastructure in order to overcome the significant physical barrier posed by the East African Rift Valley.

Nonetheless, South Africa is still considered economically important by the Tanzanian government. According to a senior Tanzanian diplomat, private firms from South Africa 'are invading' Tanzania – in particular banks, breweries and tourism companies (pers. comm., 3 February 2011). He said that the present economic dominance of South Africa resulted from the development gap between South Africa and the region. It prevented 'real competition'. Indeed, various sectors of the Tanzanian economy are affected by South African investment, ranging from farming, fishing and mining to various business services like mobile telecommunications and retail. Data provided by *Who Owns Whom* (2012) suggests that Tanzania is much more relevant for South African investment than neighbouring Malawi is. Given the predominance of South African companies,

Kenyans colloquially refer to Tanzania as 'Little Jo'burg'. Being optimistic, the diplomat I interviewed was convinced that Tanzanians will learn from South Africans and, hence, become able to develop their country themselves. He furthermore linked the future economic perspectives of his country to regional integration, which he saw as being driven by South Africa.

Adding another aspect, my interviewee argued that SADC mattered because it gave its member states a greater voice vis-à-vis the Global North and the two Asian giants. Concerning security affairs, he acknowledged that regional leadership has shifted to South Africa since 1994 and referred to South Africa's role in setting up regional institutions for jurisdiction and crisis response. At the same time, he pointed out that Britain is one of Tanzania's top trading partners. So is Kenya, which exports goods of British origin to Tanzania. China – which is providing loans for upgrading the Tanzania–Zambia Railway and the airport of Zanzibar (Hirschler and Hofmeister 2011) – and India are becoming more and more important. China is already today Tanzania's major trading partner. With regard to regional relations, my interviewee reasoned that his state – in being located at the periphery of Southern Africa – was less influenced by South Africa than other SADC countries are. He stressed that Tanzania also belongs to the EAC. Its influence reaches northwards to Somalia and South Sudan, at least from his viewpoint.

Zambia

In order to foster economic growth, SADC and South Africa are of particular relevance to Zambia. One reason for this is that the newly elected president, Michael Sata, has adopted anti-Chinese positions. A Chinese loan for the Tanzania–Zambia Railway had already been cancelled shortly before Sata became president (Erdmann 2011). Apart from that, there are structural economic reasons that tie Zambia to the regional power. A diplomat at the Zambian High Commission in Pretoria told me that companies from Europe and North America use South Africa as their springboard to East and Southern Africa, benefitting from privatisation and trade liberalisation there (pers. comm., 18 August 2010). Another Zambian diplomat, whom I met up with in Berlin, said that South Africa could stimulate economic development in the SADC region (pers. comm., 18 February 2010). He understood the criticism of South Africa's economic expansion into the continent, saying that the Zambian government should have made South African business invest in new factories and shops instead of allowing them to buy recently privatised Zambian factories and shops.

As these remarks suggest, South Africa's economic footprint in Zambia is not limited to construction, mining and transport – sectors that are implied by geographical conditions. Farming and retail are also affected. Financial services, insurance policies and software and computer services are provided by South African firms (*Who Owns Whom* 2012). They probably play an enabling role for investment in other sectors. Elaborating on South Africa's political role, the diplomat from Pretoria said that the regional power's influence had considerably limitations to it. One reason for this might be that South African politicians concentrate on domestic issues, he suggested. Apart from that, South Africa has proven unable to handle its own problems, which were comparable to those of its neighbouring countries. The idea that South Africa spearheads Africa's development has consequently vanished he said. His colleague from Berlin pointed out that South Africa is the youngest democracy in the region, which meant to him that it lacks political experience. Thus, South Africa 'is not the most qualified country' to lead the region. However, it could be politically effective by invigorating SADC and acting within its framework.

Zimbabwe

Zimbabwe is currently the most unstable state in Southern Africa. The coalition government formed by the ZANU PF and the Movement for Democratic Change in 2008 was only an interim solution. The elections of 2013 can hardly be considered to have been free and fair. The hardliners of the ZANU PF and the Zimbabwean military are not willing to relinquish power to anyone. As a mediator, South Africa plays a key role for its neighbouring state. The reason for this is that any further destabilisation in Zimbabwe will have a strong and negative impact on South Africa, as explained above. A Zimbabwean diplomat accordingly acknowledged that some member states of SADC hold for Zimbabwe an outstanding relevance in individual policy areas (pers. comm., 17 February 2010). In economic affairs, South Africa plays such a special role he said. He rejected that South Africa is particularly relevant in security affairs though, and argued instead that South Africa's military dominance 'remains to be proven'. Comparing South Africa and Zimbabwe, the diplomat said that South Africa possessed more assets of national power. Yet, it could not realise this power potential as effectively as Zimbabwe can, which benefited from its positive reputation dating back to the struggle against the apartheid regime.

My interviewee moreover criticised the regional expansion of South African businesses because it did not translate into prosperity for Zimbabwe itself. The regional dominance of South African companies was, rather, having a negative impact on his country – 'we lose because of South Africa'. From his point of view, the South African firms doing business in the region are often only conduits for companies from overseas. He recognised that Zimbabwe's economy depends upon South Africa as a transit country, but pointed out that Lobito and Walvis Bay will become alternatives as soon as appropriate railway links are built.

Beyond the regional level, Zimbabwe has been able to diversify its foreign economic relations by turning to the Far East, especially China, for investment and loans (Economist Intelligence Unit 2012). In the course of its 'Look East' strategy, visits by Chinese delegations to Harare have become frequent and bilateral economic agreements numerous. Iran and Russia are other envisaged partners of the Mugabe government. The Movement for Democratic Change is, contrariwise, rather close to the West (Kamete 2010, 2011). Because of political instability, Western sanctions and calls for further economic indigenisation, Zimbabwe continues to suffer from economic decline.

The indigenisation law – passed by parliament in 2007 but widely ignored until today – requires that 51 per cent of the shares of every firm operating in Zimbabwe be held by Zimbabweans, in practice meaning by black citizens. The indigenisation law scares off potential investors. It is highly relevant for South African businesses. Negotiations between the Mugabe government and the largest foreign investor, the South African giant Impala Platinum, stalled after the South Africans demanded to be paid at market prices for the 31 per cent of their shares that the Zimbabwean government sought to acquire. South African banks are another prime target for indigenisation, but they would also demand to be compensated at market prices – despite knowing that Zimbabwe does not possess sufficient financial capacities for that. In addition to banking and mining, South African companies have invested in chemicals, retail, tourism and transport (*Who Owns Whom* 2012). If Zimbabwe became safe again for foreign investors, much of the USD 20 billion that the country's mining facilities and related infrastructure supposedly need for their regeneration would come from South Africa, experts speculate (Economist Intelligence Unit 2012).

The Comoros, the Seychelles, Mauritius and Madagascar

Because of the recent South African-brokered introduction of a federal system to the Comoros, the political situation there has been consolidated – making foreign investment and tourism now likely to increase. Still, further support from the International Monetary Fund is additionally needed to stabilise the island state, which is suffering as a result of rising global food prices. Due to reduced aid from Europe, the current account deficit stands at 11.3 per cent of gross domestic product (Economist Intelligence Unit 2012). In other words, South Africa has played an important political role for the Comoros as a conflict mediator but global markets and international donors matter in economic and financial affairs.

For the Seychelles, Europe is equally important. Its ongoing economic crisis has led to the economic growth rate declining considerably. Less tourism from Britain, France and Italy has been offset by new tourists coming from the Far East, Russia and Switzerland though. China and India are emerging as new creditors. Seychellois emigration is directed more towards Australia, Britain and Canada than it is towards South Africa. Trade between the Seychelles and South Africa is growing rapidly. Yet, from the viewpoint of an honorary consul, a closer association with the EU makes more sense than integration in the SADC region does (pers. comm., 7 January 2010). The fight against pirates in the territorial waters of the Seychelles is mostly carried out by European navies. The honorary consul underlined the fact that the Seychelles interacts with various major powers because of the strategic location that the islands hold in the Indian Ocean. Not only the US but also China and India are interested in them as sites for transhipments and as a host country for air and naval bases. The Seychelles is an active member of the Indian Ocean Commission. According to the honorary consul, South Africa does not, contrariwise, play a politically important role for the Seychelles. The island state even ended its membership in SADC temporarily because of excessively high contributions and the organisational burden coming with common declarations and protocols.

Mauritius is much less dependent upon Europe than the Comoros and the Seychelles are, but is also highly integrated into global economic processes – most importantly those of banking and tourism. The Mauritian government seeks to foster economic ties with emerging economies, in particular China and India, which are the most important emerging economies for Mauritius according to a Mauritian diplomat (pers. comm., 19 February 2010). If this strategy succeeds, Mauritius will boost its role as a hinge between East and Southern Africa on the one side and China and India on the other. China and India have invested massively in Mauritius's financial sector, also in order to use the island as a bridge to Africa. Mauritius role as an intercontinental hinge is, according to my interviewee, based on its history of immigration from Africa, China and India. A recently set up Chinese free trade zone in Port Louis and the Indian-owned electronic derivatives exchange of Mauritius demonstrate the growing role of the two Asian giants (Treydte 2011).

In the first quarter of the year 2012, South Africa replaced France as Mauritius's top source of foreign investment (Economist Intelligence Unit 2012). Adding a political dimension to its role as an economic hinge, Mauritius is not only a member of SADC but also belongs to the Indian Ocean Commission and the Southern Asian Association for Regional Cooperation. Mauritius and its closest neighbour, Madagascar, are despite their geographical proximity economically and politically worlds apart. In the latter, the Rajoelina government still rejects the return of ousted president Marc Ravalomanana. It has lost control over most parts of the country, although there is no rebellion. Some security experts worry that Madagascar may become a failed state (Researchers at the Institute of Security Studies, pers. comm., 19 October 2011) – an assessment hardened by the mutiny of some Madagascan soldiers in July 2012. Economic growth was almost nonexistent in 2011. The projected current account deficit is high: 23.0 per cent in 2012, 16.7 per cent in 2013. The government hence faces severe budget constraints and the World Bank consequently is expecting a dramatic increase in poverty (Economist Intelligence Unit 2012).

Although one might think that Madagascar considers regional cooperation a means to deal with at least some of these challenges, a diplomat at the embassy of Madagascar in Pretoria stressed that her country's economic and political links to France are much closer than those to South Africa are (pers. comm., 26 August 2010). The Africa Growth and Opportunity Act appears to be the central pillar of her government's hope for economic consolidation. On a regional scale, Mauritius matters more than South Africa because of the former's investment in Madagascar's clothing and textile sector, and because Madagascar exports dairy products, meat and vegetables to it. Economic impulses from South Africa, which were a key motivation for Madagascar to join SADC in 2005, have not materialised. Still, South Africa is politically important for Madagascar. Another Madagascan diplomat told me that South Africa guarantees democracy and security in the SADC region (pers. comm., 21 February 2010). She referred to South Africa's role in Burundi, the Comoros, the DR Congo and Zimbabwe but did not mention South African mediation in Madagascar.

6.4 Overview and QCA

South Africa is closely economically linked to many other African countries. Starting with the impressive expansion of South African businesses into (Southern) Africa, I elaborated on the structural compatibility of the regional economies. This geographical condition has to be seen as interacting with nongeographical factors. Most importantly, the South African government pursues policies that help South African companies to gain access to regional markets, for example by pushing through economic liberalisation policies. There appears to be a pattern to the regional expansion of South African businesses: some assume the role of pioneers by constructing transport infrastructure, upgrading the local energy supply sector and providing banking and telecommunication services. These pioneers create the local business environment that other firms need in order to operate successfully.

Given the massive expansion of South African businesses into Southern Africa and beyond, South Africa's economic dominance and its pursuit of a seemingly neoliberal approach, critics argue that the regional power plays an imperialist or subimperialist role in (Southern) Africa, opening the (sub)continent up for capitalist exploitation. Others highlight the economic dynamics caused by South African–African economic interaction, and the benefits thereof for the countries that are closely tied to South Africa in economic terms. In order to delineate South Africa's economic impact on Africa, taking quantitative data on the imports and exports of African countries is the most feasible indicator. It reveals that Botswana, the DR Congo, Malawi, Namibia, Swaziland, Zambia and Zimbabwe are highly dependent upon South Africa, which accounts for a major share of the imports and/ or exports of these countries. Botswana, Namibia and Swaziland are extreme cases in this regard. Lesotho, with its globalised clothing and textile industry, constitutes a special case. Angola, Kenya, Tanzania, Uganda and the four island states form the periphery of South Africa's sphere of economic influence – Africa's economic powerhouse is an important but by far not the most important trading partner for them. Beyond this sphere of influence, South Africa is not a key trading partner for any of the other African countries.

Politically, the regime change of 1994 marked the turning point in South Africa's African agenda. Under the ANC, Southern Africa has become the primary arena for cooperative foreign policy – the premise of which has shifted from idealism under Mandela to the pursuit of national interests under Mbeki and

Zuma. In this context, SACU and SADC – two intergovernmental organisations that foster regional economic cooperation and indicate the scope of South Africa's influence as a regional power – are critically important. South Africa practically controls the customs policies of the SACU members and the monetary policy within the CMA (consisting of Lesotho, Namibia, South Africa and Swaziland). At the same time, South Africa compensates its fellow SACU members for the negative effects of market-oriented integration that they experience by contributing disproportionately to the common revenue pool and by granting protection to their nascent industries. SADC has, on account of its free trade agenda, opened up lucrative markets to South African firms. My interviews with various diplomats indicate that most governments in East and Southern Africa consider SADC to be essential for their economic development and regional security. However, it appears that integration within the framework of SADC has come to a dead end. SADC is not likely to evolve beyond a free trade area. South Africa can rather be expected to further promote the Tripartite Free Trade Area, because wider regional integration meets its economic needs. Deeper regional integration does not.

Beyond this regional focus in South Africa's foreign policy, three outstanding cases of South African regional security policy reveal the relevance therein of geographical factors. The driver of the 1998 intervention in Lesotho was the Katse Dam, which is part of the LHWP. It provides much-needed water to South Africa. The existence of the dam reflects locational, climatological and geomorphological factors. The dam itself is a manmade material structure in geographical space. South Africa's commitment to the Great Lakes region since the Mbeki era has been partly due to the economic opportunities that result from the local geology. One may also argue that stabilising the Great Lakes regions is a precondition for making the DR Congo – with its tremendous potential for hydropower generation – a supplier of electricity to South Africa. South Africa has opted for quiet diplomacy vis-à-vis Zimbabwe because its location means that instability there affects South Africa directly. Major regional transmission lines and the North–South Corridor run through Zimbabwe. Zimbabweans emigrate primarily to South Africa. Harsh criticism of the Mugabe government was and is likely to further destabilise Zimbabwe, which would threaten the considerable investments made by South African firms there.

I divide the data for the QCA gathered in this chapter into two components. Economic ties are indicated by import and export figures from Table 6.1. Kenya and Uganda are left out of the QCA because they are, at best, peripheral to South Africa's economic sphere of influence. Political links are not only measured by membership in SACU and SADC; I also take into consideration the relevance of South Africa in the chosen political strategies of the regional states, following my interviews with diplomats and the additional information presented in Chapter 6.3. These strategies are strongly influenced by current economic developments. Whilst the values for de facto existing economic ties between South Africa and the regional states derive directly from Table 6.1, the values I ascribe for political links need some additional explanation:

Table 6.2 Data for the QCA, also including economic and political outcomes

Case	Conditions						Outcome	
	Location	Physical geography			Transport	Economy	Trade	Politics
		Climate	Minerals	Movement				
Angola	0	1	1	1	0	1	0	0
Botswana	1	0	1	1	1	1	1	1
Comoros	0	–	0	0	0	0	0	0
DR Congo (except for Katanga Province)	0	1	0	0	0	0	1	1
DR Congo (Katanga Province alone)	0	1	1	1	1	1	1	1
Lesotho	1	1	0	1	1	1	0	1
Madagascar	0	–	0	0	0	0	0	0
Malawi	0	1	0	0	0	1	1	0
Mauritius	0	–	0	0	0	0	0	1
Mozambique (except for Maputo)	0	1	1	0	0	1	1	1
Mozambique (Maputo area alone)	1	0	0	1	1	1	1	1
Namibia	1	0	1	1	1	1	1	1
Seychelles	0	–	0	0	0	0	0	0
Swaziland	1	1	1	1	1	1	1	1
Tanzania	0	0	1	0	0	1	0	1
Zambia	0	1	1	1	1	1	1	1
Zimbabwe	1	1	1	1	1	1	1	1

Source: Author's own compilation.

Malawi and Tanzania are difficult to rate. My interviewees from Malawi stressed the relevance of SADC and South Africa to their country, but the development projects they described constitute centrifugal forces in the Malawian–South African relationship. I hence rate Malawi as 0. Tanzania is rated 1 because my interview revealed a clear will to foster ties with Southern Africa and South Africa. As noted, it is doubtful whether Tanzania will be able to realise these strategies, but such considerations are irrelevant for the rating. Moreover, Tanzania is not, unlike Malawi, currently pursuing any projects that may push it away from the regional power. In the case of Zimbabwe, my interview revealed much resentment being harboured towards South Africa. The diplomat I talked to recognised South Africa's outstanding role in regional economic affairs though. His comments do not indicate that South Africa is of low relevance to Zimbabwe's political strategies. Angola is different in this regard, because my interview with an honorary consul and additional data suggest that the region – including the regional power – is of low relevance to Angola's political strategies. For the politics of all other continental members of SADC, South Africa is outstandingly relevant. There do not appear to be major differences between the entire DR Congo and Katanga Province or between Mozambique as a whole and the Maputo area in this regard.

The four island countries are, once again, different. South Africa plays an important role as a political mediator in the Comoros and in Madagascar. Their economic strategies, however, aim at development through globalisation, not through regional integration. For Mauritius, South Africa does play a strategically relevant role because the island serves as a hinge between East and Southern Africa on the one side and Asia's two major emerging economies on the other. The importance of this role is boosted by the chosen policy strategies of the Mauritian government. As a consequence, the economic interaction of Mauritius and South Africa is not comparable to that of South Africa and its continental neighbours. Mauritius's advanced banking sector matters most, which is reflected by data provided by *Who Owns Whom* (2012). I thus rate the Comoros, Madagascar and the Seychelles 0 but Mauritius 1.

6.5 Interpretation of the QCA Data

The key advantage of QCA is that it enables me to simplify the numerous and complex paths that lead from initial causes or conditions to the outcome. I can reduce the complexity in the combination of location, physiogeographical factors, transport infrastructure and economic compatibility and thereby reveal which of these are necessary and/or sufficient for close economic and political relations between South Africa and its neighbouring countries. Making sense of those cases marked by close economic relations with South Africa requires the exclusion of the DR Congo beyond Katanga Province. This does not mean that this case has been wrongly classified. It rather suggests that Congolese–South African relations are of a different nature to Southern African–South African relations. Beyond Katanga Province, only favourable climatic conditions speak for close economic ties existing. The enormous potential for hydropower generation along the Congo River and its tributaries appears to compensate for the distance between the DR Congo and South Africa, natural barriers to movement, the absence of transport infrastructure and their questionable level of economic compatibility. Although Congolese–South African economic relations can, as just indicated, be explained from a geodeterminist perspective, their inclusion would distort a simplification of the QCA formula.

All remaining positive cases – meaning those that feature close economic relations with South Africa – are marked by economic compatibility with South Africa. Thus, economic compatibility should be considered a necessary condition. Intuitively, transport infrastructure appears to be the second-most important and probably also necessary condition, because it is difficult to imagine how trade could occur if means of transport were not sufficient. Concentrating on the cases that fulfil these two conditions, I eventually come to a simplified formula that indicates that economic compatibility, good transport connections and an ease of movement are, with a high degree of probability,[3] necessary conditions for a country having close economic relations with South Africa. The circumstances of the two remaining cases, Malawi and Mozambique beyond the Maputo area, do not allow a conclusive QCA formula to be generated. They suggest that climatic conditions favourable to hydropower stations and the abundance of lucrative mineral resources may account for close economic relations, even in the absence of good transport connections.

According to the formula shown by Figure 6.1, economic compatibility, good transport connections and an ease of movement are not sufficient conditions. They have to be combined with a favourable location or with climatic features and mineral assets that favour trade. The absence of favourable climatic conditions, which also appears in the final formula, does not make sense as a condition for close economic relations. Refining the final formula, the data from Table 6.2 implies that economic compatibility, good transport connections and an ease of movement are already sufficient, because whenever these three conditions are met the outcome occurs. Comparing the final formula and Table 6.2 moreover reveals that Lesotho constitutes a case hard to capture through the lens of Realist Geopolitics. As explained in Chapter 6.3, the mountain kingdom depends upon overseas markets for the sustenance of its clothing and textile industry. Nongeographical factors are the reason for these particular trade relations. Figure 6.1 shows the single steps of the simplification of the QCA formula.

---

3 Strictly speaking, the formula shown in Figure 6.1 does not mean that economic compatibility, good transport connections and an ease of movement are necessary conditions, because Table 6.2 does not comprise empirical cases for every theoretically possible combination and includes Lesotho despite it being a contradictory row.

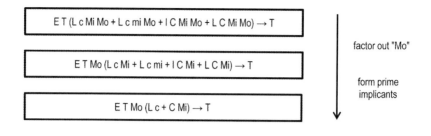

E T (L c Mi Mo + L c mi Mo + I C Mi Mo + L C Mi Mo) → T

E T Mo (L c Mi + L c mi + I C Mi + L C Mi) → T

E T Mo (L c + C Mi) → T

factor out "Mo"

form prime
implicants

Abbreviations

E = Economy   C = Climate   T = Close trade relations
T = Transport   Mi = Minerals
L = Location   Mo = Movement

Figure 6.1   Simplifying the QCA formula for close trade relations
Source: Author's own draft.

After having excluded the DR Congo beyond Katanga Province, Malawi and Mozambique beyond the Maputo area, there remain seven cases that do reach the outcome. The locational path explains three cases (Botswana, the Maputo area and Namibia); two more (Swaziland and Zimbabwe) if one omits the counterintuitive condition of unfavourable climatic features. Its coverage is 42.9 and 71.2 per cent respectively. The climate-plus-geology path explains four cases (Katanga Province, Swaziland, Zambia and Zimbabwe), or 57.1 per cent. The entire formula reaches a coverage of 100 per cent. Bringing back in the excluded cases, the coverage of the individual paths declines to 30, 50 and 40 per cent respectively. The coverage of the entire formula drops to 70 per cent. Moreover, there is also the issue of Lesotho, which features all conditions of the first path but does not maintain close economic relations with South Africa – at least according to the indicators used here. Therefore, the consistency of the first path is 83.3 per cent. It explains five cases but occurs six times. The consistency of the second path is 100 per cent. In sum, the percentages for consistency suggest that my approach – that is, Realist Geopolitics – is highly accurate. The percentages for the coverage indicate that the two paths are both relevant and, more importantly, that Realist Geopolitics can explain a lot – though not everything.

Incorporating the crude formula of the states that maintain close political relations with South Africa into a meaningful and simple formula requires the exclusion of four cases. Mauritius appears to be beyond the explanatory capacities of Realist Geopolitics. As mentioned above, the island state is linked to South Africa because it serves as a hinge between East and Southern Africa on the one side and China and India on the other. The political relevance ascribed by the Mauritian government to South Africa results from its pursued objectives

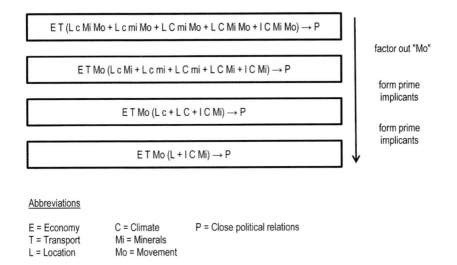

Figure 6.2   Simplifying the QCA formula for close political relations
Source: Author's own draft.

of strengthening Mauritius as a business hub and easing financial transactions. The geographical factors addressed in this study, apparently, do not matter in this particular context. With regard to the DR Congo and Mozambique, meanwhile, it is somewhat plausible to argue that the close political relations of these two states with South Africa are due specifically to the existence of Katanga Province and the Maputo area. Hence, I only take into consideration the combinations of conditions that apply to these two cases. One may also exclude the DR Congo beyond Katanga Province for the reasons stated above. The exclusion of Tanzania is more difficult to justify, but nevertheless extremely helpful for the mathematical simplification of the QCA formula. The only more or less plausible argument that comes to my mind is that my interview, which constitutes the basis of the rating of South African–Tanzanian political relations as 1, is misleading.

After having excluded these four cases, the crude formula can be simplified. Given that I have considered economic aspects an essential component of political strategies, it makes sense to extract economic compatibility and good transport connections before reducing the remaining prime implicants following Boolean algebra. Doing so eventually leads me to a final formula that reveals that economic compatibility, good transport conditions and an ease of movement are, most likely, necessary conditions for these close political relations. They must occur together with locational or climatic and geological advantages if they are to form a sufficient basis for close political relations. The absence of locational advantages as a condition for close political relations does not make sense. Data from Table 6.2 indicates that economic compatibility, good transport conditions and an ease of movement are already sufficient for the outcome. Figure 6.2 shows the single steps of the simplification of the QCA formula.

Excluding the four aforementioned cases, the locational path explains six out of eight cases (Botswana, Lesotho, the Maputo area, Namibia, Swaziland and Zimbabwe). It reaches a coverage of 75 per cent. The climate-plus-geology path explains two cases (Swaziland and Zimbabwe); two more (Katanga Province and Zambia) if one disregards the counterintuitive condition of disadvantageous location. This equals a coverage of 25 and 50 per cent respectively. Bringing the previously excluded cases back in, the coverage drops to 50, 16.7 and 33.3 per cent respectively. The complete formula covers 66.7 per cent of all cases that reach the outcome. The consistency of both paths is 100 per cent, which supports the previously drawn conclusion that hypotheses based on Realist Geopolitics are highly accurate and fairly relevant.

Chapter 7
Conclusion

Summary of the Findings on Location and Physical Geography

Oceans delimit Southern Africa as the natural sphere of influence of the regional power South Africa to the east, south and west. The East African Rift Valley forms the northeastern borderline. The northern border of Southern Africa should rather be understood as a border zone or a boundary; the valleys of the Limpopo and Zambezi Rivers are marked by escarpments. The Cunene River separates Angola from Namibia. In Angola, small valleys increase in frequency and vegetation becomes denser because of climatic conditions, hampering transport. These obstacles to human movement do not, however, include changes in elevation like the Great Escarpment does. The Lunda Uplands can be crossed without much effort. They are not a climatic boundary either; tropical influences outreach them. Yet, as soon as one reaches the river system of the Congo Basin, human movement becomes almost impossible. The northern boundary of Southern Africa hence comprises the Angolan–Congolese border region, proceeds through Katanga Province in the DR Congo and connects up with the East African Rift Valley at the Great Lakes.

Apart from that, the Great Escarpment and the characteristic features of the coastline, which hamper the construction of ports, significantly limit regional access to the global markets. South African–Southern African interaction is, contrariwise, eased by the interior plateaux because they do not pose an obstacle to movement. Physical geography thus suggests close ties existing between the countries located in continental Southern Africa but poor links with those overseas, most importantly regarding trade. Since South Africa possesses the best conditions for linking the region to the world's oceans, not only its direct neighbours but all continental SADC members can be expected to be tied to South Africa and its harbours, the latter being a kind of bottleneck between the region and its different overseas trading partners.

A striking fact about the region just described is that its countries show a high degree of complementarity in terms of agricultural potential, water supply, raw minerals and energy-related resources. This accounts, following Hartshorne's concept, for the contiguity of the continental SADC region. What is more, South Africa's outstanding position as the regional power derives, at least partly, from physical geography. The abundance and variety of mineral resources in South Africa explain the rise of its minerals–energy complex, which has expanded into neighbouring countries and accounts for South Africa's economic predominance not only in Southern Africa but throughout the entire continent (Scholvin 2011).

Physical geography also explains why South Africa depends upon its neighbouring countries. The regional powerhouse consumes 80 per cent of the water in Southern Africa but only possesses 10 per cent of that resource and thus has to look for it beyond its own borders. This dependence will continue to increase in the course of this century, not least because of ongoing climate change.

Summary of the Findings on Transport and Socioeconomic Aspects

Concerning the impact that transport infrastructure and socioeconomic factors should be expected to have on South Africa's relations with the other countries of Southern Africa, three groups of cases can be identified:

- Botswana, Namibia, Zambia and Zimbabwe are marked by good transport infrastructure connections with South Africa. Transport corridors bind these countries to South Africa and its harbours. Lesotho and Swaziland are integrated into South Africa's domestic transport infrastructure simply because of their location and size. The transport links of the DR Congo and Mozambique to South Africa are of a different nature: only the Maputo area and Katanga Province are well connected to South Africa. Almost all countries in this group are characterised by economic structures that suggest close interaction with South Africa, especially in agriculture, energy and mining. Lesotho's clothing and textile industry, which is bound to the market of the US, constitutes a unique exception. Labourers and refugees who migrate from the just mentioned countries to South Africa are another centripetal force, although migration has declined significantly since the 1980s.
- Conditions for interaction with South Africa are less favourable for the Indian Ocean island states and for the DR Congo beyond Katanga Province. In the DR Congo, the rainforest of the Congo Basin virtually swallows up the transport infrastructure. Existing and envisaged spatial development initiatives tie Katanga Province to Southern Africa and the Kivus to East Africa. Immediately accessible maritime transport links the Comoros, Madagascar, Mauritius and the Seychelles directly to their trading partners all over the world. South Africa is thus not a gateway to global markets for them, as it is for the continental members of SADC. What is more, my analysis did not reveal these island states to have any significant socioeconomic features that imply close links with South Africa. Their economies are strongly globalised, so is their out-migration. The DR Congo beyond Katanga Province appears to have no socioeconomic dimensions that imply close links to South Africa either.
- The economic geography of Angola, Mozambique and Tanzania suggests that huge potential exists for cooperation with South Africa, but the location of their resources – which are found offshore – speaks against such

ties. Malawi relies on energy imports from South Africa. Not physical but economic geography – meaning South Africa's high level of development – explains this dependence. If the current development strategies of Malawi are successfully executed, these incentives for close relations with South Africa will cease to exist. Regarding transport infrastructure, none of the countries of this group are well connected to the regional power, except for Mozambique's Maputo area. The poor transport infrastructure existing between Malawi, Mozambique, Tanzania and South Africa reflects physical geography – the East African Rift Valley and the Zambezi River to be precise. In the case of Angola, there are no significant physical barriers that separate it from South Africa. For this reason, history and not geography matters for Angolan–South African relations.

Summary of the Findings on the Economic and Political Reality of South African–African Relations

Quantitative data on the imports and exports of African states is the most feasible indicator for the de facto economic relations of these states with South Africa. It suggests that Botswana, the DR Congo, Malawi, Namibia, Swaziland, Zambia and Zimbabwe are highly dependent upon the regional power. Botswana, Namibia and Swaziland are all extreme cases in this regard. Lesotho, with its globalised clothing and textile industry, constitutes as noted a special case. Angola, Kenya, Tanzania, Uganda and the four island states form the periphery of South Africa's sphere of economic influence. Africa's economic powerhouse is an important but by far not the most important trading partner for all eight of these countries. The broader political relevance of South Africa, meanwhile, is indicated by the membership of its neighbouring countries in SACU and SADC, as well as by their chosen political strategies.

Applying QCA to economic and political relations in the SADC region verifies the first two of the three hypotheses proposed and then tested in this book: location, physical geography and material structures in geographical space that cannot be altered in the short run set a frame that guides economics and politics. Patterns behind the expansion of South Africa – that is, the directions in which it focuses its crossborder influence – result from these factors. Hence, the application of QCA confirms that Realist Geopolitics generates highly accurate and fairly relevant explanations. Realist Geopolitics as a theory has in almost no instances been proven irrelevant by the cases examined here. Its coverage is significant, but also leaves space for additional nongeographical explanations. Angola, Lesotho and Mauritius partly contradict what Realist Geopolitics suggests. Yet, at least the case of Mauritius reveals something crucial about QCA: the absence of the conditions that cause a certain outcome does not necessarily mean that the outcome does not occur (Wagemann and Schneider 2007). The relations of Angola and Lesotho with South Africa can only be explained by nongeographical factors. The DR Congo,

Malawi, Mozambique and Tanzania cause some problems for the mathematical simplification of the QCA formula. The cases themselves can, however, be explained within the framework of Realist Geopolitics.

Furthermore, the relevance of geographical factors is revealed by regional security policy. First, the reason for South Africa's intervention in Lesotho in 1998 was the Katse Dam, which provides water to its neighbour's economic heartland. The existence of the dam reflects locational, climatological and geomorphological factors; the dam itself is a manmade material structure in geographical space. Second, South Africa's commitment to the Great Lakes region during the Mbeki era was partly due to the economic opportunities that result from the local geology there. One may also argue that stabilising the Great Lakes region was and is considered a necessary precondition to making the DR Congo – with its tremendous potential for hydropower generation – a supplier of electricity to South Africa. Third, South Africa has opted for quiet diplomacy vis-à-vis Zimbabwe, because the latter's location means that any instability there directly affects South Africa; this policy choice has also been made because major regional electricity transmission lines as well as the North–South Corridor run through Zimbabwe. Harsh criticism of the Mugabe government was and is likely to further destabilise the country, which would threaten the considerable investments made by South African firms in Zimbabwe.

Yet, geography does not explain everything. In the preceding chapters, I have shown how geographical and nongeographical conditions interact with each other. The expansion of South African businesses into Southern Africa, for example, is boosted by the helpful institutional frame that was set up by the South African government through NEPAD so that access could be gained to regional markets. More generally, the regime change of 1994 marks the turning point in South Africa's regional agenda. Under the ANC, Southern Africa has become the main arena for cooperative foreign policy, with SACU and SADC being important fora for the realisation of South African interests. This has occurred even though the country's foreign policy paradigms appear to have shifted to cooperation with other emerging powers – in particular Brazil, China and India – under the Zuma presidency. My interviews with various diplomats accordingly indicate that most governments in the SADC region currently consider these two regional organisations and having good relations with South Africa as being essential for their own economic development and regional security.

Summary of the Findings on Key Projects of Regional Integration

By applying Process Tracing to three domains of regional cooperation – water, electricity and transport – I have shown that considering geographical conditions – specifically in their interplay with nongeographical ones – is necessary if some of the phenomena essential for the existence of South African regional powerhood are to be fully understood:

- Several states in the SADC region cooperate on water because aridity limits the water resources of the economically most diversified countries of the region, including of South Africa itself. Various watercourses in the region are shared by several states anyway. The LHWP exemplifies how geography provides essential conditions for regional cooperation over water: Lesotho is close to South African consumers in Gauteng and the Free State, there is a compatibility of supply and demand because Lesotho receives a significant level of rainfall and its geomorphology is suitable for building dams and artificial lakes.

- Similarly, there would be no cooperation over electricity in the SADC region if geography did not provide opportunities for that. South African energy giant Eskom can presently supply much-needed electricity to the region because of South Africa's abundant coal reserves and its high level of economic development. In future, Eskom is likely to import electricity from South Africa's neighbouring countries on account of their considerable potential for hydropower generation. Coal and natural gas will be either imported for processing in South Africa or burnt close to mining sites in order to produce electricity for the South African market.

- The Congo Basin and the East African Rift Valley constitute the natural boundaries of a region integrated by South Africa as the key transport node. On the interior plateaux south of these boundaries, geomorphology provides almost ideal conditions for transport by rail and road. The Great Escarpment and coastal geomorphology significantly limit the number of places suited to being used as harbours. Transport corridors interlink South Africa relatively well with most regional countries. Corridors that bypass the regional power are of poor quality; their future prospects are also limited. South Africa's ports are the largest and most efficient in the region. The regional power, and especially the global hub of Johannesburg, provides the best business environment in (Southern) Africa and a lucrative domestic market. The manmade geography that is being built via numerous spatial development initiatives will further boost the nodal role of South Africa.

Yet, these processes cannot be explained by geographical factors alone. As noted, one has to take into consideration the cooperative regional relations that have marked Southern African since 1994, as well as the clear will of the ANC government to engage in close economic interaction with the regional states. Moreover, geographical conditions appear to barely be able to explain the precise shape that policies take on the ground. Present-day regional cooperation on spatial development initiatives and the prior so-called 'transport diplomacy' of the apartheid regime came about in the same geographical setting; they are thus so different in nature rather because of the nongeographical – that is, historical and political – contexts that they were conceived in.

Empirical Considerations

Beyond the aforementioned findings on regional relations, projects of regional integration and the impact of geographical factors on both, this study has brought to light three aspects of South Africa's foreign relations that merit special consideration:

- Even though South Africa is labelled a 'strategic partner' of some Western states,[1] there has nevertheless been much friction between the emerging power and the West during the last decade. This calls into question whether South Africa and the West still share key norms, in particular concerning democratisation and human rights (Erdmann 2009). The height of quiet diplomacy vis-à-vis Zimbabwe probably marked also the low point of the rapport between South Africa and the West. The recent suspension of the SADC Tribunal and its subsequent limitation to resolving interstate disputes indicates that the size of common normative ground continues to be on the wane. In this context, Realist Geopolitics reveals that South African–Western disagreements are not, however, necessarily due to different norms. One may instead convincingly argue that South Africa has pursued a policy of quiet diplomacy vis-à-vis Robert Mugabe and the ZANU PF because of geographical circumstances. South African companies have invested heavily in Zimbabwe. As noted, the North–South Corridor – the region's transport backbone – and major electricity transmission lines run through the country. Zimbabwean migrants head primarily to South Africa. This means that any further destabilisation of Zimbabwe would affect South Africa directly. Whilst the distant West can safely indulge in human rights rhetoric and harsh criticism of the Mugabe government, South Africa would suffer massively if it took such an approach.
- The key importance of South Africa for its neighbouring countries is hard to refute. The regional power is the most important trading partner for Botswana, Malawi, Mozambique, Namibia, Swaziland, Zambia and Zimbabwe. As explained in Chapter 5, many regional states depend upon South African harbours. Overseas investments tend to be channelled through Cape Town and Johannesburg. Eskom's electricity sales enable many regional states to meet their own domestic demand. Yet, one may wonder how important the region is for the regional power. Basic issues of political stability aside, some recent developments suggest that SADC does not matter much to South Africa. South African banks, telecommunication providers and retailers have much more to gain in the relatively large and rapidly growing Kenyan and Nigerian markets. South Africa's major trading

---

1   It is specifically the German Federal Foreign Office and the US State Department that refer to South Africa in this way. The EU and South Africa, meanwhile, signed a strategic partnership agreement in 2007.

partners are China, the US, Germany and Japan. Politically, Brazil, Russia, India and China – as the BRIC grouping – now appear to be of greater interest to South Africa and its global aspirations than the stagnating SADC is (Researcher of the Ebert Foundation, Johannesburg, pers. comm., 12 August 2010). What my analysis has highlighted in this regard is that the SADC region does matters to South Africa. From a policy perspective, it should continue to play a primary role in South Africa's foreign policy because some of South Africa's most pressing needs – clean energy and water – can only be met through regional cooperation. By fostering its role as regional transport hub and gateway to the region, South Africa can create many jobs in the service industry – ranging from transport-related activities in the ports of KwaZulu-Natal and the Coega Industrial Development Zone to knowledge-based cooperative services in Cape Town and Johannesburg (Draper and Scholvin 2012).

- Realist Geopolitics helps to explain why regional integration in Southern Africa and beyond is currently not very extensive. A SADC customs union or common market will, most likely, not be realised in the near future. SACU will probably not expand either. This stagnation becomes understandable in looking at geographical conditions, because they reveal what matters to South Africa with regard to regional integration – namely access to energy-related resources and water in the SADC region, as well as investment opportunities for its mining and service industries both there and beyond. Regional integration is currently not achieving a greater depth because as things stand South Africa lacks incentives for pursuing that. The just-mentioned goals can be realised within the existing framework. Hence, there is not much more impetus to integration in the SADC region than that generated by trade flows. Neither a customs union nor a common market – the existence of which would call into question South Africa's current industrial policy and its selective protection of some branches of the manufacturing sector – is a necessity for the regional power itself.

Theoretical Considerations

No theory can explain everything. Realist Geopolitics only deals with the frame that geographical factors set for international relations. This frame indicates which strategies are feasible, in the sense that they can be carried out with a high probability of success ensuing. Realist Geopolitics will, therefore, lead to sound explanations of the past and accurate predictions of the future if decision makers act in a rational way, striving to achieve optimal results within the given geographical framework. My investigation has revealed that South Africa's regional relations are driven by geographical factors: if certain ones favour close links between South Africa and another regional state, there will be, in almost every case, close relations. My first two hypotheses are thus verified. The third hypothesis could not be tested because South Africa has only just begun to expand its influence beyond the limits suggested by geographical conditions such as the aforementioned East African Rift Valley. By combining both geographical and nongeographical factors, I have revealed that the former are an insufficient but necessary component of an unnecessary but sufficient cause of selected social phenomena. In other words, I have successfully applied the concept of INUS causality in order to show both that geography matters and how so.

However, the region I have analysed here appears most suited to Realist Geopolitics, meaning to moderate geodeterminist thinking. It is reasonable to argue that the level of economic development influences the relevance of geographical factors: preindustrial societies are at the mercy of nature, unable to alter the quality of soils and climatic conditions – factors which determine their agricultural productivity and, hence, their survival. Geography also influences industrialised societies because it determines the availability of minerals, and especially coal. Yet, industrialisation also brings about means to overcome a local shortage of necessary resources. Transport over long distances – by rail or steamship – supplies a poorly endowed area with whatever it needs to prosper. Postindustrial societies are even less dependent upon geography, because the rise of the tertiary sector has come along with a sharp decline in the relevance of material structures in geographical space other than those required for telecommunications: financial transactions are not impeded by mountain ranges or rivers. Many corporate and private financial services are, in fact, sold and then provided exclusively online.

It is not surprising that Realist Geopolitics explains much in a region where the transport of large quantities of mined products and the supply of water to the agricultural and industrial sectors play a crucial role. The means built by mankind to overcome physiogeographical barriers are, moreover, mostly cumulative – infrastructure from the industrial age can still be used today. Since the construction of modern infrastructure in Africa has been limited to only very few areas, the continent possesses less overall infrastructure than Europe and North America do. In addition to its infrastructural shortcomings, Africa is also behind in terms of technology. Automatic traffic management systems for urban motorways, high-speed trains that interlink major cities, process automation at airports and unmanned, fully automated container terminals are common in the developed world but rare in Africa. Hence, not only the aforementioned economic structures but also the state of local transport infrastructure and related technologies explain why the factors that matter to Realist Geopolitics play a more important role in Southern Africa than they probably do in some other parts of the world.

Topics for Further Research

Because of the aforementioned specific particularities of (Southern) Africa, a first way to advance Realist Geopolitics based on the findings of this study would be to apply it to other parts of the world. Highly-developed Europe and North

America appear to be difficult cases for that. Applying Realist Geopolitics to Central Asia and South America, however, promises to yield much insight. Central Asia is presently a political vacuum. Numerous established and emerging powers compete over natural gas and oil resources there, projecting their power through military bases, pipelines and proxy groups such as ethnic minorities and terrorist organisations (Scholvin 2009c). In South America, Brazil has assumed the role of a geographical node between the states of the Southern Cone. It is working to bind together all South American states through a shared transport infrastructure – the Initiative for the Integration of the Regional Infrastructure in South America, or IIRSA, to be precise. Distance and natural barriers explain why Brazil has close economic relations with the Southern Cone but remains a minor trading partner for the Andean countries (Scholvin and Malamud 2014).

Furthermore, a possible decline of the relevance of physiogeographical factors could be investigated for the continental SADC region. Several transport infrastructure projects now aim at overcoming the natural barriers there. The Tanzania–Zambia Railway is the most relevant case to keep an eye on in this regard. Geography suggests that Tanzania's main port at Dar es Salaam is at a disadvantage as a gateway to the global markets for Malawi, Zambia and Zimbabwe because the East African Rift Valley separates East Africa from Southern Africa. If Dar es Salaam becomes more than a gateway to the Great Lakes region, the relevance of physical geography as compared to transport infrastructure – that is, manmade geography – will have to be reassessed. Another interesting topic for Realist Geopolitics is the envisaged Tripartite Free Trade Area. Consisting of COMESA, the EAC and SADC, this might enable South Africa to expand its influence beyond the current major geographical barriers to the country's further continental reach. Geographical factors suggest that economic interaction in such a free trade zone stretching from the Cape to Cairo would be limited to investment and to the service sector. South African banks and telecommunication providers would be those most likely to benefit from its existence. From the viewpoint of Realist Geopolitics, an expansion of the EAC and not a merger of the EAC, and SADC appears likely to happen. Landlocked and oil-rich South Sudan can be expected to foster ties with the EAC and – provided the envisaged Lamu Corridor becomes a reality – to export oil to the energy-thirsty emerging economies of the Indian Ocean, including South Africa (Scholvin 2014b).

In addition to these issues related to the relevance of (physio)geographical factors, it would be worthwhile to examine those state-level decision-making processes that involve considerations of geographical factors – which I have shown matter in the context of Southern Africa for many such economic and political processes. Yet the causal chains herein, tracked with the help of Process Tracing, are analysed on the basis of the implicit assumption that decisions are – at least ultimately – rationally taken. Implicitly perceived rationality, poorly justified, is a fundamental problem of many theories that seek to explain how individual and collective human actors behave. In order to address this shortcoming, one may open the black box of decision making with the help of 'cognitive maps' (Scholvin

2015). These show how someone logically structures a specific issue, how he/she identifies obstacles as well as opportunities and how he/she links them to agendas, which then guide his/her action. Applying cognitive maps, one would be able to systematically generate knowledge not only about geographical conditions and their interplay with social conditions but also about how these conditions are transformed into subsequent courses of action.

As these proposed topics for further research imply, Realist Geopolitics can contribute much to understanding economic and political phenomena – including, as has been done here, the regional relations of emerging powers. Realist Geopolitics sheds light on those aspects that are neglected by other approaches and thus contributes to a broader, more complete picture of the functioning of the world 'out there'. Using Mackinder's own words, it is doubtful 'that a scientific analysis in human geography [...] can ever give you a complete explanation' (1916: 274). Nevertheless, Realist Geopolitics has been shown to be a special – a spatial – perspective that provides key insights that other approaches fail to uncover.

References

Adams, Martin, and John Howell. 2001. 'Redistributive Land Reform in Southern Africa'. *Natural Resource Perspectives* 64.1: 1–6.

Adelmann, Martin. 2003. *Regionale Kooperation im südlichen Afrika*. Freiburg: Arnold Bergstraesser Institut.

Adelmann, Martin. 2004. 'Quiet Diplomacy: The Reasons behind Mbeki's Zimbabwe Policy'. *Afrika Spektrum* 39.2: 249–76.

Agnew, John A. 1983. 'An Excess of National Exceptionalism: Towards a New Political Geography of American Foreign Policy'. *Political Geography Quarterly* 2.2: 151–66.

Agnew, John A., and Stuart Corbridge. 1995. *Mastering Space: Hegemony, Territory and International Political Economy*. London: Routledge.

Ahwireng-Obeng, Fred, and Patrick J. McGowan. 1998a. 'Partner or Hegemon?: South Africa in Africa I'. *Journal of Contemporary African Studies* 16.1: 5–38.

Ahwireng-Obeng, Fred, and Patrick J. McGowan. 1998b. 'Partner or Hegemon?: South Africa in Africa II'. *Journal of Contemporary African Studies* 16.2: 165–95.

Alden, Chris, and Mills Soko. 2005. 'South Africa's Economic Relations with Africa: Hegemony and its Discontents'. *Journal of Modern African Studies* 43.3: 367–92.

ANC. 2007. *52nd National Conference: Resolutions*. Polokwane: ANC.

Armijo, Leslie E. 2007. 'The BRICs Countries (Brazil, Russia, India, and China) as Analytical Category: Mirage or Insight?' *Asian Perspective* 31.4: 7–42.

Ashton, Peter. 2000. 'Southern African Water Conflicts: Are They Inevitable or Preventable?' In *Water Wars: Enduring Myth or Impending Reality*, edited by Hussein Solomon and Anthony Turton, 65–102. Pretoria: CiPS.

Ashton, Peter, and Anthony Turton. 2005. 'Transboundary Water Resource Management in Southern Africa: Opportunities, Challenges and Lessons Learned'. In *Water, Development and Cooperation: Comparative Perspectives: Euphrates-Tigris and Southern Africa*, edited by Lars Wirkus, 5–32, Bonn: BICC.

Atkins, Steve, and Alan Terry. 1998. 'The Changing Role of Sugar as a Vehicle for Economic Development within Southern Africa'. In *South Africa in Southern Africa: Reconfiguring the Region*, edited by David Simon, 129–45. Oxford: Currey.

Atuahene, Bernadette. 2011. 'South Africa's Land Reform Crisis: Eliminating the Legacy of Apartheid'. *Foreign Affairs* 90.4: 121–9.

Banda, Kelvin. 2005. 'Trade Performance Review 2005: Malawi'. Accessed 2 March 2012. http://www.sadctrade.org/files/TPR%20Malawi.pdf.

Banda, Moses, and Griffin Nyirongo. 1993. 'Zambia'. In *The Southern African Environment: Profiles of the SADC Countries*, edited by Sam Moyo, Phil O'Keefe and Michael Sill, 270–302. London: Earthscan.

Barber, James. 2005. 'The New South Africa's Foreign Policy: Principles and Practice'. *International Affairs* 81.5: 1079–96.

Barnett, Thomas P.M. 2003. 'The Pentagon's New Map'. Accessed 27 April 2009. http://www.thomaspmbarnett.com/published/pentagonsnewmap.htm.

Barnett, Thomas P.M. 2004. *The Pentagon's New Map: War and Peace in the Twenty-First Century*. New York: Berkeley.

Barnett, Thomas P.M. 2005. *Blueprint for Action: A Future Worth Creating*. New York: Berkeley.

Barrows, Harlan H. 1922. 'Geography as Human Ecology'. *Annals of the Association of American Geographers* 13.1: 1–16.

Basedau, Matthias, and Christian von Soest. 2011. 'Botswana'. In *Africa Yearbook: Politics, Economy and Society South of the Sahara in 2010*, edited by Andreas Mehler et al., 449–53. Leiden: Brill.

Benhin, James K. 2006. 'Climate Change and South African Agriculture'. *CEEPA Discussion Paper* 21.

Bennet, Mark. 2006. 'Lesotho's Export Textiles and Garment Industry'. In *The Future of the Textile and Clothing Industry in Sub-Saharan Africa*, edited by Herbert Jauch and Rudolf Traub-Merz, 165–77. Bonn: FES.

Berg-Schlosser, Dirk, et al. 2009. 'Qualitative Comparative Analysis (QCA) as an Approach'. In *Configurational Comparative Methods: Qualitative Comparative Analysis (QCA) and Related Methods*, edited by Benoît Rihoux and Charles C. Ragin, 1–18. Los Angeles: Sage.

Blumenfeld, Jesmond. 2006. 'South Africa's Evolving Foreign Trade Strategy: Coherence or Confusion?' In *State of the Nation: South Africa 2005–2006*, edited by Sakhela Buhlungu et al., 427–56. Cape Town: HSRC Press.

Bogetić, Željko. 2006. 'International Benchmarking of Lesotho's Infrastructure Performance'. *World Bank Policy Research Working Paper* 3825.

Bond, Patrick. 2002. 'A Political Economy of Dam Building and Household Water Supply in Lesotho and South Africa'. In *Environmental Justice in South Africa*, edited by David A. McDonald, 223–69. Athens: Ohio University Press.

Bond, Patrick. 2005. 'US Empire and South African Subimperialism'. In *Socialist Register 2005: The Empire Reloaded*, edited by Leo Panitch and Colin Leys, 218–38. New York: Bagchi.

Bond, Patrick. 2006. *Looting Africa: The Economics of Exploitation*. London: Zed Books.

Breslin, Shaun, et al. 2002. *New Regionalisms in the Global Economy*. New York: Routledge.

Brunhes, Jean, and Camille Vallaux. 1921. *La géographie de l'histoire: géographie de la paix et de la guerre sur terre et sur mer*. Paris: Alcan.

Brzezinski, Zbigniew K. 1986. *Game Plan: A Geostrategic Framework for the Conduct of the US–Soviet Contest*. Boston: Atlantic Monthly.

Brzezinski, Zbigniew K. 1997. *The Grand Chessboard: American Primacy and its Geostrategic Imperatives*. New York: Basic Books.

Bull, Hedley. 2002. *The Anarchical Society: A Study of Order in World Politics*. New York: Palgrave. Third edition.

Buzan, Barry. 1983. *People, States, and Fear: The National Security Problem in International Relations*. Brighton: Wheatsheaf.

Buzan, Barry, and Ole Wæver. 2003. *Regions and Power: The Structure of International Security*. Cambridge: Cambridge University Press.

Cane, Mark A., Gordon Eshel and Roger W. Buckland. 1994. 'Forecasting Zimbabwean Maize Yield Using Eastern Equatorial Pacific Sea Surface Temperature'. *Nature* 370: 204–5.

Castel-Branco, Carlos N. 2002. 'Economic Linkages between South Africa and Mozambique'. Accessed 21 August 2012. http://www.sarpn.org/documents/d0000120/P117_SA-Mozambique_Link.pdf.

Central Intelligence Agency. 2012. *World Fact Book 2012*. Washington: Central Intelligence Agency.

Centre for African Studies. 1980. 'The Constellation of Southern African States: A New Strategic Offensive by South Africa'. *Review of African Political Economy* 18.7: 102–5.

Centre for Development and Enterprise. 2010. *Water: A Looming Crisis*. Johannesburg: CDE.

Chase, Robert S., Emily B. Hill, and Paul M. Kennedy. 1996. 'Pivotal States and U.S. Strategy'. *Foreign Affairs* 75.1: 33–51.

Chase, Robert S., Emily B. Hill, and Paul M. Kennedy. 1999. *The Pivotal States: A New Framework for US Policy in the Developing World*. New York: Norton.

Chatham House. 2012. *Angola's External Relations in Africa*. Transcript of a speech by Angola's Minister for External Relations at Chatham House. London: Chatham House.

Checkel, Jeffrey T. 2005. 'It's the Process Stupid!: Process Tracing in the Study of European and International Politics'. *ARENA Working Paper*.

Chimhowu, Admos, et al. 1993. 'Namibia'. In *The Southern African Environment: Profiles of the SADC Countries*, edited by Sam Moyo, Phil O'Keefe and Michael Sill, 158–94. London: Earthscan.

Chitala, Derrick. 1987. 'The Political Economy of the SADCC and Imperialism's Response'. In *SADCC: Prospects for Disengagement and Development in Southern Africa*, edited by Samir Amin, Derrick Chitala and Ibbo Mandaza, 13–36. London: Zed Books.

Christopher, Anthony J. 1982. *South Africa*. London: Longman.

Cilliers, Jakkie. 1999. 'An Emerging South African Foreign Policy Identity?' *ISS Paper* 39.

Cilliers, Jakkie. 2007. 'The African Strategic Environment 2020: Challenges for the SA Army'. In *South African Army Vision 2020: Security Challenges Shaping the Future South African Army*, Len Le Roux, 65–82. Pretoria: ISS.

Cohen, Saul B. 1957. 'Geography and Strategy: Their Interrelationship'. *Naval War College Review* 10.4: 1–30.

Cohen, Saul B. 1963. *Geography and Politics in a World Divided*. New York: Random House.

Cohen, Saul B. 1973. *Geography and Politics in a World Divided*. New York: Oxford University Press. Second edition.

Cohen, Saul B. 2001. 'Geopolitics'. In *International Encyclopaedia of the Social & Behavioral Sciences IX*, edited by Neil Smelser and Paul Baltes, 6199–205. Amsterdam: Elsevier.

Cohen, Saul B. 2009. *Geopolitics: The Geography of International Relations*. Lanham: Rowman & Littlefield. Second edition.

Collier, Paul. 2006. 'Economic Causes of Civil Conflict and their Implications for Policy'. Accessed 16 October 2012. http://users.ox.ac.uk/~econpco/research/pdfs/EconomicCausesofCivilConflict-ImplicationsforPolicy.pdf.

Collier, Paul, and Anke Hoeffler. 1998. 'On Economic Causes of Civil War'. *Oxford Economic Papers* 50.4: 563–73.

Collier, Paul, and Anke Hoeffler. 2002. *Greed and Grievance in Civil War*. Oxford: CSAE.

Conchiglia, Augusta. 2007. 'South Africa and its Lusophone Neighbours: Angola and Mozambique'. In *South Africa in Africa: The Post-Apartheid Era*, edited by Adekeye Adebajo, Adebayo Adedeji and Chris Landsberg, 236–52. Scottsville: KwaZulu-Natal University Press.

Cooper, Andrew F., Timothy M. Shaw and Agata Antkiewicz. 2008. 'The Logic of the BRICSAM Model for Global Governance: Do Acronyms Make Sense?' Paper presented at the CPSA Conference in Vancouver, 4–6 June.

Cornish, Vaughan. 1923. *The Great Capitals: An Historical Geography*. London: Methuen.

Curchod, Corentin. 2002. 'La méthod comparative en sciences de gestion: vers une approche quail-quantitative de la réalité managerial'. *Compasss Working Paper* 28.

Curtis, Barney. 2009. 'The Chirundu Border Post: Detailed Monitoring of Transit Times'. *SSATP Discussion Paper* 10.

Dalby, Simon. 1990. *Creating the Second Cold War: The Discourse of Politics*. London: Pinter.

Daniel, John, and Jessica Luchtman. 2006. 'South Africa in Africa: Scrambling for Energy'. In *State of the Nation: South Africa 2005–2006*, edited by Sakhela Buhlungu et al., 484–509. Pretoria: HSRC Press.

Davies, Robert. 1992. 'Economic Growth in Post-Apartheid South Africa: Its Significance for Relations With Other African Countries'. *Journal of Contemporary African Studies* 11.1: 51–71.

de Beer, Geoff, and David Arkwright. 2003. 'The Maputo Development Corridor: Progress Achieved and Lessons Learned'. In *Regionalism and Uneven Development in Southern Africa: The Case of the Maputo Development Corridor*, edited by Fredrik Söderbaum and Ian Taylor, 19–31. Farnham: Ashgate.

Department of Energy. 2011. *Integrated Resource Plan for Electricity, 2010–2030*. Pretoria: Department of Energy.

Department of Finance. 1996. *Growth, Employment and Redistribution: A Macroeconomic Strategy*. Pretoria: Department of Finance.

Department of Foreign Affairs. 2003. *Strategic Plan 2003–2005*. Pretoria: Department of Foreign Affairs.

Department of Foreign Affairs. 2005. *Strategic Plan 2005–2008*. Pretoria: Department of Foreign Affairs.

Department of Foreign Affairs. 2006. *Strategic Plan 2006–2009*. Pretoria: Department of Foreign Affairs.

Department of Foreign Affairs. 2008. 'South African Foreign Policy: Discussion Document'. Accessed 11 February 2013. http://www.info.gov.za/greenpapers/1996/foraf1.htm.

Department of Minerals and Energy. 1998. *White Paper on the Energy Policy of the Republic of South Africa*. Pretoria: Department of Minerals and Energy.

Department of Minerals and Energy. 2006. *Digest of South African Energy Statistics*. Pretoria: Department of Minerals and Energy.

Department of Trade and Industry. 2010. *A South African Trade Policy and Strategy Framework*. Pretoria: Department of Trade and Industry.

Department of Water Affairs and Forestry. 2004. *National Water Resource Strategy*. Pretoria: Department of Water Affairs and Forestry.

Deudney, Daniel. 1997. 'Geopolitics and Change'. In *New Thinking in International Relations Theory*, edited by Michael W. Doyle and G. John Ikenberry, 91–123. Boulder: Westview Press.

Deudney, Daniel. 1999. 'Bringing Nature Back in: Geopolitical Theory from the Greeks to the Global Era'. In *Contested Grounds: Security and Conflict in the New Environmental Politics*, edited by Daniel Deudney and Richard A. Matthew, 25–57. New York: State University of New York Press.

Diamond, Jared. 2003. *Guns, Germs, and Steel: The Fates of Human Societies*. New York: Norton. Second edition.

Diamond, Jared. 2005. *Collapse: How Societies Choose to Fail or Succeed*. New York: Viking.

Dion, Douglas. 1998. 'Evidence and Inference in the Comparative Case Study'. *Comparative Politics* 30.1: 127–45.

Dollar, Evan, and Andrew S. Goudie. 2000. 'Environmental Change'. In *The Geography of South Africa in a Changing World*, edited by Roddy Fox and Kate Rowntree, 31–59. Oxford: Oxford University Press.

Draper, Peter, and Sören Scholvin. 2012. 'The Economic Gateway to Africa?: Geography, Strategy and South Africa's Regional Economic Relations'. *SAIIA Occasional Paper* 121.

Drescher, Axel. 1998. *Sambia*. Gotha: Klett-Perthes.

Dzimbiri, Lewis, and Tiyesere M. Chipaka-Jamali. 2010. 'Malawi'. In *Africa Yearbook: Politics, Economy and Society South of the Sahara in 2009*, edited by Andreas Mehler et al., 465–72. Leiden: Brill.

Dzimbiri, Lewis, and Tiyesere M. Chipaka-Jamali. 2011. 'Malawi'. In *Africa Yearbook: Politics, Economy and Society South of the Sahara in 2010*, edited by Andreas Mehler et al., 467–75. Leiden: Brill.

Economic Development Department. 2010. 'The New Growth Path: The Framework'. Accessed 11 February 2013. http://www.info.gov.za/view/Down loadFileAction?id=135748.

Economist Intelligence Unit. 2012. 'Country Analysis'. Accessed 23 July 2012. http://country.eiu.com.

Energy Information Administration. 2011a. 'South Africa'. Accessed 3 April 2012. http://www.eia.gov/EMEU/cabs/South_Africa/pdf.

Energy Information Administration. 2011b. 'Angola'. Accessed 9 November 2011. http://www.eia.gov/emeu/cabs/Angola/pdf.

Ercolano, Vincent. 1995. 'Comoros'. In *Indian Ocean: Five Island Countries*, edited by Helen Chapin Metz, 137–97. Washington, DC: US Government Printing Office. Third edition.

Erdmann, Gero. 2009. 'Südafrika: Regionaler Hegemon, Mittel- oder Zivilmacht?' In *Neue Führungsmächte: Partner deutscher Außenpolitik?* edited by Jörg Husar et al., 99–121. Baden-Baden: Nomos.

Erdmann, Gero. 2010. 'Verantwortung oder Interesse?: Südafrikas Rolle in der Region'. In *Konsolidierungsprojekt Südafrika: 15 Jahre Post-Apartheid*, edited by Werner Distler and Kristina Weissenbach, 209–25. Baden-Baden: Nomos.

Erdmann, Gero. 2011. 'Zambia'. In *Africa Yearbook: Politics, Economy and Society South of the Sahara in 2010*, edited by Andreas Mehler et al., 525–34. Leiden: Brill.

Eriksson, Patrick. 2000. 'The Geological Template'. In *The Geography of South Africa in a Changing World*, edited by Roddy Fox and Kate Rowntree, 257–83. Oxford: Oxford University Press.

Eskom. 2006. *Annual Report*. Johannesburg: Eskom.

Eskom. 2010. *New Build Programme*. Johannesburg: Eskom.

Fairgrieve, James. 1917. *Geography and World Power*. London: University of London Press.

Fairgrieve, James, and Ernest Young. 1956. *The British Isles*. London: Philip. Second edition.

Fearon, James D. 2004. 'Why Do Some Civil Wars Last So Much Longer than Others?' *Journal of Peace Research* 41.3: 275–301.

Febvre, Lucien. 1922. *La terre et l'évolution humaine*. Paris: Renaissance du livre. Second edition.

Fig, David, and Sören Scholvin. 2015. 'Fracking the Karoo: Barriers to Shale Gas Extraction in South Africa Based on Experiences from Europe and the US'. In *A New Scramble for Africa?: The Rush for Energy Resources*, edited by Sören Scholvin. Farnham: Ashgate, forthcoming.

Fine, Ben, and Zavareh Rustomjee. 1996. *The Political Economy of South Africa: From Minerals-Energy Complex to Industrialisation*. London: Hurst.

Flemes, Daniel. 2007. 'Conceptualising Regional Power in International Relations: Lessons from the South African Case'. *GIGA Working Paper* 53.

Flemes, Daniel, and Douglas Lemke. 2010. 'Findings and Perspectives of Regional Power Research'. In *Regional Leadership in the Global System: Interests, Ideas and Strategies of Regional Powers*, edited by Daniel Flemes, 313–33. Farnham: Ashgate.

Flemes, Daniel, and Detlef Nolte. 2010. Introduction to *Regional Leadership in the Global System: Interests, Ideas and Strategies of Regional Powers*, edited by Daniel Flemes, 1–14. Farnham: Ashgate.

Flemes, Daniel, Sören Scholvin and Georg Strüver. 2011. 'Aufstieg der Netzwerkmächte'. *GIGA Focus Global* 2/2011.

Gallup, John L., and Jeffrey D. Sachs. 2000. 'The Economic Burden of Malaria'. *CID Working Paper* 52.

Gallup, John L., Jeffrey D. Sachs and Andrew D. Mellinger. 1998. 'Geography and Economic Development'. *NBER Working Paper* 6849.

Gamba, Virginia. 2007. 'Regional Security'. In *South African Army Vision 2020: Security Challenges Shaping the Future South African Army*, Len Le Roux, 93–106. Pretoria: ISS.

Games, Dianna. 2004. 'The Experience of South African Firms Doing Business in Africa: A Preliminary Service and Analysis'. *SAIIA Business in Africa Report* 1.

Geldenhuys, Deon. 1991. *Some Foreign Policy Implications of South Africa's 'TNS' with Particular Reference to the 12 Point Plan*. Johannesburg: SAIIA.

George, Alexander L., and McKeown, Tim. 1985. 'Case Studies and Theories of Organizational Decision Making'. In *Advances in Information Processing in Organizations 2*, edited by Robert F. Coulam and Richard A. Smith, 21–58. London: JAI Press.

George, Alexander L., and Andrew Bennett. 2004. *Case Studies and Theory Development in the Social Sciences*. Cambridge: MIT Press.

German Advisory Council on Global Change. 1996. *Welt im Wandel: Herausforderungen für die deutsche Wissenschaft*. Bremerhaven: German Advisory Council on Global Change.

German Advisory Council on Global Change. 1998. *Welt im Wandel: Strategien zur Bewältigung globaler Umweltrisiken*. Bremerhaven: German Advisory Council on Global Change.

German Advisory Council on Global Change. 2007. *Welt im Wandel: Sicherheitsrisiko Klimawandel*. Berlin: Springer.

Gleave, Micheal B. 1992. 'The Dar es Salaam Transport Corridor: An Appraisal'. *African Affairs* 363: 249–67.

Gibb, Richard A. 1991. 'Imposing Dependence: South Africa's Manipulation of Regional Railways'. *Transport Reviews* 11.1: 19–39.

Gibb, Richard A. 2002. 'Regional Economic Integration'. In *Geography and Economy in South Africa and its Neighbours*, edited by Anthony Lemon and Christian M. Rogerson, 273–91. Farnham: Ashgate.

Gibb, Richard A. 2006. 'The New Southern African Customs Union Agreement: Dependence with Democracy'. *Journal of Southern African Studies* 32.3: 583–603.

Good, Kenneth, and Skye Hughes. 2002. 'Globalization and Diversification: Two Case Studies in Southern Africa'. *African Affairs* 402: 39–59.

Gottmann, Jean. 1951. 'Geography and International Relations'. *World Politics* 3.2: 153–73.

Gray, Colin S. 1988. *The Geopolitics of Super Power*. Lexington: University Press of Kentucky.

Gray, Colin S. 1991. 'Geography and Grand Strategy'. *Comparative Strategy* 10.4: 311–29.

Gray, Colin S. 1996. 'The Continued Primacy of Geography: A Debate on Geopolitics'. *Orbis* 40.2: 247–59.

Gray, Colin S. 1999. 'Inescapable Geography'. In *Geopolitics, Geography and Strategy*, edited by Colin S. Gray and Geoffrey R. Sloan, 161–77. London: Cass.

Grobbelaar, Neuma. 2004. 'Every Continent Needs an America: The Experience of South African Firms Doing Business in Mozambique'. *SAIIA Business in Africa Report* 2.

Grobbelaar, Neuma, and Kaemete Tsotetsi. 2005. 'Africa's First Welfare State: The Experience of South African Firms Doing Business in Botswana'. *SAIIA Business in Africa Report* 5.

Grygiel, Jakub J. 2006. *Great Powers and Geopolitical Change*. Baltimore: Johns Hopkins University Press.

Gulick, Edward V. 1955. *Europe's Classical Balance of Power: A Case History of the Theory and Practice of One of the Great Concepts of European Statecraft*. Ithaca: Cornell University Press.

Gwebu, Thando. 2008. 'Contemporary Patterns, Trends and Development Implications of International Migration from Botswana'. In *International Migration and National Development in Sub-Saharan Africa: Viewpoints and Policy Initiatives in the Countries of Origin*, edited by Adepoju, Aderanti, Ton van Naerssen and Annelies Zoomers, 117–40. Leiden: Brill.

Hall, Peter G., 1966. *The World Cities*. London: Weidenfeld and Nicolson.

Hanlon, Joseph. 1986. *Beggar your Neighbours: Apartheid Power in Southern Africa*. Bloomington: Indiana University Press.

Hanlon, Joseph. 2010. 'Mozambique'. In *Africa Yearbook: Politics, Economy and Society South of the Sahara in 2009*, edited by Andreas Mehler et al., 481–91. Leiden: Brill.

Hartnady, Chris J. 2010. 'South Africa's Diminishing Coal Reserves'. *South African Journal of Science* 106.9–10.

Hartshorne, Richard. 1935a. 'Recent Developments in Political Geography I'. *American Political Science Review* 29.5: 785–804.

Hartshorne, Richard. 1935b. 'Recent Developments in Political Geography II'. *American Political Science Review* 29.6: 943–66.

Hartshorne, Richard. 1950. 'The Functional Approach in Political Geography'. *Annals of the Association of American Geographers* 40.2: 95–130.

Hartshorne, Richard. 1954. 'Political Geography'. In *American Geography: Inventory and Prospect*, edited by Preston E. James and Clarence F. Jones, 167–225. Syracuse: Syracuse University Press.

Hartshorne, Richard. 1959. 'The Role of the State in Economic Growth: Contents of the State Area'. In *The State and Economic Growth: Papers of a Conference Held on October 11–13 1956 under the Auspices of the Committee on Economic Growth*, edited by Hugh G. Aitken, 287–324. New York: SSRC.

Hartshorne, Richard. 1960. 'Political Geography in the Modern World'. *Journal of Conflict Resolution* 4.1: 52–66.

Hartshorne, Richard. 1966. *Perspective on the Nature of Geography*. Chicago: McNally. Fourth edition.

Haushofer, Karl. 1928. 'Grundlagen, Wesen und Ziele der Geopolitik'. In *Bausteine zur Geopolitik*, edited by Karl Haushofer et al., 29–48. Berlin: Vowinckel.

Haushofer, Karl et al. 1928. 'Über die historische Entwicklung des Begriffs Geopolitik'. In *Bausteine zur Geopolitik*, edited by Karl Haushofer et al., 3–28. Berlin: Vowinckel.

Hay, Simon I. 2002. 'Climate Change and the Resurgence of Malaria in the East African Highlands'. *Nature* 6874: 905–9.

Hentz, James J. 2005a. 'South Africa and the Political Economy of Regional Cooperation in Southern Africa'. *Modern African Studies* 43.1: 21–51.

Hentz, James J. 2005b. *South Africa and the Logic of Regional Cooperation*. Bloomington: Indiana University Press.

Heseltine, Nigel. 1971. *Madagascar*. London: Pall Mall.

Hettne, Björn, and Fredrik Söderbaum. 2000. 'Theorising the Rise of Regionness'. *New Political Economy* 5.3: 457–73.

Hettne, Björn, András Inotai and Osvaldo Sunkel. 2000. *The New Regionalism and the Future of Security and Development*. New York: Palgrave.

Heyns, Piet. 2002. 'The Interbasin Transfer of Water between SADC Countries: A Developmental Challenge for the Future'. In *Hydropolitics in the Developing Word: A Southern African Perspective*, edited by Anthony Turton and Roland Henwood, 157–76. Pretoria: CiPS.

Heyns, Piet. 2005. 'Strategic and Technical Considerations in the Assessment of Transboundary Water Management with Reference to Southern Africa'. In

Water, Development and Cooperation: Comparative Perspectives: Euphrates-Tigris and Southern Africa, edited by Lars Wirkus, 55–81. Bonn: BICC.

Hirschler, Kurt, and Rolf Hofmeier. 2010. 'Tanzania'. In *Africa Yearbook: Politics, Economy and Society South of the Sahara in 2009*, edited by Andreas Mehler et al., 395–407. Leiden: Brill.

Hirschler, Kurt, and Rolf Hofmeier. 2011. 'Tanzania'. In *Africa Yearbook: Politics, Economy and Society South of the Sahara in 2010*, edited by Andreas Mehler et al., 399–412. Leiden: Brill.

Homer-Dixon, Thomas F. 1991. 'On the Threshold: Environmental Changes as Causes of Acute Conflict'. *International Security* 16.2: 76–116.

Homer-Dixon, Thomas F. 1994. 'Environmental Scarcities and Violent Conflict: Evidence from Cases'. *International Security* 19.1: 5–40.

Homer-Dixon, Thomas F. 1996. 'Strategies for Studying Causation in Complex Ecological-Political Systems'. *Journal of Environment Development* 5.2: 132–48.

Homer-Dixon, Thomas F. 1999. 'Threshold of Turmoil: Environmental Scarcities and Violent Conflict'. In *Contested Grounds: Security and Conflict in the New Environmental Politics*, edited by Daniel Deudney and Richard A. Matthew, 61–90. New York: State University of New York Press.

Horvei, Tore. 1998. 'Powering the Region: South Africa in the Southern African Power Pool'. In *South Africa in Southern Africa: Reconfiguring the Region*, edited by David Simon, 146–63. Oxford: Currey.

Hudson, Judy. 2007. 'South Africa's Economic Expansion into Africa: Neo-Colonialism or Development?' In *South Africa in Africa: The Post-Apartheid Era*, edited by Adekeye Adebajo, Adebayo Adedeji and Chris Landsberg, 128–49. Scottsville: KwaZulu-Natal University Press.

Humphrey, John, and Dirk Messner. 2005. 'The Impact of the Asian and Other Drivers on Global Governance'. Accessed 23 March 2008. http://www.ids.ac.uk/ids/global/pdfs/AsianDriversGovernancepaper05.pdf.

Humphrey, John, and Dirk Messner. 2006. 'Instabile Multipolarität: Indien und China verändern die Weltpolitik'. *DIE Analysen und Stellungnahmen* 1/2006.

Huntington, Samuel P. 1996. *The Clash of Civilizations and the Remaking of World Order*. New York: Simon & Schuster.

Huntington, Samuel P. 1999. 'The Lonely Superpower'. *Foreign Affairs* 78.2: 35–49.

Hurrell, Andrew. 2006. 'Hegemony, Liberalism and Global Order: What Space for Would-Be Great Powers?' *International Affairs* 82.1: 1–20.

Hurrell, Andrew. 2007. 'One World? Many Worlds?: The Place of Regions in the Study of International Society'. *International Affairs* 83.1: 127–46.

Husar, Jörg, et al. 2008. 'Neue Führungsmächte als Partner deutscher Außenpolitik: Ein Bericht aus der Forschung'. *SWP Studie* 36/2008.

Husar, Jörg, and Günther Maihold. 2009. 'Neue Führungsmächte: Forschungsansätze und Handlungsfelder'. In *Neue Führungsmächte: Partner deutscher Außenpolitik?* edited by Jörg Husar et al., 7–30. Baden-Baden: Nomos.

International Panel on Climate Change. 2007. *Climate Change 2007: Impacts, Adaptation and Vulnerability*. Cambridge: Cambridge University Press.

Jarrett, Harold R. 1979. *Africa*. Plymouth: MacDonald and Evans. Fifth edition.

Jenkins, Carolyn. 2002. 'The Politics of Economic Policy-Making after Independence'. In *The Economic Decline of Zimbabwe: Neither Growth nor Equity*, edited by Carolyn Jenkins and John Knight, 18–59. New York: Palgrave.

Jonasson, Johanna. 2011. 'The Sicomines Agreement: Change and Continuity in the Democratic Republic of Congo's International Relations'. *SAIIA Occasional Paper* 97.

Jones, Stephen B. 1954. 'A Unified Field Theory of Political Geography'. *Annals of the Association of American Geographers* 44.2: 111–23.

Joomun, Gilles. 2006. 'The Textile and Clothing Industry in Mauritius'. In *The Future of the Textile and Clothing Industry in Sub-Saharan Africa*, edited by Herbert Jauch and Rudolf Traub-Merz, 193–211. Bonn: FES.

Jourdan, Paul. 1998. 'Spatial Development Initiatives (SDIs): The Official View'. *Development Southern Africa* 15.5: 717–25.

Kabemba, Claude. 2007. 'South Africa in the DRC: Renaissance or Neo-Imperialism?' In *State of the Nation: South Africa 2007*, edited by Sakhela Buhlungu et al., 533–51. Cape Town: HSRC Press.

Kagwanja, Peter. 2006. 'Power and Peace: South Africa and the Refurbishing of Africa's Multilateral Capacity for Peacemaking'. In *South Africa's Role in Conflict Resolution and Peacemaking in Africa*, edited by Roger Southall, 27–58. Pretoria: HSRC Press.

Kamete, Amin Y. 2010. 'Zimbabwe'. In *Africa Yearbook: Politics, Economy and Society South of the Sahara in 2009*, edited by Andreas Mehler et al., 537–47. Leiden: Brill.

Kamete, Amin Y. 2011. 'Zimbabwe'. In *Africa Yearbook: Politics, Economy and Society South of the Sahara in 2010*, edited by Andreas Mehler et al., 534–45. Leiden: Brill.

Kaplan, Robert D. 2012. *The Revenge of Geography: What the Map Tells Us about Coming Conflicts and the Battle Against Fate*. New York: Random House.

Kaplinsky, Raphael. 2005. 'The Impact of Asian Drivers on the Developing World'. Accessed 11 April 2009. http://www.ids.ac.uk/download.cfm?object id=F94F67DC-5056-8171-7B34DA4FE3ACD9D8.

Katerere, Yemi, Sam Moyo and Peter Ngobese. 1993. 'Zimbabwe'. In *The Southern African Environment: Profiles of the SADC Countries*, edited by Sam Moyo, Phil O'Keefe and Michael Sill, 303–40. London: Earthscan.

Kelly, Philip L. 1997. *Checkerboards and Shatterbelts: The Geopolitics of South America*. Austin: University of Texas Press.

Kelly, Philip L. 2006. 'A Critique of Critical Geopolitics'. *Geopolitics* 11.1: 24–53.

Kenny, Bridget, and Charles Mather. 2008. 'Der Melker der Region?: Südafrikanisches Kapital und die sambische Milchindustrie'. *Afrika Süd* 37.4: 21–4.

Khanna, Parag. 2008. *The Second World: Empires and Influence in the New Global Order*. London: Allen Lane.

Kissinger, Henry A. 1979. *The White House Years*. London: Weidenfeld and Nicolson.

Kjellén, Rudolf. 1916. *Staten som livsform*. Stockholm: Geber.

Klare, Michael T. 2002. *Resource Wars: The New Landscape of Global Conflict*. New York: Holt.

Klare, Michael T. 2004. *Blood and Oil: The Dangers and Consequences of America's Growing Petroleum Dependency*. London: Penguin.

Klare, Michael T. 2009. *Rising Powers, Shrinking Planet: The New Geopolitics of Energy*. New York: Holt.

Klimm, Ernst, et al. 1994. *Das südliche Afrika II: Namibia-Botswana*. Darmstadt: Wissenschaftliche Buchgesellschaft.

Koen, Michael, and Aisha Bahadur. 2010. *Eskom: Business as Usual in Africa*. Amsterdam: SOMO.

Kristof, Ladis. 1960. 'The Origins and Evolution of Geopolitics'. *Journal of Conflict Resolution* 4.1: 15–51.

Kruger, Andries C., and Stephen Shongwe. 2004. 'Temperature Trends in South Africa: 1960–2003'. *International Journal of Climatology* 24.15: 1929–45.

Kuder, Manfred. 1971. *Angola: Eine geographische, soziale und wirtschaftliche Länderkunde*. Darmstadt: Wissenschaftliche Buchgesellschaft.

Kuder, Manfred. 1975. *Moçambique: Eine geographische, soziale und wirtschaftliche Länderkunde*. Darmstadt: Wissenschaftliche Buchgesellschaft.

Lacoste, Yves. 1976. *La géographie, ça sert, d'abord, à faire la guerre*. Paris: Maspero.

Lacoste, Yves. 1993. Préambule to *Dictionnaire de géopolitique*, edited by Yves Lacoste, 1–35. Paris: Flammarion.

Landsberg, Chris. 2006. 'South Africa'. In *Security Dynamics in Africa's Great Lakes Region*, edited by Gilbert M. Khadiagala, 204–34. London: Lynne Rienner.

Larmer, Miles. 2005. 'Tafelsilber verkauft: Die Privatisierung des Bergbaus in Sambia'. *Afrika Süd* 34.4: 23–4.

Le Billon, Philippe. 2001a. 'Angola's Political Economy of War: The Role of Oil and Diamonds 1975–2000'. *African Affairs* 398: 55–80.

Le Billon, Philippe. 2001b. 'The Political Ecology of War: Natural Resources and Armed Conflicts'. *Political Geography* 20.5: 561–84.

Le Billon, Philippe. 2004. 'The Geopolitical Economy of "Resource Wars"'. *Geopolitics* 9.1: 1–28.

Le Pere, Garth. 2009. 'South Africa's Post-Apartheid Foreign Policy: The Past as Prologue'. Paper presented at a workshop on New Directions in the South, Rio de Janeiro, 23–24 June.

Lee, Margaret C. 2003. *The Political Economy of Regionalism in Southern Africa*. Boulder: Rienner.

Lesufi, Ishmael. 2004. 'South Africa and the Rest of the Continent: Towards a Critique of the Political Economy of NEPAD'. *Current Sociology* 52.5: 809–29.

Lesufi, Ishmael. 2006. *Nepad and South African Imperialism*. Johannesburg: JSA.

LHWP. 2011a. 'Sales to Eskom'. Accessed 16 November 2011. http://www.lhwp. org.ls/Reports/PDF/Electricity%20Sales%20-%20ESKOM.pdf.

LHWP. 2011b. 'Water Sales'. Accessed 16 November 2011. http://www.lhwp.org. ls/Reports/PDF/Water%20Sales.pdf.

Lienau, Cay. 1981. *Malawi: Geographie eines unterentwickelten Landes*. Darmstadt: Wissenschaftliche Buchgesellschaft.

Lipton, Merle. 2009. 'Understanding South Africa's Foreign Policy: The Perplexing Case of Zimbabwe'. *South African Journal of International Affairs* 16.3: 331–46.

Lundahl, Mats, Colin L. McCarthy and Lennart Petersson. 2003. *In the Shadow of South Africa: Lesotho's Economic Future*. Farnham: Ashgate.

Mackie, John L. 1974. *The Cement of the Universe*. Oxford: Clarendon Press.

Mackinder, Halford J. 1887. 'On the Scope and Methods of Geography'. *Proceedings of the Royal Geographical Society* 9.3: 141–60.

Mackinder, Halford J. 1890. 'The Physical Basis of Political Geography'. *Scottish Geographical Magazine* 6.2: 78–84.

Mackinder, Halford J. 1900a. 'The Great Trade Routes I: Their Connection with the Organization of Industry, Commerce and Finance'. *Journal of the Institute of Bankers* 21: 1–6.

Mackinder, Halford J. 1900b. 'The Great Trade Routes II: Their Connection with the Organization of Industry, Commerce and Finance'. *Journal of the Institute of Bankers* 21: 137–46.

Mackinder, Halford J. 1904. 'The Geographical Pivot of History'. *Geographical Journal* 23.4: 421–44.

Mackinder, Halford J. 1905. 'Manpower as a Measure of National and Imperial Strength'. *National and English Review* 265: 136–45.

Mackinder, Halford J. 1909. 'Geographical Conditions Affecting the British Empire'. *Geographical Journal* 33.4: 462–78.

Mackinder, Halford J. 1916. 'Presidential Address to the Geographical Association'. *Geographical Teacher* 8: 271–7.

Mackinder, Halford J. 1919. *Democratic Ideals and Reality: A Study in the Politics of Reconstruction*. New York: Holt.

Mackinder, Halford J. 1922. *Britain and the British Seas*. Oxford: Clarendon Press. Second edition.

Mackinder, Halford J. 1943. 'The Round World and the Winning of Peace'. *Foreign Affairs* 21.4: 595–605.

MacLean, Sandra J. 2002. 'Mugabe at War: The Political Economy of Conflict in Zimbabwe'. *Third World Quarterly* 23.3: 513–28.

Mahan, Alfred T. 1890. *The Influence of Sea Power Upon History, 1660–1783*. London: Low.

Makoa, Francis K. 1999. 'Foreign Military Intervention in Lesotho's Election Dispute: Whose Project'. *Strategic Review for Southern Africa* 21.1.

Maminirinarivo, Ralaivelo. 2006. 'The Textile and Clothing Industry of Madagascar'. In *The Future of the Textile and Clothing Industry in Sub-Saharan Africa*, edited by Herbert Jauch and Rudolf Traub-Merz, 178–92. Bonn: FES.

Mandela, Nelson. 1993. 'South Africa's Future Foreign Policy'. *Foreign Affairs* 72.5: 86–97.

Manshard, Walther. 1988. *Afrika: Südlich der Sahara*. Frankfurt: Fischer. Third edition.

Matlosa, Khabele. 1998. 'Changing Socio-Economic Setting of the Highlands Region as a Result of the Lesotho Highlands Water Project'. *Transformation* 37: 29–45.

Matondo, Emanuel. 2005. 'Öldiplomatie'. *Afrika Süd* 34.4: 16.

Matyszak, Derek. 2009. 'Die Verhandlungen und das Abkommen zur Teilung der Macht in Simbabwe'. *KAS-Auslandsinformationen* 1/2009: 97–129.

Maull, Otto. 1936. *Das Wesen der Geopolitik*. Leipzig: Teubner.

Maupin, Agathe. 2015. 'Energy and Regional Integration: The Grand Inga Project in the DR Congo'. In *A New Scramble for Africa?: The Rush for Energy Resources*, edited by Sören Scholvin. Farnham: Ashgate, forthcoming.

Mayer, Hartmut. 2009. 'Declining Might in the Limelight: European Responses to New Regional Powers'. *South African Journal of International Affairs* 16.2: 195–214.

McCarthy, Colin. 1994. 'Revenue Distribution and Economic Development in the Southern African Customs Union'. *South African Journal of Economics* 62.3: 167–87.

McCarthy, Colin. 1999. 'SACU and the Rand Zone'. In *Regionalisation in Africa: Integration & Disintegration*, edited by Daniel C. Bach, 159–68. Oxford: Currey.

McDonald, David. 2009. 'Electric Capitalism: Conceptualising Electricity and Capital Accumulation in (South) Africa'. In *Electric Capitalism: Recolonising Africa on the Power Grid*, edited by David McDonald, 1–49. Cape Town: HSRC Press.

McKinley, Dale T. 2004. 'South African Foreign Policy towards Zimbabwe under Mbeki'. *Review of African Political Economy* 100: 357–64.

Mdluli, Funekile. 1993. 'Swaziland'. In *The Southern African Environment: Profiles of the SADC Countries*, edited by Sam Moyo, Phil O'Keefe and Michael Sill, 195–233. London: Earthscan.

Meining, Donald W. 1956. 'Heartland and Rimland in Eurasian History'. *Western Political Quarterly* 9.3: 553–69.

Melber, Henning. 2011. 'Namibia'. In *Africa Yearbook: Politics, Economy and Society South of the Sahara in 2010*, edited by Andreas Mehler et al., 493–501. Leiden: Brill.

Mellinger, Andrew D., Jeffrey D. Sachs and John L. Gallup. 1999. 'Climate, Water Navigability, and Economic Development'. *CID Working Paper* 24.

Messner, Dirk. 2007. 'Global Governance: Emerging Powers in Energy and Climate Change Regimes'. Paper presented at the Conference on Emerging Powers in Global Governance, Paris, 6–7 July.

Mhone, Guy, and Austin Nguria. 1993. 'Malawi'. In *The Southern African Environment: Profiles of the SADC Countries*, edited by Sam Moyo, Phil O'Keefe and Michael Sill, 92–125. London: Earthscan.

Middlemas, Keith. 1987. *Cabora Bassa: Engineering and Politics in Southern Africa*. London: Weidenfeld & Nicolson.

Miles-Mafafo, Miranda. 2002. 'Swaziland: Changing Economic Geography'. In *Geography and Economy in South Africa and its Neighbours*, edited by Anthony Lemon and Christian M. Rogerson, 218–30. Farnham: Ashgate.

Mills, Greg. 2008. 'Bricks, Mortar, Policy and Development: Aid and Building African Infrastructure'. In *Africa Beyond Aid*, edited by Gerhard Wahlers, Greg Mills and Holger B. Hansen, 102–22. Johannesburg: Brenthurst Foundation.

Ministry of Defence. 1996. *Defence in a Democracy: White Paper on National Defence for the Republic of South Africa*. Pretoria: Ministry of Defence.

Mohr, Steve H., and Geoffrey M. Evans. 2009. 'Forecasting Coal Production until 2100'. *Fuel* 88.11: 2059–67.

Mongula, Benedict S., and Chiselebwe Ng'andwe. 1987. 'Limits to Development in Southern Africa: Energy, Transport and Communications in SADCC Countries'. In *SADCC: Prospects for Disengagement and Development in Southern Africa*, edited by Samir Amin, Derrick Chitala and Ibbo Mandaza, 85–108. London: Zed Books.

Morgenthau, Hans J. 1954. *Politics among Nations: The Struggle for Power and Peace*. New York: Knopf. Second edition.

Mpotokwane, Masego, Sandra Shaw and Richard Segodi. 1993. 'Botswana'. In *The Southern African Environment: Profiles of the SADC Countries*, edited by Sam Moyo, Phil O'Keefe and Michael Sill, 32–64. London: Earthscan.

Mthembu-Salter, Gregory. 2012. 'South Africa in Africa: Your Hinterland Is There'. *Africa Report* 46.10: 53–6.

Mudge, Dirk. 2004. 'Land Reform in Perspective'. In *Who Should Own the Land?: Analyses and Views on the Land Question in Namibia and Southern Africa*, edited by Justine Hunter, 100–103. Windhoek: KAS.

Muller, Mike, et al. 2009. 'Water Security in South Africa'. *DBSA Development Planning Division Working Paper* 12.

Musyoki, Agnes, and Micheal B. Kwesi Darkoh. 2002. 'Adjustments to Globalisation: The Changing Economic Geography of Botswana'. In *Geography and Economy in South Africa and its Neighbours*, edited by Anthony Lemon and Christian M. Rogerson, 187–204. Farnham: Ashgate.

Ndlela, Daniel B. 1987. 'The Manufacturing Sector in the East and Southern African Subregion with Emphasis on the SADCC'. In *SADCC: Prospects for Disengagement and Development in Southern Africa*, edited by Samir Amin, Derrick Chitala and Ibbo Mandaza, 37–61. London: Zed Books.

Neethling, Theo. 2003. 'Pursuing a Functional Security Community in Southern Africa: Is it Possible after All?' *Strategic Review for Southern Africa* 25.1.

Nel, Etienne, and Peter Illgner. 2001. 'Tapping Lesotho's "White Gold"'. *Geography* 86.2: 163–7.

Nel, Philip, and Matthew Stephen. 2010. 'The Foreign Economic Policies of Regional Powers in the Developing World: Towards a Framework of Analysis'. In *Regional Leadership in the Global System: Ideas, Interests and Strategies of Regional Powers*, edited by Daniel Flemes, 71–90. Farnham: Ashgate.

Nevin, Tom. 1998. 'The Impossible Dream Comes True'. *African Business* 236: 9–11.

New, Mark, et al. 2006. 'Evidence of Trends in Daily Climate Extremes over Southern and West Africa'. *Journal of Geophysical Research* 111: 1–11.

Newman, Harold R. 2011. 'The Mineral Industry of Botswana'. In *2010 Minerals Yearbook*, edited by US Geological Survey. Accessed 3 March 2012. http://minerals.usgs.gov/minerals/pubs/country/2010/myb3-2010-bc.pdf.

Nolte, Detlef. 2006. 'Macht und Machthierarchien in den internationalen Beziehungen: Ein Analysekonzept für die Forschung über regionale Führungsmächte'. *GIGA Working Paper* 29.

Norbrook, Nicholas. 2012. 'Buried Treasure'. *Africa Report* 38.2: 78–9.

Nuvunga, Milissão. 2008. 'Region-Building in Central Mozambique: The Case of the Zambezi Valley Spatial Development Initiative'. In *Afro-Regions: The Dynamics of Cross-Border Micro-Regionalism in Africa*, edited by Fredrik Söderbaum and Ian Taylor, 74–89. Uppsala: Nordiska Afrikainstitutet.

O'Neill, Jim. 2001. 'Building Better Global Economic BRICs'. *Goldman Sachs Global Economics Paper* 66.

O'Neill, Jim, et al. 2005. 'How Solid are the BRICs?' *Goldman Sachs Global Economics Paper* 134.

Ó Tuathail, Gearóid. 1989. 'Critical Geopolitics: The Social Construction of Space and Place in the Practice of Statecraft'. PhD diss., Syracuse University.

Ó Tuathail, Gearóid. 1992. 'Putting Mackinder in his Place'. *Political Geography* 11.1: 100–118.

Ó Tuathail, Gearóid. 1996. *Critical Geopolitics: The Politics of Writing Global Space*. Minneapolis: University of Minnesota Press.

Ó Tuathail, Gearóid. 1999. 'Understanding Critical Geopolitics: Geopolitics and Risk Society'. In *Geopolitics, Geography and Strategy*, edited by Colin S. Gray and Geoffrey R. Sloan, 107–24. London: Cass.

Ó Tuathail, Gearóid, and John A. Agnew. 1992. 'Geopolitics and Discourse: Practical Geopolitical Reasoning in American Foreign Policy'. *Political Geography* 11.2: 190–204.

Ó Tuathail, Gearóid, and Simon Dalby. 1998. 'Rethinking Geopolitics: Towards a Critical Geopolitics'. In *Rethinking Geopolitics*, edited by Gearóid Ó Tuathail and Simon Dalby, 1–15. London: Routledge.

Olivier, Gerrit. 2003. 'Is Thabo Mbeki Africa's Saviour?' *International Affairs* 79.4: 815–28.

Østerud, Øyvind. 1992. 'Regional Great Powers'. In *Regional Great Powers in International Politics*, edited by Iver B. Neumann, 1–15. London: St. Martin's.

Palmer, Robin. 2000. 'Mugabe's "Land Grab" in Regional Perspective'. In *Land Reform in Zimbabwe: Constraints and Prospects*, edited by Tanya Bowyer-Bower and Colin Stoneman, 15–23. Farnham: Ashgate.

Parliament of the Republic of South Africa. 1994. *White Paper on Reconstruction and Development*. Cape Town: Parliament of the Republic of South Africa.

Pazvakavambwa, Simon C. 2005. 'The Politics of Water Use and Water Access: How National Water Development Plans Affect Regional Cooperation (Focus on Zimbabwe and South Africa)'. In *Water, Development and Cooperation: Comparative Perspectives: Euphrates-Tigris and Southern Africa*, edited by Lars Wirkus, 122–35. Bonn: BICC.

Pearson, Mark, and Bo Giersing. 2012. *Revamping the Regional Railway Systems in Eastern and Southern Africa*. Pretoria: TradeMark Southern Africa.

Peters-Berries, Christian. 2001. 'Southern Africa Development Community (SADC): Regionale Integration und Kooperation in Afrika südlich der Sahara III'. *SWP Studie* 16/2001.

Petters, Sunday W. 1991. *Regional Geology of Africa*. Berlin: Springer.

Phimister, Ian, and Brian Raftopoulos. 2004. 'Mugabe, Mbeki and the Politics of Anti-Imperialism'. *Review of African Economy* 101: 385–400.

Price, Robert M. 1984. 'Pretoria's Southern African Strategy'. *African Affairs* 330: 11–32.

Radelet, Steven C., and Jeffrey D. Sachs. 1998. 'Shipping Costs, Manufactured Exports, and Economic Growth'. Paper presented at the annual meeting of the American Economic Association, Chicago, 4 January.

Ragin, Charles C. 1987. *The Comparative Method: Moving Beyond Qualitative and Quantitative Strategies*. Berkeley: University of California Press.

Ragin, Charles C. 1998. 'Comparative Methodology, Fuzzy Sets, and the Study of Sufficient Causes'. *Newsletter of the APSA Organized Section in Comparative Politics* 9.1: 18–22.

Ragin, Charles C. 2000. *Fuzzy Set Social Science*. Chicago: University of Chicago Press.

Ragin, Charles C. 2006. 'Set Relations in Social Research: Evaluating Their Consistency and Coverage'. *Political Analysis* 14.3: 291–310.

Raimundo Oucho, Inês. 2008. 'Migration Management: Mozambique's Challenges and Strategies'. In *International Migration and National Development in Sub-Saharan Africa: Viewpoints and Policy Initiatives in the Countries of Origin*, edited by Adepoju, Aderanti, Ton van Naerssen and Annelies Zoomers, 91–116. Leiden: Brill.

Ranganathan, Rupa, and Vivian Foster. 2011. 'The SADC's Infrastructure: A Regional Perspective'. *World Bank Policy Research Working Paper* 5898.

Raphael, Lois A. 1973. *The Cape to Cairo Dream: A Study in British Imperialism*. New York: Octagon.

Rappaport, Jordan, and Jeffrey D. Sachs. 2003. 'The United States as a Coastal Nation'. *Journal of Economic Growth* 8.1: 5–46.

Ratzel, Friedrich. 1897. *Politische Geographie*. München: Oldenbourg.

Ratzel, Friedrich. 1899. *Anthropogeographie I: Grundzüge der Anwendung der Erdkunde auf die Geschichte*. Stuttgart: Engelhorn. Second edition.

Rautenbach, George, and Waldemar Vrey. 2010a. 'South Africa's Foreign Policy and Africa: The Case of Burundi'. In *The Burundi Peace Process: From Civil War to Conditional Peace*, edited by Henri Boshoff, Waldemar Vrey and Rautenbach, George, 11–34. Pretoria: ISS.

Rautenbach, George, and Waldemar Vrey. 2010b. 'The Implementation of South African Foreign Policy in Burundi'. In *The Burundi Peace Process: From Civil War to Conditional Peace*, edited by Henri Boshoff, Waldemar Vrey and Rautenbach, George, 35–49. Pretoria: ISS.

Reilly, Rosemary C. 2010. 'Process Tracing'. In *Encyclopedia of Case Study Research*, edited by Albert J. Mills et al., 734–6. Thousand Oaks: Sage.

Rihoux, Benoît, and Charles C. Ragin. 2004. 'Qualitative Comparative Analysis (QCA): State of the Art and Prospects'. Paper presented at the Annual Meeting of the American Political Science Association, Chicago, 2–5 September.

Rihoux, Benoît, and Gisèle De Meur. 2009. 'Crisp Set Qualitative Comparative Analysis (csQCA)'. In *Configurational Comparative Methods: Qualitative Comparative Analysis (QCA) and Related Techniques*, edited by Benoît Rihoux and Charles C. Ragin, 33–68. Los Angeles: Sage.

Roberts, Clayton. 1996. *The Logic of Historical Explanation*. University Park: Pennsylvania State University Press.

Rogerson, Christian M. 2001. 'Spatial Development Initiatives in Southern Africa: The Maputo Development Corridor'. *Tijdschrift voor Economische en Sociale Geografie* 92.3: 324–46.

Rogerson, Christian M. 2004. 'Towards the World-Class African City: Planning Local Economic Development in Johannesburg'. *Africa Insight* 34.4: 12–21.

Ross, Michael L. 2003. 'Oil, Drugs, and Diamonds: How Do Natural Resources Vary in their Impact on Civil War?' In *Beyond Greed and Grievance: The Political Economy of Armed Conflict*, edited by Karen Ballentine and Jake Sherman, 47–70. Boulder: Lynne Rienner.

Sachs, Jeffrey D. 1999. 'Resource Endowments and the Real Exchange Rate: A Comparison of Latin America and East Asia'. In *Changes in Exchange Rates in Rapidly Developing Countries: Theory, Practice, and Policy Issues*, edited by Takatoshi Ito and Anne O. Krueger, 133–54. Chicago: University of Chicago Press.

Sachs, Jeffrey D., and Andrew M. Warner. 1997a. 'Sources of Slow Growth in African Economies'. *Journal of African Economies* 6.3: 335–76.

Sachs, Jeffrey D., and Andrew M. Warner. 1997b. *Natural Resource Abundance and Economic Growth*. Cambridge: HIID.

Sachs, Jeffrey D., and Andrew M. Warner. 1999. 'The Big Push, Natural Resource Booms, and Growth'. *Journal of Development Economics* 59.1: 43–76.

Sachs, Jeffrey D., and Andrew M. Warner. 2001. 'The Curse of Natural Resources: Natural Resources and Economic Development'. *European Economic Review* 45.4–6: 827–38.

SACU. 2002. *2002 Southern African Customs Union (SACU) Agreement.* Windhoek: SACU.

SADC. 1996. 'Towards Enhanced Trade and Investment in the Southern African Development Community (SADC)'. Communiqué of the SADC Consultative Conference on Trade and Investment, Johannesburg, 1–4 February.

SADC. 2000. *Revised Protocol on Shares Water Courses.* Gaborone: SADC.

SADC. 2001. *Protocol on Politics, Defence and Security Co-operation.* Gaborone: SADC.

Samset, Ingrid. 2002. 'Conflict of Interests or Interests in Conflict?: Diamonds and War in the DRC'. *Review of African Political Economy* 29.3–4: 463–80.

Sandrey, Ron, et al. 2005. 'Lesotho: Potential Export Diversification Study'. Accessed 19 April 2012. http://www.tralac.org/wp-content/blogs.dir/12/files/2011/uploads/20050913_Lesotho_export_diversity.pdf.

Schirm, Stefan. 2005. 'Führungsindikatoren und Erklärungsvariablen für die neue internationale Rolle Brasiliens'. *Lateinamerika Analysen* 11: 107–30.

Schleicher, Hans-Georg. 2006. *Regionale Sicherheitskooperation im südlichen Afrika: SADC und OPDSC.* Leipzig: Institut für Afrikanistik.

Schoeman, Maxi. 2003. 'South Africa as an Emerging Middle Power, 1994–2003'. In *State of the Nation: South Africa 2003–2004*, edited by John Daniel et al., 349–67. Cape Town: HSRC Press.

Schoeman, Maxi, and Chris Alden. 2003. 'The Hegemon that Wasn't: South Africa's Foreign Policy towards Zimbabwe'. *Strategic Review for Southern Africa* 25.1.

Schöller, Peter. 1957. 'Wege und Irrwege der Politischen Geographie und Geopolitik'. *Erdkunde* 11.1: 1–20.

Scholvin, Sören. 2009a. 'Politik mit Stellvertretern: Neuere außenpolitische Konzepte setzen auf Core States und Ankerländer'. *iz3w* 312: 12–14.

Scholvin, Sören. 2009b. 'Scheitern an der Zweiten Welt'. *iz3w* 315: 47.

Scholvin, Sören. 2009c. 'Ein neues Great Game um Zentralasien'. *GIGA Focus Global* 2/2009.

Scholvin, Sören. 2011. 'The Economics of Southern Africa from a Geopolitical Perspective: Why and How Geography Matters'. In *Monitoring Regional Integration in Southern Africa 2010*, edited by Anton Bösl et al., 93–114. Stellenbosch: TRALAC.

Scholvin, Sören. 2012. 'Regional Powers as Driver of Regional Cooperation?: The Case of South Africa'. *Beiträge zur Internationalen Politik und Sicherheit* 1/2012: 10–23.

Scholvin, Sören. 2013. 'From Rejection to Acceptance: The Conditions of Regional Contestation and Followership to Post-Apartheid South Africa'. *African Security* 4.2: 133–52.

Scholvin, Sören. 2014a. 'Nigeria and West Africa 1990–2003: A Regional Power Without (Many) Followers'. *World Affairs* 18.1: 106–23.

Scholvin, Sören. 2014b. 'Eigennützige Integration: Südafrika, Kenia und Äthiopien wollen Ostafrika nach ihren Interessen gestalten'. *iz3w* 337: 14–16.

Scholvin, Sören. 2014c. 'South Africa's Energy Policy: Constrained by Nature and Path Dependency'. *Journal of Southern African Studies* 40.1: 185–202.

Scholvin, Sören. 2015. 'Energy from Across the Border: Explaining South Africa's Regional Energy Policy'. In *A New Scramble for Africa?: The Rush for Energy Resources*, edited by Sören Scholvin. Farnham: Ashgate, forthcoming.

Scholvin, Sören, and Andrés Malamud. 2014. 'Is there a Geoeconomic Node in South America?: Geography, Politics and Brazil's Role in Regional Economic Integration'. *ICS Working Paper* 2/2014.

Schröder, Bernd. 2005. 'Cahora Bassa: Ein Staudamm im Wandel der Zeit'. *Afrika Süd* 34.5: 28–30.

Schubert, Jon. 2010. 'Angola'. In *Africa Yearbook: Politics, Economy and Society South of the Sahara in 2009*, edited by Andreas Mehler et al., 431–42. Leiden: Brill.

Schubert, Jon. 2011. 'Angola'. In *Africa Yearbook: Politics, Economy and Society South of the Sahara in 2010*, edited by Andreas Mehler et al., 435–45. Leiden: Brill.

Schultz, Jürgen. 1983. *Zambia*. Darmstadt: Wissenschaftliche Buchgesellschaft.

Seawright, Jason, and John Gerring. 2008. 'Case Selection Techniques in Case Study Research: A Menu of Qualitative and Quantitative Options'. *Political Research Quarterly* 61.2: 294–308.

Seiffert, Bernd. 1997. *'Der Staudamm nützt nur der Regierung – nicht uns!': Geschichte und Auswirkungen des Lesotho Hochland Wasserbauprojektes.* Berlin: Hilbert.

Semple, Ellen C. 1903. *American History and its Geographic Conditions*. Boston: Mifflin.

Sidaway, James, and Richard A. Gibb. 1998. 'SADC, COMESA, SACU: Contradictory Formats for Regional "Integration" in Southern Africa'. In *South Africa in Southern Africa: Reconfigurating the Region*, edited by David Simon, 164–84. Oxford: Currey.

Simon, David. 2000. 'Geographies of Mobility and Accessibility'. In *The Geography of South Africa in a Changing World*, edited by Roddy Fox and Kate Rowntree, 233–54. Oxford: Oxford University Press.

Singer, Max, and Aaron Wildavsky. 1993. *The Real World Order: Zones of Peace/Zones of Turmoil*. Chatham: Chatham House.

Smith, Hampton, Tim Merrill and Sandra W. Meditz. 1994. 'The Economy'. In *Zaire: A Country Study*, edited by Sandra W. Meditz and Tim Merrill, 135–99. Washington, DC: US Government Printing Office. Fourth edition.

Smith, Jose. 1988. 'The Beira Corridor Project'. *Geography* 73.3: 258–61.

Söderbaum, Fredrik. 2002. *The Political Economy of Regionalism in Southern Africa*. Göteborg: PADRIGU.

Söderbaum, Fredrik, and Ian Taylor. 2001. 'Transmission Belt for Transnational Capital or Facilitator for Development?: Problematising the Role of the State in the Maputo Development Corridor'. *Journal of Modern African Studies* 39.4: 675–95.

Southall, Roger. 2006. 'A Long Prelude to Peace: South African Involvement in Ending Burundi's War'. In *South Africa's Role in Conflict Resolution and Peacemaking in Africa*, edited by Roger Southall, 105–33. Pretoria: HSRC Press.

Spence, John E. 2007. 'Change and Continuity in Global Politics and Military Strategy'. In *South African Army Vision 2020: Security Challenges Shaping the Future South African Army*, edited by Len Le Roux, 35–63. Pretoria: ISS.

Sprout, Harold, and Margaret Sprout. 1965. *The Ecological Perspective on Human Affairs: With Special Reference to International Politics*. Princeton: Princeton University Press.

Spykman, Nicholas J. 1938a. 'Geography and Foreign Policy I'. *American Political Science Review* 32.1: 28–50.

Spykman, Nicholas J. 1938b. 'Geography and Foreign Policy II'. *American Political Science Review* 32.2: 213–36.

Spykman, Nicholas J. 1942. *America's Strategy in World Politics: The United States and the Balance of Power*. New York: Harcourt.

Spykman, Nicholas J. 1944. *The Geography of the Peace*. Hamden: Harcourt.

Spykman, Nicholas J., and Abbie A. Rollins. 1939a. 'Geographic Objectives in Foreign Policy I'. *American Political Science Review* 33.3: 391–410.

Spykman, Nicholas J., and Abbie A. Rollins. 1939b. 'Geographic Objectives in Foreign Policy II'. *American Political Science Review* 33.4: 591–614.

Stamm, Andreas. 2004. 'Schwellen- und Ankerländer als Akteure einer globalen Partnerschaft: Überlegungen zu einer Positionsbestimmung aus deutscher entwicklungspolitischer Sicht'. *DIE Discussion-Papers* 1/2004.

Stephan, Harry, and Angus Fane Hervey. 2008. 'New Regionalism in Southern Africa: Functional Developmentalism and the Southern African Power Pool'. *Politeia* 27.3: 54–76.

Stige, Lief C., et al. 2006. 'The Effect of Climate Variation on Agro-Pastoral Production in Africa'. *Proceedings of the National Academy of Science* 103.9: 3049–53.

Stock, Robert. 1995. *Africa South of the Sahara: A Geographical Interpretation*. New York: Guilford Press.

Stratfor. 2012. 'The Geopolitics of Angola: An Exception to African Geography'. Accessed 8 August 2012. http://www.stratfor.com/sample/analysis/geopolitics-angola-exception-african-geography.

Swatuk, Larry A. 2000. 'Power and Water: The Coming Order in Southern Africa'. In *The New Regionalism and the Future of Security and Development*, edited by Björn Hettne, andrás Inotai and Sunkel, Osvaldo, 210–47. New York: Palgrave.

Tabirih, Ina. 1993. 'Lesotho'. In *The Southern African Environment: Profiles of the SADC Countries*, edited by Sam Moyo, Phil O'Keefe and Michael Sill, 65–91. London: Earthscan.

Tadross, Mark, Chris Jack and Bruce Hewitson. 2005. 'On RCM-Based Projections of Change in Southern African Summer Climate'. *Geophysical Research Letters* 32.23.

Tartter, Jean. 1995. 'Seychelles'. In *Indian Ocean: Five Island Countries*, edited by Helen Chapin Metz, 199–248. Washington, DC: US Government Printing Office. Third edition.

Taylor, Peter J. 1985. *Political Geography: World-Economy, Nation-State and Locality*. London: Longman.

Taylor, Peter J. 1993. 'Geopolitical World Orders'. In *Political Geography of the Twentieth Century: A Global Analysis*, edited by Peter J. Taylor, 31–61. London: Belhaven.

Taylor, Peter J., and Colin Flint. 2000. *Political Geography: World-Economy, Nation-State and Locality*. London: Prentice Hall. Fourth edition.

The Presidency. 2005. *Accelerated and Shared Growth Initiative: South Africa (ASGISA): A Summary*. Pretoria: The Presidency of the Republic of South Africa.

The Presidency. 2007. *ASIGSA Annual Report 2006*. Pretoria: The Presidency of the Republic of South Africa.

The Presidency. 2008. *ASGISA Annual Report 2007*. Pretoria: The Presidency of the Republic of South Africa.

The Presidency. 2009. *ASGISA Annual Report 2008*. Pretoria: The Presidency of the Republic of South Africa.

Thomas, Wolfgang. 2006. *South Africa's Foreign Direct Investment in Africa: Catalytic Kingpin in the NEPAD Process*. Pretoria: AISA.

Thompson, Carol. 2000. 'Regional Challenges to Globalisation: Perspectives from Southern Africa'. *New Political Economy* 5.1: 41–57.

Thompson, Madeleine C., et al. 2003. 'El Niño and Drought in Southern Africa'. *Lancet* 9355: 437–8.

Thompson, William R. 1973. 'The Regional Subsystem: A Conceptual Explication and Propositional Inventory'. *International Studies Quarterly* 17.1: 89–117.

Toth, Anthony. 1995. 'Mauritius'. In *Indian Ocean: Five Island Countries*, edited by Helen Chapin Metz, 89–135. Washington, DC: US Government Printing Office. Third edition.

TradeMark Southern Africa. 2012a. *North South Corridor Pilot Aid for Transport Programme: Surface Transport*. Pretoria: TradeMark Southern Africa.

TradeMark Southern Africa. 2012b. *Regional Solutions to Providing Electricity in the COMESA–EAC–SADC Tripartite Region*. Pretoria: TradeMark Southern Africa.

TradeMark Southern Africa. 2012c. *North–South Corridor Roads*. Pretoria: TradeMark Southern Africa.

Teravaninthorn, Supee, and Gaël Raballand. 2008. 'Transport Prices and Costs in Africa: A Review of the Main International Corridors'. *AICD Working Paper* 14.

Treydte, Klaus-Peter. 2011. 'Mauritius'. In *Africa Yearbook: Politics, Economy and Society South of the Sahara in 2010*, edited by Andreas Mehler et al., 479–82. Leiden: Brill.

Troll, Carl. 1947. 'Die geographische Wissenschaft in Deutschland in den Jahren 1933 bis 1945'. *Erdkunde* 1.1: 3–48.

Tull, Denis M. 2010. 'Democratic Republic of the Congo'. In *Africa Yearbook: Politics, Economy and Society South of the Sahara in 2009*, edited by Andreas Mehler et al., 241–55. Leiden: Brill.

Tull, Denis M. 2011. 'Democratic Republic of the Congo'. In *Africa Yearbook: Politics, Economy and Society South of the Sahara in 2010*, edited by Andreas Mehler et al., 243–5. Leiden: Brill.

Turner, Frederick J. 1920. *The Frontier in American History*. New York: Holt.

Turton, Anthony, et al. 2004. 'A Hydropolitical History of South Africa's International River Basins'. *WRC Report* 1220.

Tyson, Peter D. 1981. 'Climate and Desertification in Southern Africa'. *GeoJournal* (Supplement) 5.2: 3–10.

Tyson, Peter D. 1986. *Climatic Change and Variability in Southern Africa*. Cape Town: Oxford University Press.

Tyson, Peter D. 1991. 'Climatic Change in Southern Africa: Past and Present Conditions and Possible Future Scenarios'. *Climatic Change* 18.2–3: 241–58.

UN Conference on Trade and Development. 2011. 'Liner Shipping Connectivity Index: 2004–2011'. Accessed 4 February 2012. http://unctadstat.unctad.org/TableViewer/tableView.aspx?ReportId=92.

Usman, Mohammad T., and Chris J. Reason. 2004. 'Dry Spell Frequencies and Their Variability over Southern Africa'. *Climate Research* 26.3: 199–211.

Väyrynen, Raimo. 1984. 'Regional Conflict Formations: An Intractable Problem of International Relations'. *Journal of Peace Research* 21.4: 337–59.

Vale, Peter, and Sipho Maseko. 1998. 'South Africa and the African Renaissance'. *International Affairs* 74.2: 271–87.

Vletter, Fion de. 2006. *Migration and Development in Mozambique: Poverty, Inequality and Survival*. Cape Town: Idasa.

Vogel, Walther. 1921. *Das neue Europa und seine historisch-geographischen Grundlagen*. Bonn: Schroeder.

Wagao, Jumanne H. 1987. 'Trade Relations among SADCC Countries'. In *SADCC: Prospects for Disengagement and Development in Southern Africa*, edited by Samir Amin, Derrick Chitala and Ibbo Mandaza, 147–80. London: Zed Books.

Wagemann, Claudius, and Carsten Q. Schneider. 2007. 'Standards of Good Practice in Qualitative Comparative Analysis (QCA) and Fuzzy Sets'. *Compasss Working Paper* 51.

Waites, Bryan. 2000. 'The Lesotho Highlands Water Project'. *Geography* 85.4: 369–74.

Waller, Peter. 1988. 'Das Verkehrssystem im südlichen Afrika: Kann die Abhängigkeit von Südafrika abgebaut werden?' *Geographische Rundschau* 40.12: 44–9.

Waltz, Kenneth N. 1979. *Theory of International Politics*. Boston: McGraw-Hill.

Waltz, Kenneth N. 2000. 'Structural Realism after the Cold War'. *International Security* 25.1: 5–41.

Weigert, Hans. 1949. 'The Heartland and the Expansion of the USSR'. In *New Compass of the World: A Symposium on Political Geography*, edited by Hans Weigert et al., 80–90. New York: Macmillan.

Whitaker, Donald P. 1983. 'The Economy'. In *Zimbabwe: A Country Study*, edited by Harold D. Nelson, 135–84. Washington, DC: Library of Congress. Second edition.

Whittlesey, Derwent S. 1922. 'Geographic Factors in the Relations of the United States and Cuba'. *Geographical Review* 12.2: 241–56.

Whittlesey, Derwent S. 1933. 'Trans-Pyrenean Span: The Val d'Aran'. *Scottish Geographical Magazine* 49.4: 217–28.

Whittlesey, Derwent S. 1934. 'Andorra's Autonomy'. *Journal of Modern History* 6.2: 147–55.

Whittlesey, Derwent S. 1944. *The Earth and the State: A Study in Political Geography*. New York: Holt.

Who Owns Whom. 2012. 'Africa Inc.: List of Investments'. Accessed 15 August 2012. http://www.whoownswhom.co.za/.

Wight, Martin. 1978. *Power Politics*. London: Leicester University Press.

Wilson, Dominic, and Roopa Purushothaman. 2003. 'Dreaming with BRICs: The Path to 2050'. *Goldman Sachs Global Economics Paper* 99.

Wilson, Dominic, and Anna Stupnytska. 2007. 'The N-11: More Than an Acronym'. *Goldman Sachs Global Economics Paper* 153.

World Bank. 2010. 'Review of Maritime Transport International LPI: Ranking'. Accessed 6 August 2012. http://info.worldbank.org/etools/tradesurvey/mode 1b.asp?sorder=lpirank&cgroup=r6.

Wyk, Jo-Ansie van. 1997. 'The Case for Benign Hegemony'. *Global Dialogue* 2.3: 10–12.

Index

THE INTERNATIONAL POLITICAL ECONOMY OF NEW REGIONALISMS SERIES

Other titles in the series

Exploring the New South American
Regionalism (NSAR)
Edited by Ernesto Vivares

China's Diplomacy in Eastern and
Southern Africa
Edited by Seifudein Adem

Regionalism and Regional Security
in South Asia
The Role of SAARC
Zahid Shahab Ahmed

Comparative Regionalisms for
Development in the 21st Century
Insights from the Global South
*Edited by Emmanuel Fanta,
Timothy M. Shaw and Vanessa T. Tang*

Mapping Agency
Comparing Regionalisms in Africa
*Edited by Ulrike Lorenz-Carl and
Martin Rempe*

The EU and the Eurozone Crisis
Policy Challenges and Strategic Choices
Edited by Finn Laursen

China-Africa Relations in an Era of Great
Transformations
*Edited by Li Xing with Abdulkadir
Osman Farah*

The European Union Neighbourhood
Challenges and Opportunities
Edited by Teresa Cierco

The New Democracy Wars
The Politics of North American
Democracy Promotion in the Americas
Neil A. Burron

The European Union after Lisbon
Polity, Politics, Policy
Edited by Søren Dosenrode

Roads to Regionalism
Genesis, Design, and Effects of
Regional Organizations
*Edited by Tanja A. Börzel,
Lukas Goltermann, Mathis Lohaus
and Kai Striebinger*

New Regionalism or No Regionalism?
Emerging Regionalism in the
Black Sea Area
Edited by Ruxandra Ivan

Our North America
Social and Political Issues beyond NAFTA
Edited by Julián Castro-Rea

Community of Insecurity
SADC's Struggle for Peace and Security
in Southern Africa
Laurie Nathan

Cruising in the Global Economy
Profits, Pleasure and Work at Sea
Christine B.N. Chin

Beyond Regionalism?
Regional Cooperation, Regionalism and
Regionalization in the Middle East
*Edited by Cilja Harders
and Matteo Legrenzi*

The EU-Russian Energy Dialogue
Europe's Future Energy Security
Edited by Pami Aalto

Regionalism, Globalisation
and International Order
Europe and Southeast Asia
Jens-Uwe Wunderlich

EU Development Policy
and Poverty Reduction
Enhancing Effectiveness
Edited by Wil Hout

An East Asian Model for Latin
American Success
The New Path
Anil Hira

European Union and New Regionalism
Regional Actors and Global Governance
in a Post-Hegemonic Era
Second Edition
Edited by Mario Telò

Regional Integration and Poverty
*Edited by Dirk Willem te Velde
and the Overseas Development Institute*

Redefining the Pacific?
Regionalism Past, Present and Future
*Edited by Jenny Bryant-Tokalau
and Ian Frazer*

Latin America's Quest for Globalization
The Role of Spanish Firms
*Edited by Félix E. Martín
and Pablo Toral*

Exchange Rate Crises
in Developing Countries
The Political Role of the Banking Sector
Michael G. Hall

Globalization and Antiglobalization
Dynamics of Change in the
New World Order
Edited by Henry Veltmeyer

Twisting Arms and Flexing Muscles
Humanitarian Intervention and
Peacebuilding in Perspective
*Edited by Natalie Mychajlyszyn
and Timothy M. Shaw*

Asia Pacific and Human Rights
A Global Political Economy Perspective
Paul Close and David Askew

Demilitarisation and Peace-Building
in Southern Africa
Volume I – Concepts and Processes
*Edited by Peter Batchelor
and Kees Kingma*

Demilitarisation and Peace-Building
in Southern Africa
Volume II – National and
Regional Experiences
*Edited by Peter Batchelor
and Kees Kingma*

Persistent Permeability?
Regionalism, Localism, and Globalization
in the Middle East
*Edited by Bassel F. Salloukh
and Rex Brynen*

The New Political Economy of
United States-Caribbean Relations
The Apparel Industry and the
Politics of NAFTA Parity
Tony Heron

The Nordic Regions and
the European Union
*Edited by Søren Dosenrode
and Henrik Halkier*